FOUNDATIONS OF BUSINESS INFORMATION SYSTEMS

APPROACHES TO INFORMATION TECHNOLOGY

Series Editor
Thomas F. Carbery, *Strathclyde Business School*
University of Strathclyde
Glasgow, Scotland

Foundations of Business Information Systems
Andrew Doswell

FOUNDATIONS OF BUSINESS INFORMATION SYSTEMS

Andrew Doswell
University of Strathclyde
Glasgow, Scotland

PLENUM PRESS • NEW YORK AND LONDON

Library of Congress Cataloging in Publication Data

Doswell, Andrew.
Foundations of business information systems.

(Approaches to information technology)
Bibliography: p.
Includes index.
1. Information storage and retrieval systems—Business. 2. Business—Data processing. I. Title. II. Series.
HF5548.2.D62 1985 658.4′038 85-3689

ISBN-13: 978-0-306-41796-2 e-ISBN-13: 978-1-4613-2395-2
DOI: 10.1007/978-1-4613-2395-2

Softcover reprint of the hardcover 1st edition 1985

A Division of Plenum Publishing Corporation
233 Spring Street, New York, N.Y. 10013

For my mother and the memory of my father

FOREWORD

A few years ago there were no books on information technology and business, now there are a great many. To add to that flow calls for courage and judgment on the part of both a potential author and publisher. Andrew Doswell and Plenum Press are justified in bringing this work into the market.

The main reason is that Andrew Doswell has brought to the work some simple yet formidable attributes. The first of these is that he knows what he is talking about. He was trained as an electrical engineer; he then was employed in business, drawing on and fortifying that training, where he moved into an administrative position. Later still he moved into teaching, first in Ireland, then in Scotland, but while employed in education he has not become an academic recluse. On the contrary, he has continued to maintain his links with business, doing so by engaging in both research and consultancy. Within the University he has been at the forefront of our thrust into office automation and office information systems.

The second great attribute that Andrew Doswell brings to this work is that he speaks and writes in a language that ordinary men and women can understand. This is refreshing. Most writers in this area fall into one of two categories. The first group consists of advanced computer scientists and electronic engineers who are so accustomed to speaking to others of their own kind that they cannot speak about their own subjects other than in an "elitist" language or jargon, or, variant on a theme, they presuppose greater prior knowledge than most would-be students and readers possess. The other group consists of professional writers, frequently journalists, who write with lucidity but with no great understanding of the subject.

The language used by Andrew Doswell in this work can be understood and followed by all, including backbench M.P.'s, trade union leaders, retired Brigadiers, junior, middle, and senior executives, and high-IQ students.

O that there were yet more books on this subject that were written with such a happy combination of knowledge and lucidity!

THOMAS F. CARBERY
Strathclyde Business School
University of Strathclyde
Glasgow

PREFACE

The purpose of this book is to provide an introduction to information systems in their business setting. I have tried to indicate what information technology is, and how it will impact business in terms of the products and services business provides, and the processes used to provide and support the provision of business products and services.

I have assumed the reader to have no prior knowledge concerning the mechanics of business, let alone the mechanics of processing information. Therefore, ideas about both business and information processing are developed from scratch. For the reader who does know something already, there are, hopefully, enough signposts provided to indicate which parts of the book can be safely left out.

All books of this kind are intended for students. There are, however, two broad groups of students. First, there are those who are actually working in business and feel the need for a book to provide some guidance as to what is going on around them. If you are one of this group, I hope to have written a book that is practical enough for your needs. In particular, Part IV deals with the uses and effects of information technology without going into the reasons why.

You may, on the other hand, belong to the second group—a full-time student with perhaps no knowledge either of business or computer-based information processing. For you I hope to have written a book that combines an explanation of the theoretical reasons *why* with practical explanations of *what*. The material is meant to be useful to both the student specializing in either computer science or technology in general who knows nothing of business, and to the student specializing in some aspect of business who knows nothing of computers or technology.

ACKNOWLEDGMENTS

There are many people who help during the process of writing a book. There is the home support from wife and family and also the help from teaching colleagues who provide information. Perhaps most importantly there is the help from others who are working in the same subject area but who are not nearby. Since information technology is far beyond the comprehension of one mind I would like to take this opportunity to acknowledge the work of others—the many books and articles—which has helped me to form my understanding of business information technology. Most of these can be found in the references at the back of the book.

There is another important contributor in this book—the illustrator. In this case the drawings were done by a friend, Les Lambert, who combines the ability to draw beautiful illustrations with many other talents.

Usually the last, but not least, acknowledgment is reserved for the typist. In an age of information technology, that acknowledgment must disappear since the author is the word processing operator!

CONTENTS

I

INTRODUCTION

"In a simple society, . . . Speech supplies adequate communication . . . Our world has far outgrown the reach of the voice or the comprehension of any one mind." John R. Pierce, *Communication*, W. H. Freeman, San Francisco, 1972.

SUMMARY: Signposts to the contents of the book.

1

STRUCTURE

INTRODUCTION

The processing of information is a fundamentally important activity. We can do nothing without information. In business not only do we need information for the business to function, but also many of the products of business involve information technology—and so information systems and information technology are intertwined.

What Is Information Technology?

Information technology is the combined use of computers and telecommunications. Although both computers and telecommunications have been around for quite a long time now, the advent of the microprocessor and the falling cost of microprocessor-based information technology have resulted in an explosive growth in the use of computers and communications. This book, therefore, is primarily concerned with the microprocessor aspects of information technology and systems.

Who Can Use Information Technology and Systems?

The application of the microcomputer is at an early stage. But even now it is apparent that many, perhaps most, businesses could afford and would benefit from computer-based help. This help might be in accounting, word processing, stock control, tax returns, or some other administrative activity, but the application of information systems is not limited solely to administrative work. Information systems are equally useful on the shop floor controlling production machines and manufacturing processes, and in some cases information technology is the product or service that the business provides. Certainly in Europe there is growing concern that European companies will miss out on the rapidly developing sector concerned with providing information technology. To show that this concern is not just a lot of talk, the EEC has allocated a billion U.S. dollars to fund the ESPRIT information technology research program.

So this book is concerned with information technology and systems not just as they apply to the manager in the office. We deal with information technology as a product in its own right as well as system effects on the production and administrative processes.

The Two Faces of Information Technology

Information technology is a mixed blessing. The changes that occur with the introduction of information systems exact a price just as any other changes do. Hopefully, this book will help in providing an understanding of information technology and systems so that those businesses which do adopt new information technology can avoid the fate of those which do not, for the latter will pay the price of certain failure.

Information technology is not a panacea, and its application needs to be worked at, hard.

The principles of information technology are universal. However, the application of these principles is not. In our world the majority of people live in poor surroundings eking out a meager existence. For these people utilities such as a stable supply of electricity are a luxury, not the necessity that they are in order for our information technology to work.

Even in those parts of the world where information processing is a dominant concern of society, there are considerable variations. Most notably information technology prices and costs in the United States and Canada are considerably lower than, by about half, those for Western Europe. Clearly, in trying to write a book that is not confined to a single country, the very important business factors of how much equipment costs and what the value of information is, have to be dealt with in generalized rather than in specific terms. The reader will have to apply the figures appropriate for his or her own country.

STRUCTURE OF THE VOLUME

Chapter 2

The book starts properly in the next chapter. Chapter 2 is concerned with establishing why the application of technology to information processing is important. The idea of the activity system is introduced as a foundation for understanding both information processing activities and performance measurements such as productivity. We look briefly at the ways in which one business will be different from another in order to make the point that it is the business context of information technology that is as important as the technology itself.

Part II

It is no good knowing about the principles of technology if the principles of business are not established, and in the second part of the book we do this.

Chapter 3

In Chapter 3 a brief eye is cast over business. A description of business in terms of management functional activities is provided together with the relationship between specialization and organization. The chapter is completed by looking at communication and how it affects organizational structure. Communication is important since information systems are mostly concerned with communication.

Chapter 4

Chapter 4 starts with a discussion of information in terms of its properties and presents a model of the use of information in decision making. The areas of application of information technology in products, services, production, and administration processes, are then briefly reviewed.

Part III

Part III deals with the technology of information systems.

Chapter 5

Chapter 5 is a review of current conventional information technology, paper and microforms, and how they are used.

Chapter 6

Chapter 6 deals with the principles of digital electronics, how digital devices are made and work, and the development of their performance since the 1960s. The operation of the computer is briefly discussed before looking at the characteristics of telecommunication processes.

Chapter 7

Chapter 7 looks in more detail at how the computer works and at the interactions between people and computers through various peripheral devices.

Part IV

Having described information technology, information systems and their use of information technology in business are considered in Part IV.

Chapter 8

Four headings are used to examine the general application of information technology: products, services, production processes, and administrative processes. Under these four headings typical applications, developments, and drawbacks are discussed.

Chapter 9

To conclude the book, information technology is reviewed by a discussion of various topics ranging from the societal effects of information technology to the key points for the successful implementation of information technology in a business.

2

PREVIEW

INTRODUCTION

Changes in Employment

One apparently inevitable result of the development of society seems to be of the form shown in Illustration 2.1.

Increasing Administrative Costs

Besides the changes in working patterns shown in Illustration 2.1 being an interesting sociological phenomenon, there is an important implication for business—the overheads of running a business have become ever greater (Illustration 2.2).

Quite simply Illustration 2.2 shows that the costs of nonproductive information overheads have risen to very high levels compared to costs earlier in this century. There are very many possible reasons for this growth. It is not just a simple question of inefficiency. However, it would clearly be prudent to try to minimize the costs of information overheads. One way to try to do this is to use technology.

BUSINESS APPLICATIONS OF INFORMATION TECHNOLOGY

No one knows the full extent to which the technology of computers and telecommunications may develop, but it is quite clear that the developments

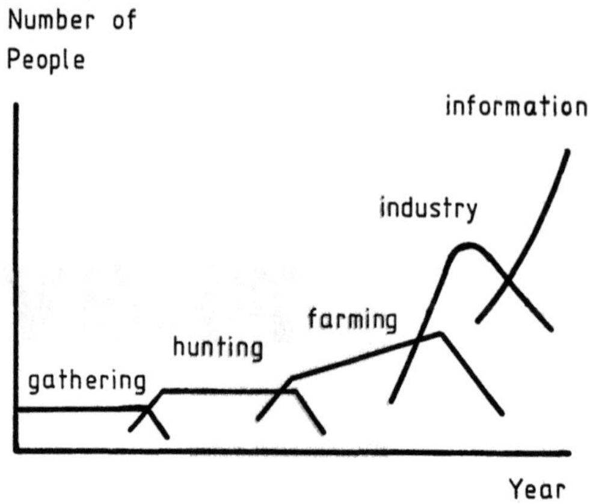

Illustration 2.1. Employment evolution

We have to eat in order to live. Until fairly recently almost all of us worked directly at getting food by either gathering it, hunting for it, or farming it. Even today, for most people in the world, direct production of food by farming is the way that life is maintained.

However, as countries develop they start to industrialize, and from then on the economic importance of the production of food as a source of employment diminishes. Not only does farming become less important as an employer, but also industralization means that in a given land area, more people can be kept alive.

The graph above shows the typical way in which employment evolves. The graph is meant to be a very general one applicable to any country. Because different countries are at different stages of employment evolution and are evolving at different rates, it is not possible to put specific values to the time scale. Similarly, it is not possible to put values on the percentage of people in any particular employment sector. However, a general point seems to be that the period of dominance of any particular form of employment becomes progressively less. Change in society becomes more rapid as societies evolve.

Although the graph is meant to be a general one, to give some idea of values, the situation applying to the United States: Farming dominant until 1910; industry dominant until 1960; information dominant since 1960.

will have a tremendous effect. There are four major ways in which information technology is currently being used to help business:

- data processing;
- information storage and retrieval;
- control; and
- electronic communications.

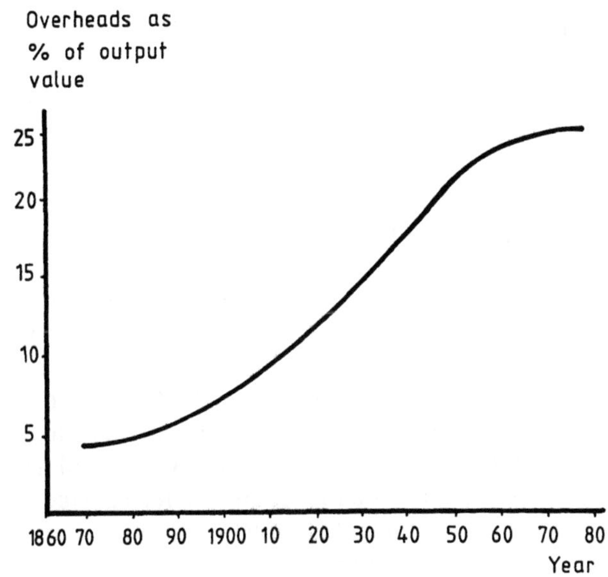

Illustration 2.2. Overhead costs

A simple estimate of the cost of information processing overheads can be made by calculating the ratio of information workers to others. For the United States this produces the picture shown here. A similar situation applies to other countries.

The vertical scale measures the cost of overheads as a percentage of the value of the output. The values, given in the figure, are approximate but show the same trend as found by others (see, for example, Kalthoff, and Lee 1981).

The message is that for the past 100 years it has cost more and more to provide the administrative support needed to support the production of goods and services. What the message *means* is open to interpretation. Some people, thinking along the lines of economist Milton Friedman, will say that it shows the effect of a burgeoning bureacracy. Others (Jones and Lakin, 1977) will say that it just demonstrates the built-in drive of people to create interesting but nonproductive administrative jobs in business for themselves. Others will talk in terms of the need to develop such overhead but essential activities as marketing if a business is to survive in a complex world.

It is noticeable, although maybe only coincidental, that since the mid-1950s to early 1960s, and with the ever widening use of computers, there has been only a slight increase in the relative costs of overheads.

Data Processing

Although computers are expected to be good at arithmetic, what they are really good at are jobs that seem to be full of drudgery to us—the repetition of the same routine over and over again. This kind of work is involved in preparing bills or wage slips. Each time there are a few pieces of information to be used and a few calculations to be done. When we perform this kind of work we make mistakes and easily get bored. A computer does neither.

Information Storage and Retrieval

In addition to being used for performing a few simple operations over and over again, the computer can also be used to carry out the very simple operation of searching through stored information to find out if a particular symbol or word appears in it. Although we can do this by reading, it takes us time, and we might forget to read each word, or we might turn over two pages at once. The computer would never do anything as slipshod as that. Even a very slow computer, such as a word processor, can read a page of writing in a few seconds and not miss anything. Examples of this kind of use could be for checking the credit rating of customers or the criminal records of previous offenders.

Control

In addition to providing us with information we can use, computers can be used to provide information to other machines. This information is used to control the machine's activities. So instead of having people operating paint spray units or welding guns, we can use robots, which are just computer-controlled machines, to do the job. Robots never tire and do not go on strike—they are ideally docile.

Electronic Communication

Finally, information that is in one place is generally wanted somewhere else. By harnessing computers and telecommunications together we can develop sophisticated but cheap methods for transmitting information from one place to another very rapidly. This can allow us to develop machines that not only tell us how much we have just spent on groceries in the supermarket but which can order replacement stock from the warehouse, draw out money from our bank account, and pay it into the shop's account. All this can be done without any human intervention.

Products and Processes

Information technology can be used in businesses in two distinct ways.

First, information technology can be incorporated into the products and services that a business provides. The reason for carrying out this incorporation would be to provide a new and, hopefully, better product or service. The better quality might be perceived by the customer as being improved reliability, increased usefulness, or lower cost. For the business providing the product the better quality will mean either lower operating costs, perhaps because the product is more reliable or easier to assemble, or higher income, perhaps from an increased market share.

The second, alternative, approach to the use of information technology is to incorporate it into the business organization itself, thus altering the way in which the business itself functions by changing either the *methods* of production and/or the *methods* of administration.

Both of these two approaches—products and processes—will be examined in this book.

ACTIVITY SYSTEMS: CONCEPTS

One fundamental concept that will appear and reappear throughout this book is that of the activity system. This idea is very simple and very powerful. Any process that produces something, e.g., cars from a production line, documents from an office, or leaves from a tree in the park, can be represented as an activity block (Illustration 2.3). Using this simple activity block it is possible to build up a representation of a business in terms of the various combinations of people and machines taking inputs, and then processing the inputs into outputs. The development of an activity-based representation for a business is shown in Illustration 2.4.

Performance Measurements

Given the activity system concept as a starting point to understand a business, features of prime concern that immediately make themselves apparent are the outputs from and the inputs to the business system. In everyday terms we would ask ourselves: "Has the business done what it was supposed to have done?" and "How well has it done it?"

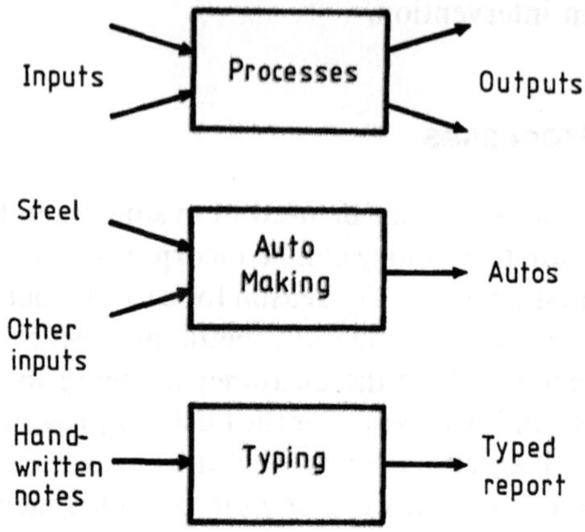

Illustration 2.3. Idea of an activity

The basic idea of an activity is that inputs are changed by processes into outputs.

This idea can be applied in any circumstances where something is produced, whether the process is a manufacturing one such as auto making or is an office routine such as letter typing.

Usually there are many inputs and outputs for any process, but in any particular case we are only interested in a few. There is not enough time to identify, let alone deal with, all the inputs and outputs. This process of selectivity has to apply and is usually satisfactory. However, problems do occur when previously disregarded inputs or outputs become important, for example, the impact of human input on production processes or the output of pollution from manufacturing processes.

These questions can be answered in many ways, but one particularly useful way is by considering the efficiency, the effectiveness, and, finally, the productivity, of the business.

Efficiency

With efficiency we are concerned with the quantity of resources that have had to be consumed in order to get the output. Efficiency can therefore be measured in terms of

$$\text{Efficiency} = \frac{\text{value of actual output}}{\text{cost of input}}$$

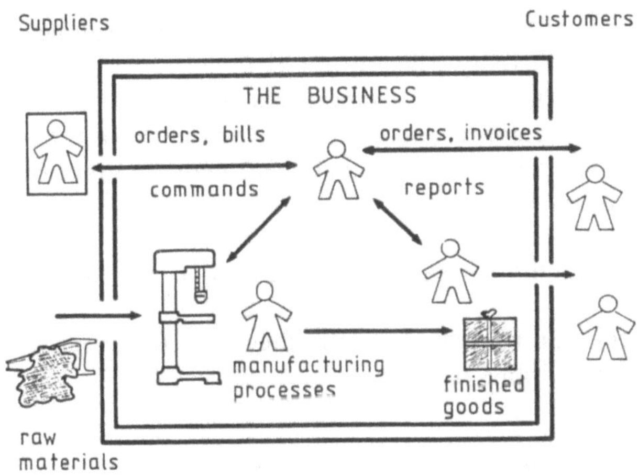

Illustration 2.4. Principles of a business system

A business consists of a vast number of interconnected activities, i.e., a system of activities. In this illustration we try to hint at some of that complexity.

Production is "simple." It consists of taking raw materials and transforming them by the manufacturing process into finished goods. But in order to get the raw materials transformed, there will be information and communication processes involving the operators who control the machines and the various supervisors and managers. In addition, there will be all the communications that are necessary in order to sell products, take orders, pay bills, get the sales receipts in, and so on.

A failure in the communication processes can obviously have far-reaching effects on the business.

Effectiveness

With effectiveness we are concerned with quality—how good or appropriate is the output? This can be expressed as

$$\text{Effectiveness} = \frac{\text{value of actual output}}{\text{value of best output}}$$

Effectiveness is more difficult to determine since it is concerned with qualitative rather than quantitative factors. In essence quality can only be judged in hindsight by realizing what could have been compared to what actually was.

Productivity

The two measures of efficiency and effectiveness can be combined into a measure of productivity (Illustration 2.5).

In addition to these standard measures, further indicators can be used to assess system performance. An increasingly popular measure is that of added value. Added value measures the increment between input cost and output value and can be expressed as

$$\text{Added value} = \text{value of actual output} - \text{cost of input}$$

and clearly this can be related to efficiency and effectiveness since they are determined by the same factors.

ACTIVITY SYSTEMS: APPLICATIONS

In writing a book we are dealing with generalized statements. The drawback to generalizations is that they are only generalizations, and we are trying to cover a wide range of different types and sizes of business. Although the activity system concept is a valid one, the way in which any business actually exists will vary because of the effects of size, business sector, and individuals involved.

Effects of Size

In the one-person business all activities will naturally be carried out by one person, not by different divisions or departments as in the large organization. In the small business many of the activities will be carried out informally; there will be no memoranda flowing between the men and women in sales and those in manufacturing. But in the large organization there will likely be vast amounts of communication on paper and over telephone lines, as well as face-to-face communication between individuals who are employed in different functions.

Type of Business

Even if we disregarded the factor of size by concentrating on one particular size of company, there would be differences dependent upon the *kind* of business that is being considered. A large oil company does things in a different way compared with a large electronics company. A small jobbing

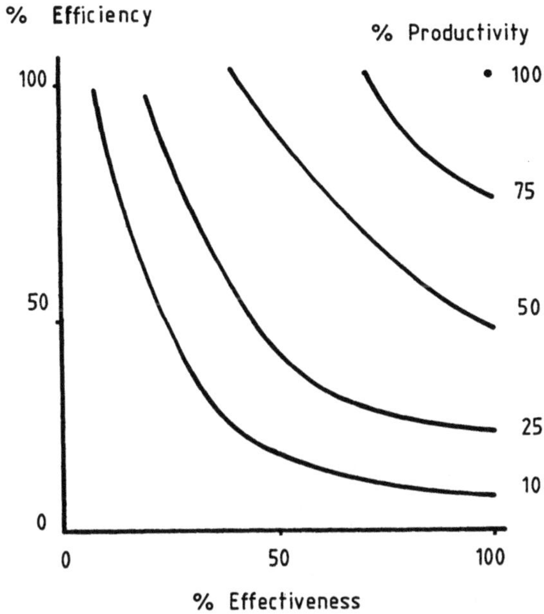

Illustration 2.5. Productivity, effectiveness, and efficiency

Productivity is a measure that takes into account both efficiency and effectiveness. Efficiency measures how well the existing activities transform inputs into outputs. Efficiency is not concerned with whether the output is wanted; this is measured by effectiveness. Effectiveness measures the value of what is currently being produced and compares it to the value of what else could be done.

So while it is true that efficiency is important, it is not true that efficiency is everything. There is no point in running a business that is very *efficient* at producing goods that few customers want. The business must be *effective* by producing goods that meet a need.

By using the relationship

Productivity = efficiency × effectiveness

both efficiency and effectiveness are taken into account.

The major stumbling block in performing measurements of productivity is establishing a value for effectiveness. It is extremely difficult to assess the values of other courses of action until they have been tried out. However, in business, there is rarely time or money enough to actually try out various possibilities: a single choice has to be made.

engineering business has different information needs compared with a small warehousing operation or an attorney's office.

Effects of People

Finally, even if we tried to disregard the effect of different business types as well as size by dealing only with businesses of similar size and type we would discover differences because of the differences between individual people. Not only are there variations to deal with because of different national characteristics, but there are also variations because of local characteristics.

All of these considerations should make us realize that we are dealing with a complex and complicated problem. It would be foolish to think that there is one simple remedy for all of a business's problems.

SUMMARY

For a large part of this century it appears that the amount of resources, time, money, and people expended on processing information has increased relentlessly. We have reached a stage where it almost seems that no longer is information processing simply an adjunct to the real operations activity of a business, but rather that information *is* the business activity, and operations are merely a way of generating enough money in order to support it! But in spite of this there is as yet little overall control of the information processing activities of businesses. The concept of the administrative or information manager who is responsible for the information resources of the business remains, on the whole, a strange idea. Still, most businesses do not realize the importance of information and how it can be used to help develop a business.

In order to try to come to grips with the information needs of a business, it is extremely useful to think in terms of the activity of information processing. This activity consists of input, process, and output. Using this concept, ideas concerning efficiency, effectiveness, and productivity can be brought into focus. However, there are severe practical difficulties that can prevent the establishment of anything like accurate values for information processing effectiveness and hence information processing productivity.

Although the activity concept is powerful, the actual way that any particular business is organized will depend on a variety of factors including size, business sector, and the characteristics of the individuals concerned. The application of information technology as a solution to the problems of a business is not simple. Local needs and individual variations have to be taken into account if information technology is to be successfully implemented.

There is no guaranteed easy solution. In order to get a long-term profit from using information technology, both hard work and understanding are required.

DISCUSSION QUESTIONS

1. With the introduction of computers into general office work, what will happen to unneeded workers? (Increasing efficiency has meant that in many countries only a relatively few people are needed to produce all the food that is necessary for the whole population. Historically, the surplus labor from the agricultural revolution transferred to industrial production, but increasing production automation means that now fewer people are needed to make things. This labor surplus has transferred to office work since the 1940s).

2. Analyze what could be wrong, in terms of an input process–output activity model when a typical office machine, say a photocopier, goes "wrong."

3. What would be the problems in attempting to measure the productivity of a college? How do these difficulties compare to those of measuring the performance of a manufacturing business?

II

BUSINESS AND INFORMATION

"As just about everyone knows, the business of American business is going to meetings–what-are-we-going-to-do meetings, meet-the-other-guy meetings,... probably even why-are-we-having-so-many-meetings." Walter Kiechel III, Teleconferencing to stardom, *Fortune,* May 2, 1983.

SUMMARY: How business is organized into specialisms and their functions. Decision making and information. The use of information in business.

3

FUNCTIONS, COMMUNICATION, AND ORGANIZATION

INTRODUCTION

Structure of the Chapter

In this chapter we start by providing a description of the typical business in terms of the three major functions of production operations, marketing, and accounting. In addition, the importance of office/administrative information processing support for these activities is pointed out. The existence of these three different functions creates specialization. Because of specialization communication is required. As a business grows in size, there will be increasing amounts of communication, and, in order to prevent chaos, organization has to occur. Organization and communication go hand in hand. There are a variety of factors to consider when thinking about organizational communication: the type of business sector, the size of business, and the preferences of the individuals within the business.

This chapter is concluded by the inclusion of a program listing of a computer-based simulation of a business that can be used to get some feeling of what running a real business is like.

The Growth of Organization

Each of us individually has wants, needs, and desires. Rarely can any of these be met without help from others. The combination of people's efforts to meet our needs means that organization of some kind is necessary. But we tend to look at our dependence on organization in a mixed light because to a large extent organization work consists of managing and administrating rather than "doing."

> The wealth of our society is largely a product of our ability to organise. By coordinating a multitude of activities widely separated in time and space, we can employ physical resources with greater economy and create artefacts of a size and complexity previously beyond our ambitions; by pooling our resources we may reduce dramatically the risks which individuals face and increase amazingly the wealth and variety of satisfactions which each person can obtain. The benefits of organisation are great but the work it involves is often regarded as wasteful.
>
> No wonder! because organisation is achieved not by doing things but by talking and writing about them: transmitting and processing information. (Stamper, 1973)

FUNCTIONS

Business Objectives

It would seem obvious that businesses overall have fairly well-defined objectives. One attempt to define business objectives might be: to provide goods and services in order to make profits.

Constraints

There are, of course, certain constraints—that goods and services should be legally permitted, for example—to add to the simple statement of objectives, nevertheless the general principles are clear enough.

Activity Model

Using the simple idea of business objectives, a simple activity system model of a business can be formed as shown in Illustration 3.1.

Business Functions. The simple model can be developed by identifying three major functional areas: production, marketing, and accounting (Illustration 3.2).

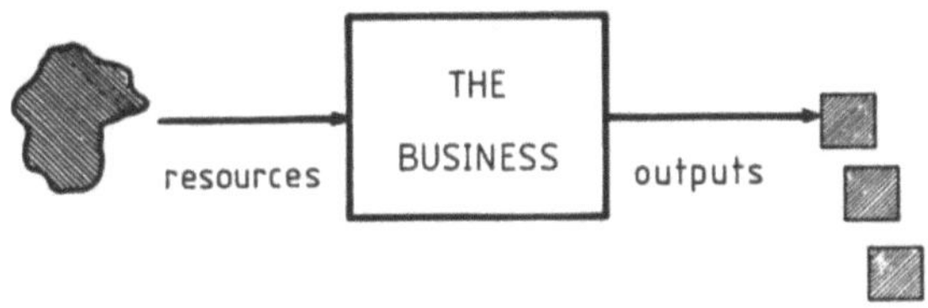

Illustration 3.1. A basic business system

In the simplest terms, a business takes in raw materials and turns out products.

The resources are raw materials. The raw materials might be food, or minerals, or ingots of metal, or sheets of paper. The raw material might literally be raw—potatoes or rice out of the ground—or they may have been partially processed before by some other business, e.g., steel ingots for an automobile company.

Converting the raw materials will involve a number of different activities and processes. These will not only be directly concerned with production but will also include all the other processes supporting production.

It is convenient to think in terms of the business output as being *products*, physically real things that can be picked up, and *services* which are anything that are not products. Even though we can distinguish between physical products and nonphysical services, no one actually buys a product. Customers buy the service a product can provide.

Operations. Production operations are concerned with the conversion of raw input materials into finished products. This is mainly an area of technical knowledge and deals with problems that are of a technical nature, although clearly the human side in terms of operators' needs and requirements are not just technical matters, and this illustrates the difficulties of taking all factors into account when considering a system.

Marketing. Having made the products, we then become concerned with *marketing* them: distributing the products to the right places, charging the right price, advertising them appropriately, and so on. Certainly until the 1940s almost all businesses worked in precisely this manner of first making the products and then selling them. However, since the end of the second world war, there has been an increasing emphasis on the distinct function of marketing. Now it is generally no longer sufficient just to make a product and then sell it. Now it is much more likely that what kind of product is required will be considered first and then the production facilities set up subsequently. So although in terms of our simple model here, the business's products flow from production to marketing, that does not mean that is necessarily the order in which decisions are taken within the business.

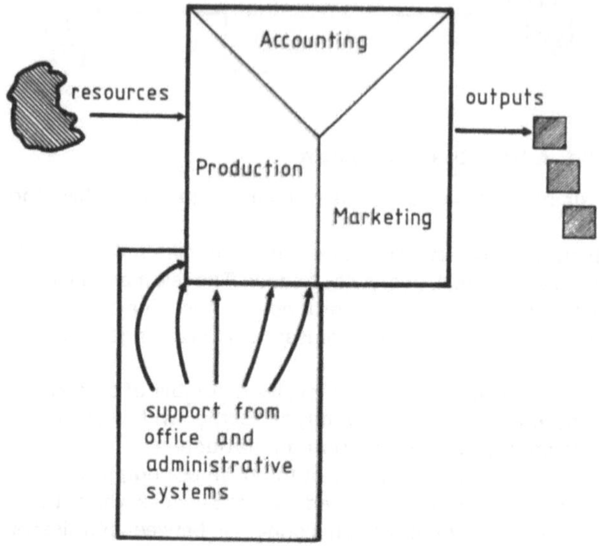

Illustration 3.2. Main functions of the ideal business

Any business can be split into three main functions.

Production (or *operations)* is concerned with the production of goods and services. Operations cover a wide range of tasks from drilling holes in pieces of metal to cutting holes in people. Operations are performed by a vast range of people from unskilled laborers to highly skilled surgeons. The chief concern of operations management is to provide efficient operations.

Marketing is concerned with establishing what customers want. The effect of marketing is to determine the effectiveness of the business.

Accounting is concerned with monitoring the performance of the business. While operations are concerned with efficiency and marketing with effectiveness, accounting provides the data from which the *values* of efficiency, effectiveness, and productivity can be determined.

Supporting these three main functions there are, of course, a host of other activities. One general support activity, however, is particularly important and is that given by the office and administrative support systems. A moment's thought will indicate that in any particular functional activity it is likely that only a minority of the people employed there will actually have any expertise in that particular function. The main expertise of employees in these three main functions, as well as other functions, will be in processing information with the various information processing machines that are at hand: the telephone, the copier, and the typewriter.

Accounting. The third business function is the monitoring of the success or failure of the various products. This is carried out by the accounting function: all the costs of running the business are accounted for and set against all the income from the business activities. Based on this information various reports are prepared and actions taken if and when necessary.

We have so far discussed a simple representation of the business. It is now time to develop this idea further.

Production

Before the 1750s the production of goods was based on specialized domestic outworking. From the 1750s onward, especially in the textile industry, various people (Hargreaves, Arkwright, and Crompton, in particular) started to invent machines that speeded up the production process and simultaneously introduced uniformity into the manufacturing process. In 1785 Cartwright's invention of the power loom started a trend whereby rather than taking work to the workers, the workers had to come to where the work was. This was because the machines were expensive (and so could not be afforded by the majority of outworkers who had little capital) and depended on being driven by power sources (rivers) that could not be easily moved. And so the factory system started.

The advent of centralized and expensive equipment meant that in order to achieve a full financial return, planning and control to an extent not seen before was necessary. This planning and control evolved over the next 200 years into production (or operations) management.

Today it is generally accepted that there are essentially three types of production processes: job, batch, and flow (although different names may be used, the ideas are the same).

Although the factory system of production was initially limited to the physical production of goods, today many production operations that are not primarily, if at all, concerned with production engineering, are conducted on a factory system—institutes of education, film making companies, and insurance companies, for example, all use factory systems.

In job production single items are produced. Job production on a big scale is associated with project work such as building a bridge or a space vehicle, or making a film, or writing a book. In any case, whether big or small, job production is concerned with bringing together all the materials and parts necessary to produce a single item.

For batch production, each operation is carried out in one step on all the items that are to be processed in a particular batch. With completion of a particular operation, all the items in a batch are then taken on to the next step in the process. Batch production techniques are often applied to the processing of data for payrolls and bank accounts, and, of course, an obvious engineering example is that of the production of microprocessors (where the batch will be the wafer of silicon).

Finally, there is flow production. Here we are dealing with input which is either actually physically continuous—oil in a refinery, for example—or which consists of so many individual yet identical items—automobiles, for example—as to be practically the same as a physically continuous stream.

Each of the different types of approach to production tends to go with a particular type of organization structure. Typical organization characteristics are shown in Illustration 3.3.

It is possible for all three types of production process to be encountered in one business; they are not mutually exclusive. In an engineering context, job production could be used for the preparation of a prototype of a new design, batch production for trial production prior to full production, and flow production for the main-line production activity. Similar arrangements could be found in almost any other kind of business.

Generally speaking, it is more likely that small-sized businesses will use job or batch production techniques rather than flow production processes since flow production implies considerable financial investment, which would normally be beyond the scope of a small business.

In a business dealing with a single product or service, life might be simple, but very few businesses are in this position. Generally, there are a range of items to produce, each requiring planning and control so that all the production resources are used efficiently. Given a certain amount of production capacity the work that is to be done must be arranged so as to achieve the most profitable turnover. This is where conflict between the production and accounting functions can arise because the volume of production is not necessarily related to profit. It is too easy to increase production of an unprofitable but high-demand item. From the production viewpoint it is desirable, of course, to keep to long-time sequences of doing the same thing so as to minimize the amount of time spent setting up and closing down a particular production activity.

Marketing

Marketing is concerned with identifying, enlarging, and satisfying the demand for the goods and services output by a business.

Marketing has developed since the 1950s with increased business competition arising from better communication and transportation, meaning that the earlier marketing strategy of making items because they could always be sold has had to be replaced by one where the needs of the customer have to

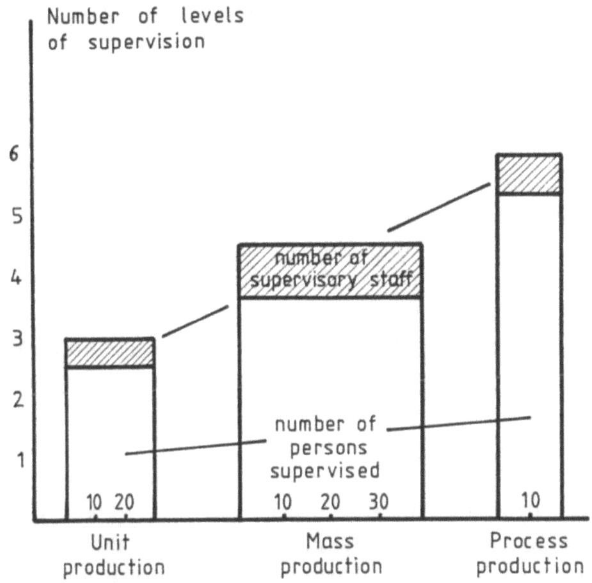

Illustration 3.3. Typical characteristics of operations organization

Operations type	Unit	Mass	Process
Number made	1	Many	Continuous
Number of levels of authority	3	4	6
Number of persons controlled	25	45	15
Percent of supervisory staff	4	6	11

Although Woodward's work (Woodward, 1970), which this illustration is based upon, was carried out on engineering manufacturing businesses, the findings are applicable to other kinds of business.

The unit business is concerned with the individual customer order and works on a project basis. There are few levels of authority and people work in medium-sized groups with relatively few supervisory staff.

In mass production there are more levels of authority, much bigger groups of people, and more supervisors. Generally speaking, there is more organization. The greater degree of organization is needed in order to keep the operation functioning efficiently.

In process operations there are even more levels of authority and greater numbers of supervisors. This reflects the greater technically based nature of the work and the even greater need to keep the operation function efficient.

To the extent that process operations tend to reflect the more computer-based automated businesses, the process-based organization indicates the way that information technology affects business: more levels of control, more controllers, and smaller working groups.

be taken into account. Although fairly obvious common sense it is only within the past 30 or so years that marketing has really become an established function.

For most businesses, income from sales is the major source of cash. If products are not sold there will be no cash and hence, shortly afterward, no business. But it is found from experience that all products go through a life cycle consisting of a build-up to a maximum sales volume and income, followed by a decline (Illustration 3.4).

Therefore, in order to maintain or expand income, new products are constantly required in order to replace declining old products. And it is the function of marketing to establish what the new products should be, and, subsequently, how they should be promoted and distributed to customers.

For all small businesses and for those businesses concerned with job production (where the business produces individual items to meet particular customer orders) the concept of marketing, that is, providing the customer with what is required by the customer, has always been applied and is obvious common sense. However, for larger businesses dealing with flow production and mass markets, it is apparently more difficult for the business to identify what it is that the customer requires. And so it is quite common to see some large businesses get completely out of touch with customer requirements and produce what is not wanted—several American and European automobile manufacturers fall into this category—while rival companies expand or new companies are founded in order to meet actual customer requirements, e.g., Japanese automobile manufacturers, the new wave of personal computer companies.

In terms of long-range strategic planning it is also obviously necessary from the viewpoint of the senior management of a business to define the business's market orientation: What need is the business offering to satisfy for potential customers? Having identified this need and thus defined its primary objective, the methods by which the business will achieve these objectives can then be considered. In order to establish which of a range of technically possible products would be most successful, market research would be conducted to determine likely customer reactions to either hypothetical or actual test products.

Accounting

The basis of any successful business is that income is greater than outgoings. The income has to support the day-to-day running costs, the capital requirements, and payment of taxes and dividends, etc., to the government and shareholders. These financial matters can be split into two

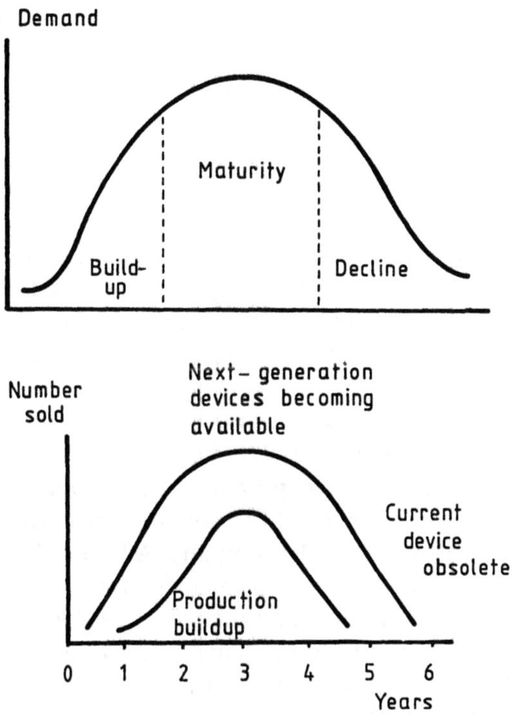

Illustration 3.4. Product life cycle

All products and services appear to go through the life cycle shown here.

The values on the time scale and degree of popularity varies from product to product. Some products are ephemeral, because of fashion, while others are long-lasting, staple food products.

However, as all products do go through a life cycle it is clearly important for a business to identify where each of its products is in the life cycle. This is the function of market research.

In addition, market research will be used to assess how well future products will perform and to help in the development of new products.

In a technical field such as microprocessor manufacture, the development of new products is primarily determined by technical drive rather than by market demand. The problem for most users is to usefully employ the computing power they already have rather than to worry about the lack of computing power that will be overcome by a forecasted tenfold increase in microprocessor power over the next ten years.

As we are interested in information technology in particular, the product life cycle for a typical microprocessor is shown.

divisions within the broad category of accounting: there is financial accounting and there is management accounting.

Financial accounting is concerned with the recording of the transactions that occur within the business and organizing their conduct so that the company's cash flows smoothly. Invariably, there are legal requirements for the production of an annual report of this aspect of the business's activities. Financial accounting is concerned with the provision of accounting information for people, such as central and local government, lenders, and stockholders, who are in some way external to the business.

The financial accountant records the occurrence of each and every transaction that the business is involved in. From this detail it is possible to determine how well the company is performing and whether it is necessary to reduce stock levels, refuse customer credit, speed up payments by outstanding customers, and so on.

Management accounting is concerned with providing people who are internal to the business—the business's managers—with accounting information relating costs and profits to products. Specifically, the management accountant's task is to relate expenditure and income to the products (goods or services) that are provided by the company. A little reflection leads one to the conclusion that it is impossible to provide figures of the *exact* expenditure on any particular product because it is simply not possible to produce accurate figures for everything—the allocation of overheads for different products can be carried in different ways depending on taste—and because there are so many items to produce figures for that the cost of such accounting would be prohibitively high. To overcome these kinds of difficulties techniques such as standard costing are introduced so that rather than looking at all the costing information, only those item costs which vary from previously set standards are investigated, thus saving much time and effort.

ORGANIZATION

The specialism of functions exists because of inherent economic advantages that accrue from specialization. But in order for these separate specialist contributions to have an effect they must be coordinated. Coordination is achieved by organization.

What Is Organization?

Organization is the way in which the people and other resources of the business are utilized to achieve the various business tasks. The utilization of people is particularly affected by the organizational structure which, as well as indicating who has what power and what authority, determines the "how" and "what" of the communication processes that are at the heart of the business.

Varieties of Organization

From even the briefest of studies of business it becomes apparent that instead of there being just one business structure there are many. Are some good and some bad? Why are they different?

Clearly, some will be good, and some will be bad. Those businesses with bad structures are those that do not do as well as they could. Besides the obvious importance of the effect of the competence of the individual persons involved, there are other reasons why there are different business structures: the size of the business, for instance. The manufacturing technology and processes used. The routineness of the tasks that the business has to deal with. These and other factors affect the business structure.

Effects of Organization

The business structure, in its turn, affects the morale, happiness, and efficiency (among other features) of the people working in the business, and it may be that to achieve a high order of morale or an efficient workforce, a structure that is appropriate on technical grounds may have to be abandoned in favor of something less technically sound. This is a lesson that should be learned early and not forgotten: people are not used best as just the filling between inflexible machine processes.

Business Size

To give this discussion of organization a bit more substance we consider various aspects of business. First, we look at business size. While the size of businesses varies from country to country the typical situation is as shown in Illustration 3.5.

It is apparent that although most businesses are small, most people work for big businesses. Although the actual numbers change for countries other than England, for which the figures of Illustration 3.5 actually apply, the same story is true. So most of us work for businesses with hundreds or thousands of co-employees, although the majority of businesses have typically no more than thirty or forty employees and often considerably less.

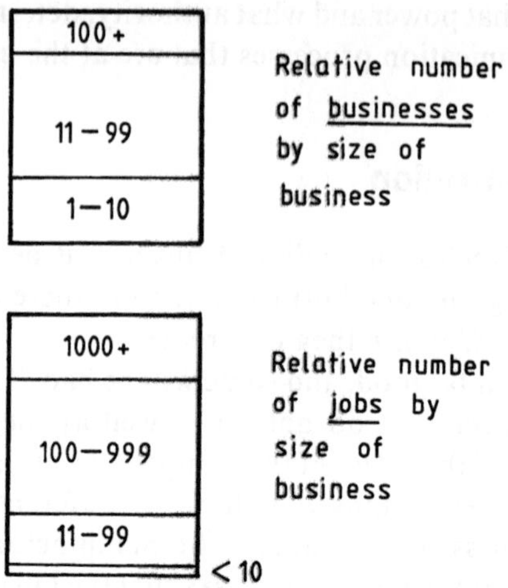

Illustration 3.5. Size of business

Average number of employees	Percent of businesses	Percent of all jobs
2000	2	35
300	15	46
35	45	17
5	38	2

Using four size categories—1-10, 11-99, 100-199, and 1,000+—it is found that most businesses are small, employing less than 100 people. Businesses of this type account for 83% of all businesses.

However, when we look at the number of jobs rather than the number of businesses, we find that most jobs are in big businesses. Businesses with 100+ employees employ 81% of the work force.

Why are some businesses very large while others are small? The reasons for these different sizes stem from the balance between the advantages and disadvantages of size and the type of business that is being pursued. The advantages of being big are: special production machines and improved processes together with division and specialization of labor at all levels. Finance is cheaper and more readily available. Acquisition of stock is cheaper. Top-level managers can be afforded.

The disadvantages of being big are that shareholding and management become separated, legal requirements become more stringent, and flexibility and adaptability are often lost.

The advantages of being small are personal involvement, control, and reward. The disadvantages are limited resources and less legal protection.

When considering real businesses we will have to distinguish between large and small businesses as they will have different kinds of information processing problems to deal with. For big businesses there is the problem that managers of resources are, at least in a psychological sense and perhaps even literally, remote from the resources that they have to control.

Problems of Growth

There is a tendency for businesses to grow in size. This means that in addition to the problems of pure size, there is often a problem of growth to deal with. Managers have to accommodate themselves to a situation where their life is getting increasingly difficult as they have to face increasingly more complex problems caused by the growth in business size (Illustration 3.6).

We will complete this section by dealing with a concrete, although imaginary, example. We will imagine the development of a business starting with one person.

Consisting of a single person business life is at least simple, in some ways. There are no problems of division of labor and responsibility to deal with. One person does everything: gets and pays for the raw materials used, makes and provides the products and services, sells the products, writes the bills, and so on. On the other hand, life is clearly hectic: there are a whole range of others to deal with—suppliers, customers, and government agencies, and the one-person business has to be able to deal with them all. Of course, almost nobody works completely by themselves, and even the one-man business will use the specialist services of others—legal advisers and accountants, for example—from time to time.

With success comes business growth—a second person will be employed and business life will never again be the same as it was, it will never again be so simple. Clearly, with two people in the business, it has to be decided, Who is going to do what? Are both people going to do everything that there is to be done or will there be some degree of specialization, some division of work? Inevitably each of the two people will do different work, even in the most equal of businesses. Specialization appears. Each of the two will have slightly different functions and in order for it to be clear who is doing what, there will have to be communication between the two people.

Communication is the dramatically new factor.

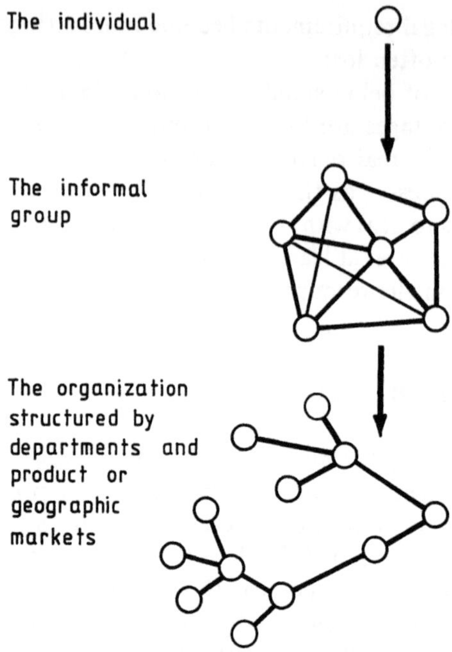

Illustration 3.6. Problems of growth of business size

As organizations grow in size they tend to develop from the informal entrepreneurial grouping of nearly everyone talking and communicating with everyone else, to a formally centralized structure with functional responsibilities, which in its turn develops into a formally decentralized structure. The decentralization will be based on the market requirements of either a product or a geographic area.

For the individual in the small business, there are few communication and organization problems. Probably the major difficulty will arise from forgetting information because of a lack of formal information systems.

As the business grows, communication and organization problems develop. These may be problems caused by the sheer size of the business, preventing information from getting from one part to another.

Certainly managers who have grown with the company will likely find difficulties arising from their changing roles. No longer will they be concerned with the immediate day-to-day activities, for these will be delegated to lower levels of management. Now the prime concern of higher management will be with longer-term strategic thinking and planning. Specialization of labor which occurs everywhere also affects management.

There is a tendency for there to be a hierarchy of management problems, with the problems being described in terms of their intrinsic nature and the time scale that is available to handle them in. Typically, at the top of the organization, managers have to decide what resources to have, and these kinds of decisions have to be made on an irregular basis for a long time ahead. At the other end of the management hierarchy, the problems are how to use the resources available. These decisions have to be made periodically, every Monday morning, for example; they have to be solved in real time, that is, *now,* and they have to be solved quickly.

COMMUNICATION

With just two people the specialization can be quite slight although it may be very marked, as with the difference between boss and secretary. Either way, with just two people, the communication process can be relatively free and easy. The two will probably just chat to each other as and when the need arises. However, this informal process cannot be kept up as the business continues to expand.

Communication and Chaos

If, as more and more people came to work for the business, the informal direct contact between individuals was allowed to continue, chaos rather than organization would ensue (Illustration 3.7).

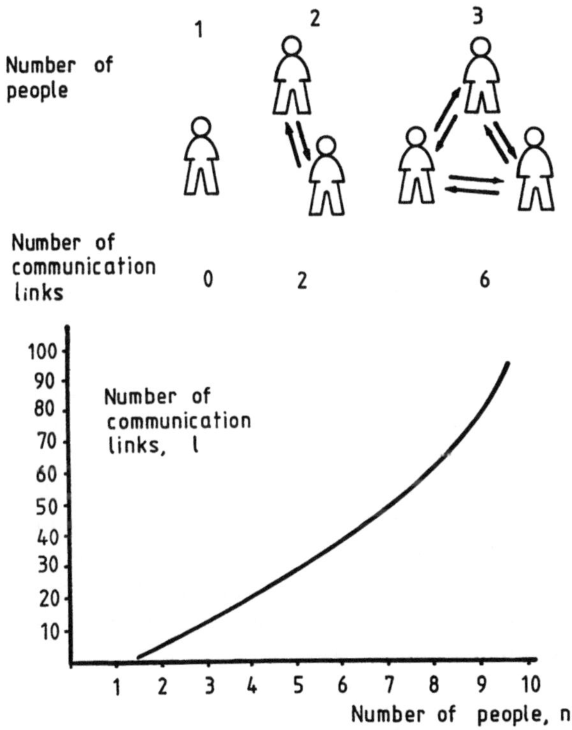

Illustration 3.7. Fully interconnected communication networks

The relationship between the number of people in an organization and the number of potential communication links that could be made is such that, as organizations grow in size, the addition of one extra person increases the number of potential communication links enormously.

	Number of people			
	1	2	3	4
Number of communication links	0	2	6	12

If each individual is involved in interactional communication, the number of communication links l is given by the relationship

$$l = n \times (n - 1) = n^2 - n$$

As n gets larger, then approximately $l = n^2$

n	n^2	$l\ (= n^2 - n)$
0	0	0
1	1	0
2	4	2
3	9	6
10	100	90
20	400	380

This is why there simply has to be organization—to prevent all time being spent on communicating rather than doing things.

Some degree of formality has to be introduced in order to allow individuals to get on with their tasks of making and producing rather than simply communicating with others. So businesses are characterized by the lack rather than by the presence of communication between people. The organization is constructed by the removal of communication links, which is discussed in Illustration 3.8.

Of course, the business organization does not simply consist of the presence or absence of communication links. It is rather a question of degree. Some communication links will be very strong with lots of communication taking place, while others will be very weak with little if any communication taking place (Illustration 3.9). Rarely, if ever, however, will there be a rule forbidding communications to occur.

Forms of Communication

As well as considering the degree of communication, there is the question of how the communication takes place and what form it takes. There are a range of possible ways of communicating information, from the very formal

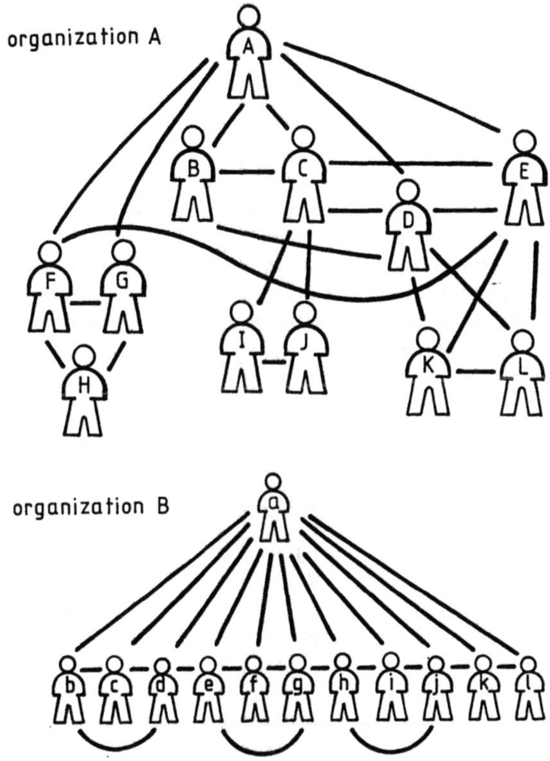

Illustration 3.8. Organization

Although there are 12 people in this organization, there are only 48 communication links instead of the theoretically possible 120.

Of course, different organizational arrangements can be made that will either increase or decrease the number of communication links. But different organizational arrangements can be made with the same number of communication links.

However, the simple counting either of the number of employees or of the number of communication links is not enough. To gain an insight into how the organization works, some idea of the degree of centralization is required. Organization A has a completely different method of working compared to Organization B. Different organizational structures have different effects upon morale, happiness, and efficiency. Some of these structures will clearly be good, others bad. Even with good structures, there is variation dependent on business size, the operations technology being used, and the kind of people working in the organization.

The difference between the shape of the two organizational structures shown here can be expressed numerically by the control ratio, where

$$\text{Control ratio} = \frac{\text{Number of (superiors/subordinates)}}{\text{Number of employees} - 1}$$

Note that everyone except the boss at the top has one, and only one superior. The initial relationship for the control ratio can then be simplified to

$$\text{Control ratio} = \frac{1}{\text{number of superiors}}$$

which, for A, gives a control ratio of 0.16 and for B a value of 1.

For ease of illustration the 48 communication links have been shown as 24 two-way links rather than 48 one-way links.

For Organization B the calculation of the control ratio is achieved by identifying the superiors. In addition, just to confirm the agreement between the two possible methods for calculating the ratio, the details of the calculation of the first method is shown below.

Superiors	Subordinates	Number of subordinates
A	B,C,D,E,G	5
B	F	1
C	I,J	2
D	K	1
E	L	1
F	H	1
6		11

printed document to the informal raising of an eyebrow. There are various factors that affect this aspect including how far apart the communicators are (Illustration 3.10) and what kind of people are involved in the communication processes. Different organizations will emerge depending on what mode of communication is being studied (Illustration 3.11).

The Communications Gap

In the early and mid-sixties work was carried out in identifying the "communications gap" that illustrates well the problems involved in running an organization. The idea is to establish within a business how well each level perceives itself to be communicating with another. The picture that invariably emerges is that people at each level say their superiors do not understand their problems well, while simultaneously they say they understand their subordinates' problems well (Illustration 3.12).

EXERCISE

Many readers may have no appreciation of the problems facing a business manager. In order to partially overcome this problem, a listing of a computer program that carries out a business simulation is provided below in which the reader has to take on the role of being a manager.

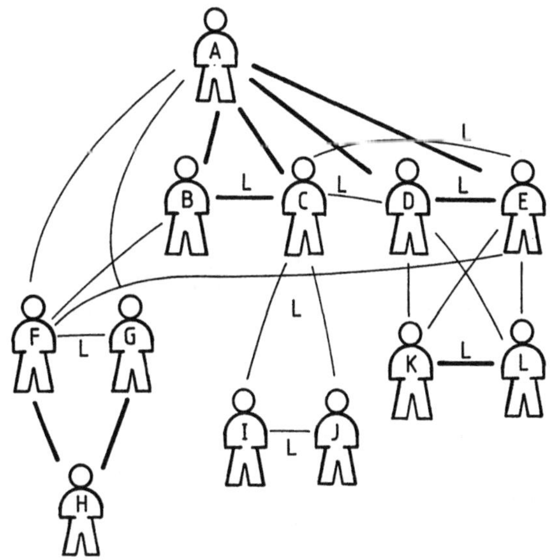

Illustration 3.9. Analysis of organizational communication

Number of communication links = 48. Control ratio = 0.16

Thickness of line indicates the amount of communication. Compare with 3.8.

Sixteen of the forty-eight communication links are lateral, marked with an L. These represent the transfer of information between people at the same level of authority and are therefore not command instructions. Most of the communications occur between the small group at the top, A, B, C, D, and E.

The low control ratio might be thought to automatically mean a relatively small degree of management control from the top. However, analysis of the volume of communications shows that four out of the seven high-volume communication links are from the group leader to her four subordinates. This might suggest a picture of a high degree of central control with relatively little lateral coordination occurring. For example, perhaps a particular project or emergency is being dealt with that requires a high volume of high-level discussion.

It is always dangerous to use only one tool to analyze an organization with.

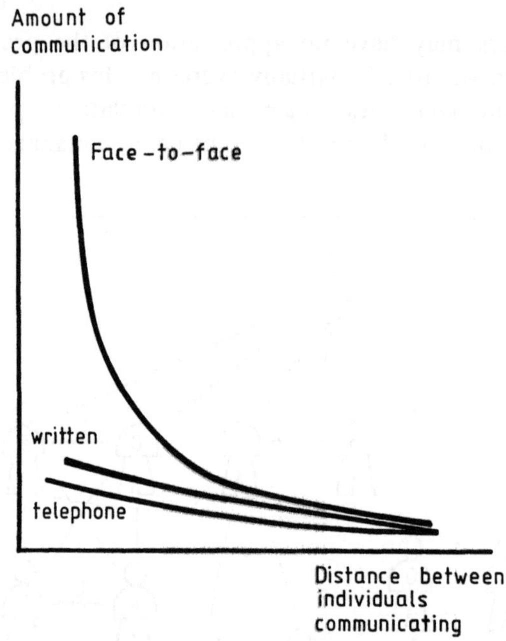

Illustration 3.10. The effect of distance on modes of communication

It is apparent that face-to-face communication is predominant over short distances, but as the separation distance increases the total amount of communication decreases and face-to-face communication then is no more popular than any other method.

The popularity of different methods of communication depends, of course, on the methods available. For most businesses, face-to-face communication is easier over short distances. But the culture of the organization also has a strong effect. People working within a bureaucratic organization will rely more on symbolic, written communication.

Communication survey results, such as those shown here, only record the number of communications occurring, not their duration nor their importance.

Required Decisions

For each month of the simulation the player will have to make three decisions:

(i) how much to spend on advertising;
(ii) how many items to make; and
(iii) what price to sell at.

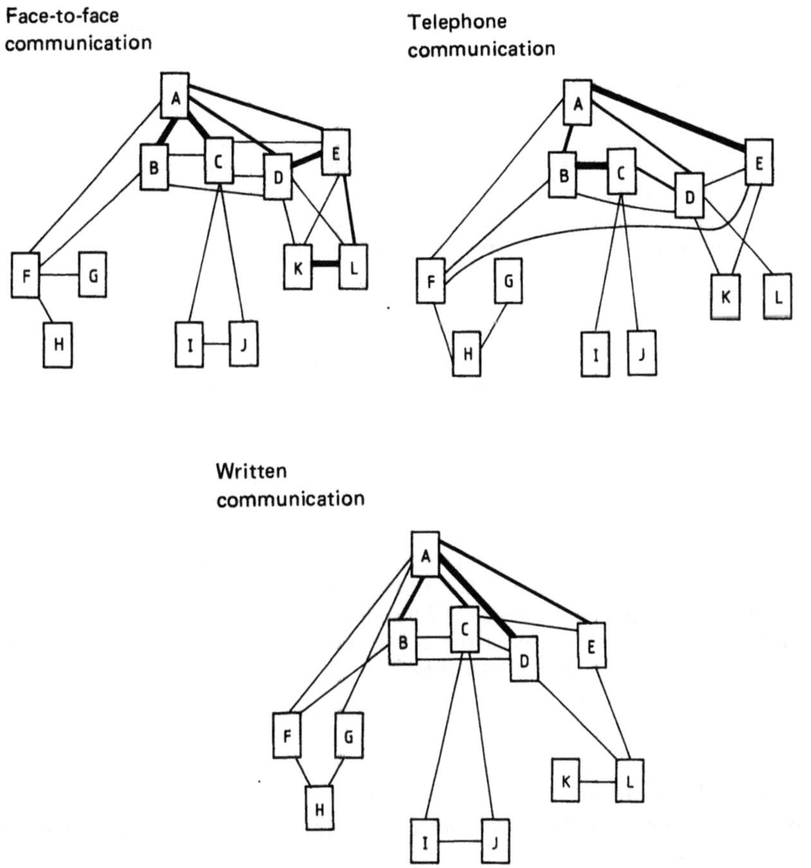

Illustration 3.11. Variation of amount of communication with communication mode

The type and degree of communication does not depend solely on distance between the communicators. Here the number of communications between different individuals are shown. For example, although D and E have strong face-to-face contact between themselves, A prefers telephone contact with E and written contact with D. Separating the total communications record into its components may reveal very different types of organization.

Clearly, in this case, face-to-face contact is preferred overall as the means of communication.

Illustration 3.12. The communications gap

Mann and Revans were two among several people who in the early 1960s investigated the "communications gap." The communications gap (see Handy, 1976 and Revans, 1965) refers to the difference between how subordinates assess their superiors' understanding of their problems and how superiors themselves assess their own understanding of their subordinates' problems. There is a considerable difference! By multiplying the values of understanding at different levels together, a measure of communication transparency can be formed. It appears that most people at the top of the organization think that they know the problems at the bottom while most people at the bottom consider that their bosses have little idea of what their real problems are [see Mann (1961) and Revans (1965)].

Level	Percent of subordinates that say superiors understand	Percent of superiors that say they understand subordinates
1	28–35	
2	43–51	88–95
3	59–60	90–94

Multiplying these figures together produces an upward understanding of between $(28 \times 43 \times 59 =)$ 7% and $(35 \times 51 \times 60 =)$ 11%. The downward understanding is not better than between $(100 \times 90 \times 88 =)$ 79% and $(100 \times 94 \times 95 =)$ 89%. No one knows which, if any, of these figures is true, but the fact that differences of opinion exist suggests that there is a communications gap of some kind.

These decisions are conveyed by typing in the appropriate numbers one by one, checking that they are correct and then pressing the ENTER key.

Objectives

The idea presumably is to make more money and expand the company. If there is enough money available, more production machines can be bought.

However, no one can say what the best decisions are because there is an element of randomness built into the game. It is extremely unlikely that any two people will ever face exactly the same decision situation. Also, what the best decision is depends on who is making the judgment; this reflects the problems that can be encountered when dealing with quasi-subjective measurements like effectiveness.

In general, however, it can be seen that for each decision there is an optimum value. If you do not spend enough on advertising you will be left with unsold items. If you spend too much you will just be spending money unnecessarily. If you operate your machine(s) at too high an output level there is a danger of the machinery breaking down and your losing output. If you underutilize your machinery your per unit manufacturing costs will be too high. If you offer your items for sale at too low a price you will be losing revenue. If you try to sell them at too high a price you will be left with stock in the warehouse.

Constraints

Surrounding these considerations there are some real constraints. Generally you cannot spend more on advertising than you have as cash in hand. There is an exception to this rule that occurs if the business runs up a negative bank balance. In this case the limit on advertising expenditure is £2000 per month. The operation of this limitation shows quite effectively the problems that a business can get into and how difficult it can be to get out. You cannot make more than 1000 units per machine. The more units that are made on a machine the more likely it is that it will break down or suffer from other technical problems that will cut production output.

You can offer items for sale at any price that you like. However, even when sold, payment may not always be forthcoming because of bad debts or slow payers. There is nothing that can be done about this aspect of the business in this game. The price of raw materials will fluctuate and again there is nothing that can be done. Unsold products are automatically warehoused, they cannot be dumped, but they may be sold later if demand is sufficiently high.

Although running the business may appear to be simple, beware! Unless you have a real understanding of what is going on, it is very easy to turn what appears to be a very successful business almost overnight into bankruptcy. (There is actually no limit applied to the amount of money that can be borrowed, but the reader is advised to call a halt when debts go above -£50,000.)

Just playing the game solitaire will give some idea of the kinds of problems that managers running businesses have to deal with. Probably the most valuable lesson to be learned will be that in the real world, unlike the school world, there is no absolutely right or wrong decision, just some that are better and some that are worse. Clearly going bankrupt is not so good as staying in business, but then how much profit could be made? Could the business be doing better?

Communication with Other People

The simulation can be made to be more realistic by having several persons rather than just one making decisions. One person could take on the task of deciding what price to sell the units at, while another decides how many to make. In order for sensible decisions to be made, how much communication between the two is necessary? How do they come to a mutual agreement, or is it necessary for someone else to make a decision for them and tell them what is going to be done, after they have presented their arguments? These are all important questions that have to be dealt with when running a business.

A Business Simulation Program

```
1 REM (c) Andrew Doswell, 1983.
2 REM This program is written in BASIC.
3 REM The BASIC is compatible with both Microsoft
and Sinclair
1000 LET month=0: LET machines =1: LET money = 9900:
LET stock = 0
1001 LET sales = 1000: LET oldprice = 12: LET
y$="y": LET adv =3000
1002 LET price = 0: LET prod = 0
1999 LET r = 1 - RND
2000 PRINT "Month "; month ;" you have"
2010 PRINT "Money $ ";money
2020 PRINT "Machines "; machines
2030 PRINT "Stock ";stock
2035 PRINT: PRINT
2040 PRINT "Last month you sold ";sales;" at £ ";
oldprice;" and the advertising cost was $ ";adv
3000 LET month=month+1
3005 IF month<2 THEN GO TO 3030
3010 INPUT "Type in y if you want another go";y$
3020 IF y$<>"y" THEN GO TO 5000
3030 IF money < 10000 THEN GO TO 3070
3035 INPUT "Type in y if you want another machine";y$
3040 IF y$<>"y" THEN GO TO 3070
3050 LET machines=machines+1
3060 LET money=money-10000
3070 PRINT "Type in values for Advertising budget,
Production level, and Selling price."
3074 INPUT adv,prod,price
```

```
3080 LET prod=INT (prod)
3090 IF prod <1 THEN PRINT "Sorry you must produce
something!"
3095 IF money ≤0 AND adv > 2000 THEN PRINT "Bank
manager won't allow ad. budget!!"
3100 IF money > 0 THEN IF adv > money THEN PRINT "Ad.
budget too big!!!"
3200 IF prod > 1000*machines THEN PRINT "Can't make
this many!!!!"
3201 IF prod < 1 THEN GOTO 3070
3202 IF money ≤0 AND adv > money THEN GOTO 3070
3203 IF money > 0 AND adv > money THEN GOTO 3070
3204 IF prod > 1000*machines THEN GOTO 3070
3205 IF prod/(machines*1000) > (1.95-r) THEN GOSUB
4800
3206 IF r < machines/(machines+9) THEN GOSUB 4800
4000 LET sales = ((prod/(100*machines))*(sales/
(2+r))*(old price/price))
4001 LET sales = INT (sales 3*(14/price) 3*(adv/
(prod+stock)))
4010 IF sales > (prod+stock) THEN LET sales =
(prod+stock)
4400 LET stock = stock+prod-sales
4600 LET money = int (money - 4000 - stock*5 -machines
*2000 - adv + r * sales * price)
4610 LET oldprice=price
4700 GOTO 1999
4800 PRINT "Technical problems reduce production!"
4805 LET prod = int ((1-r)*prod)
4810 RETURN
5000 STOP
```

SUMMARY

What Is a Business?

A business is an activity system concerned with the production of goods or services. This production is carried out through three major functions: production operations, marketing, and accounting. All of these major functions are supported by the general office and administrative support functions.

Differences and Similarities between Businesses

Although there are many features that are common to different businesses, there are also many differences that are determined not only by the size of the business and the sector that it is in but also by the nature of the particular individuals who work in that particular business.

Success and Communication

All successful businesses have to cope with the problems of success. The major problem is that of communication. Business organization structure can be seen essentially as the removal of some of the potential communication links. However, communication is not something that is either present or absent. It is present to different degrees between individuals depending on their needs and positions within the business structure. Additionally, the amount of communication between two individuals will vary with the type of communication mode being considered. The amount of written communication between two individuals may, for example, be totally different from the amount of spoken communication between them.

Management Information

Although this book is concerned with the business application of information technology in production processes and in products as well as the use of information technology in management information systems, clearly the use of information technology to help in the management of a business is of major importance. To this end the computer-based management simulation exercise was included at the end of this chapter. As well as providing some inkling of the problems that face a manager of a business, it is hoped that the exercise will have illustrated some of the inflexibilities and drawbacks of a computer-based information system. While running the exercise many questions may come to mind concerning the fluctuations in income, the cost of storage, etc. These questions, however, will have to remain unanswered because the system was not designed to provide this information.

Dependence on Expertise

It is never too early to learn that in using computer-based information technology information systems, the user is restricted to what the information analyst decides should be provided. In the analyst's defense the prospective user should develop some of his or her own expertise in the form of asking pertinent questions.

DISCUSSION QUESTIONS

1. How can it be that in almost any organization the heads of different departments will have different and possibly opposite views as to what is the best way to achieve success for the organization? (Remember that as businesses grow in size and complexity areas of functional specialism appear.)

2. Illustrations 3.10 onward show that there are different preferred methods of communication between different people. What is the implication of this finding for the use of a standardized computer-based communication system?

3. (Try this question after running the business simulation.) What are the technical problems of running a business? How are these problems exacerbated by the need for different managers to communicate their aims and decisions to other decision makers rather than simply being able to take and execute all decisions themselves?

4

INFORMATION, DECISIONS, PRODUCTS, AND PROCESSES

INTRODUCTION

The Study of Information

Naturally, it is only when things present us with problems that we study them. Science—as we understand it today—did not emerge until the 15th century; economics did not appear until the 18th century; and the study of information, semiotics, has really only started to appear in the latter half of this century.

Why has the study of information taken so long to become established? After all, both economics and science, together with everything else, involves the processing of information, and surely there must have been information problems encountered in the 15th and 18th centuries? The answer seems to be that until very recently all information processing was done on a small, familiar, human scale, and this smallness and humanity prevented people from seeing and recognizing the information processing problems for what they were.

> We take information for granted... Problems about information—its nature, the processes whereby it is communicated and stored, and the ways in which it reveals its meaning, are regarded as either technical problems for the telephone engineer, or philosophical problems having little to do with practical matters. This is a mistaken view. There is little we can do without information. There is no organisation controlling the flows of materials and energy, or the work of people and machines, which does not make elaborate use of information; so why has its study been neglected? One reason is that, until recently, information has presented us with few technical difficulties. Until the days of the telegraph, communication was always either direct over short distances, or by some physical form of transport over longer distances, and therefore if the physical problems of contact or transport could be solved, problems of transferring information took care of themselves. Until the computer came along there existed no creature or machine which could seriously challenge the ability of a human being to handle information. It is also true that, until recently, cooperative human endeavour has been on a small scale, or very simple or slow, these limitations being imposed by the speeds at which physical communication could be accomplished.
>
> The kind of world we live in today probably owes more to our newly found ability to transmit information accurately by electromagnetic impulses at the speed of light, rather than by messenger at the speed of a horse or steam locomotive, than to any other innovation. We are at last being forced, by the way our society is developing, to make a thorough study of information. (Stamper, 1973)

The Difficulties of Communication

To repeat the point made by Stamper, until the advent of electromagnetism, communication with others had to involve either a short-distance direct communication whereby you walked to someone and then talked to them face-to-face, or a long-distance physical transportation, perhaps employing messengers carrying pieces of knotted string or rolls of parchment. In either case the transmission process was on a human scale and of human dimensions. The tools used were human operated.

Because of the lengths of time that would have been involved in long-distance communication, much communication was simply not carried out. Large businesses operating in a coordinated manner in large international markets simply did not exist. Illustration 4.1 gives some idea of transmission times and how they have altered.

Technological developments have altered the scale of things so that many things are now possible. But, of course, just because things are technically possible does not make them humanly necessary or desirable.

In any case, to discover what business can now, and will likely be able to do in the future, we need to know what information is and what it is used for.

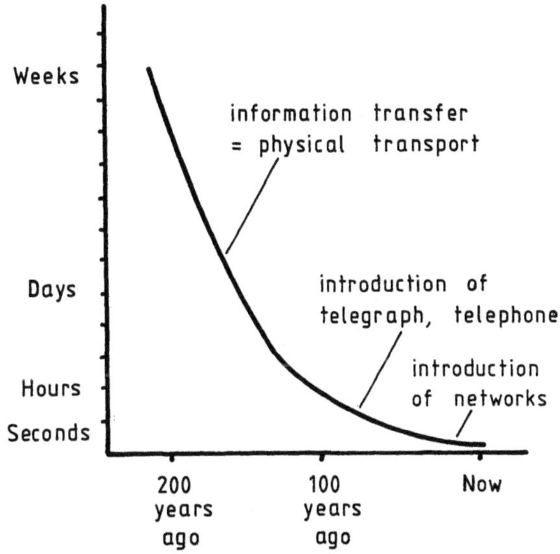

Illustration 4.1. The time taken to transmit information

The graph shows typical values for information transmission times over the past 200 years. The values are for a particular country, Great Britain, and so can only be approximations for any other country, but they are reasonably typical for any industrialized nation.

An important point to note is the difference between the physical transportation of information, which until the 1840s was effectively the only way to transmit information, and the more recent telecommunications of information.

Because of the reliance on the physical transportation of information some 200 years ago Glasgow, which is 500 miles away from London, was some 10 to 15 days away in terms of normal communication methods. Clearly the two cities were to a large extent decoupled from each other. Many of the things that happened in London had no effect in Glasgow simply because of the time it took information to be communicated. This decoupling also applied, only even more so, to communications between countries. Regular communication between Britain and the U.S.A. took two to three months.

Running a multinational business would have simply been impossible in terms that we use today. In communication terms nowhere in our solar system need now be as far away as Glasgow was from London.

Today in order to get two to three months away in terms of telecommunication time, it would be necessary to be well on the way to Alpha Proxima, the nearest star outside our solar system.

SEMIOTICS

The study of information is called semiotics. The basic proposition of semiotics is that information is made up from signs. The modern foundations of semiotics were laid by the American Charles S. Pierce (1839–1914) who, among other achievements, realized the potential of using simple electric circuits to represent the ideas behind simple words such as "and" and "or." Although the ideas of "and" or "or" are simple, they are also powerful. In fact, the terms "AND" and "OR" are the foundation of today's electronic computer.

As soon as we start using electronic currents and voltages to represent "ideas," then obviously we are talking about the use of signs (or signals, if you prefer) to represent information. Using the word "sign" as a substitute for the word "information" makes it easier to study and understand information. No one is bothered about questions such as: How well do the signs work in conveying instructions? How quickly can the signs be generated, remembered, taught? How cheaply can the signs be stored, transmitted and so on? whereas similar questions with the word "information" being used instead not only cause some people's minds to go blank but also lead to the generation of various information experts who all seem to find it necessary to speak in the peculiar jargons of applied social science.

Signs have a variety of characteristics, some of which are dealt with in Illustration 4.2.

Social Context of Signs

Concentrating on a study of signs, as opposed to information, it comes as no surprise that different signs work in different ways in different settings. The social and cultural environment surrounding signs are important in determining the effect of signs. It simply is not possible to sensibly discuss the technical aspects of sign manipulation without taking into account the human setting of the signs.

The emphasis on the machine aspects of information processing makes it too easy to forget that business information processing rests fundamentally on the resolution of conflicting human judgments. In the end, only humans decide. Computers are there to do what they are told.

Undue Formalism

Overemphasis on the computer aspects of processing signs tends to lead to an overemphasis on the formal, symbolic side of signs:

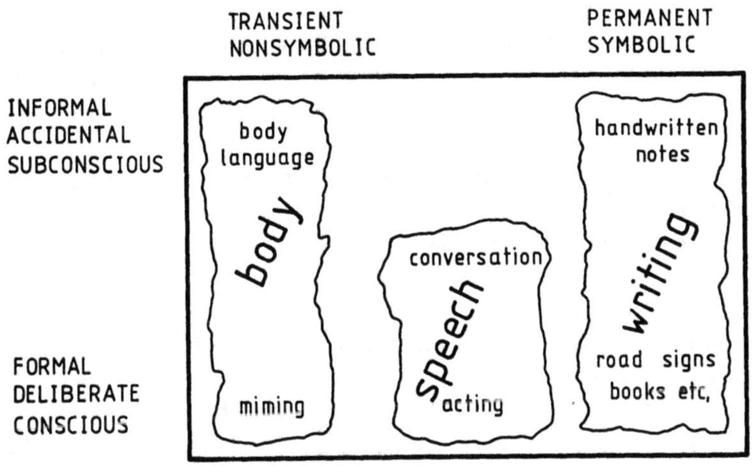

Illustration 4.2. Some characteristics of signs

One way to analyze signs is in terms of their transience or permanence. This aspect of signs is shown along the top of the drawing. Additionally, signs can be looked at in terms of their informality or formality. Formal signs tend to be permanent, while informal signs tend to be transient. Although transient informal signs can be powerful—a smile, for example, may only be brief, but it can create a lasting impression. A textbook may be fairly permanent, but it may have little effect.

The location of the signs in the diagram is not precise. There may be considerable variation in the degree of formality, for example of a conversation.

There are other properties that can be used to analyze and characterize signs: accuracy and precision, for example.

> The information specialist . . . is very likely to exaggerate the importance of written information compared with face-to-face conversation, and ignore the messages which are transmitted nonverbally. (Stamper, 1973)

As long as we remember that information and information processing are simply concerned with handling signs and signals, then it will be possible to retain a balanced view of business information technology.

THE PROPERTIES OF SIGNS

As indicated above in Illustration 4.2, signs have various characteristics. Of particular importance in business are the properties of form and accuracy.

Form

Signs come in a variety of forms, but particularly important are numeric signs. Numeric information is important for three reasons, the first two of which are connected with the managerial and administrative side of information processing:

First, numbers are used by accountants as the primary method of conveying information concerning how well the business is performing, and financial performance and financial criteria often predominate when making business decisions.

Second, numbers are important because they were the door through which computers, and hence, by current definition, information technology, slipped into business life.

Finally, the machines that we use that are the products of business invariably are designed and constructed by people—engineers and designers—who have a numeric background. These people are numerically literate—they are numerate.

Because of this underswell of numbers, it is sometimes thought that computers and information technology in general are concerned solely with numbers. The truth, of course, could hardly be more different. The machines of information technology are indifferent as to whether they are handling numbers or letters, and the letters could just as easily be English or Chinese.

Pulses, not Numbers

What computers actually handle are electronic pulses, not numbers. But because of their feelings of innumeracy many people build up a barrier convincing themselves that information technology is too difficult. Because of this, there is a great temptation to surrender to the "expert" who designs and builds inflexible juggernauts of information systems rather than building information systems that actually help people in the business.

Quantification of Opinions

It is important to realize that much of the information that we use in a numeric form is simply quantified opinion. This is clearly true for statements that relate to the future, for example, a sales forecast. A sales forecast is just an opinion no matter how sophisticated the technique used for constructing it. But many statements about the past are also quantified opinions. For example, the value of a company is an opinion, expressed perhaps according to some convention, but none the less an opinion rather than an objective fact. This arrangement of quantifying opinions and treating them as if they were objective facts is perfectly satisfactory as long as the differences between the two are recognized. However, there can be trouble when a quantified opinion is turned into a numerical reality.

Accuracy and Precision

Accuracy is not precision. Precision relates to the amount of detail provided. A lot of detail corresponds to high precision, but high precision does not necessarily, in information terms, correspond to high accuracy. I could supply precise details of someone's height, weight, and age, and be totally wrong in every detail (Illustration 4.3).

The achievement of accuracy and precision consumes resources, particularly money. Information, therefore, should not be provided either more accurately or more precisely than is needed. And, of course, it is nonsensical to provide precision that is not founded on accuracy.

When information is transmitted it is possible for corruptions to creep in and destroy the original accuracy. This form of corruption is shown by the message "Send reinforcements, we're going to advance" being changed in transmission from one person to another to "Send three or four pence, we're going to a dance". This kind of corruption can be combatted by sending more information than is actually necessary. Normal written and spoken language is full of redundancy as this following example, in which some of the letters in the text have been removed, shows:

> N+t s+ the +ptical character rec+gniti+n c+mputer—it scans every detail +f the text, and in the pr+cess is very easily f++led by ink bl+bs, misprints, and +ther min+r irritants. Ch+ng+ th+ f+++nt +nd th+ c+mp+t+r m+st r+c++v+ +r l++rn + n+w l+br+ry +f ch+r+ct+r f++t+r+s. (Dale and Williamson, 1980)

Redundancy of Information

The built-in excess of signs is called redundancy. Many, possibly most, signs are redundant, not needed, most of the time. They are useful, however, should anything happen to some of the text for then they can be used as clues in order to help decide what the information was originally. In computer and telecommunications technology there are various techniques used to guard against signs being changed accidentally, and although these guards may sometimes fail—it is difficult to guard against the total failure of everything—most of the time accuracy will be maintained.

Illustration 4.3. Accuracy and precision

	Precise	Accurate	Accurate and precise
Height	5′ 2″	About 6′	5′ 11″
Weight	100.73 lb	About 160 lb	157.3 lb
Age	57 yr 3 mo 2 days	About 40	37 yr 7 mo

The three columns are intended to show the difference between precision and accuracy. Precise information contains detail. Accurate information is correct. Precise information may be wrong. In many cases high precision is not required since the information is constantly changing. In this example, while height is a fairly stable fact, weight may vary considerably and age is increasing continuously. Accurate precision about weight and age may well be unnecessary.

DECISIONS

We use information to make decisions concerning our environment. Our decisions are shown by the actions and reactions that we make (Illustration 4.4).

The decisions our ancestors in prehistory had to make may have been

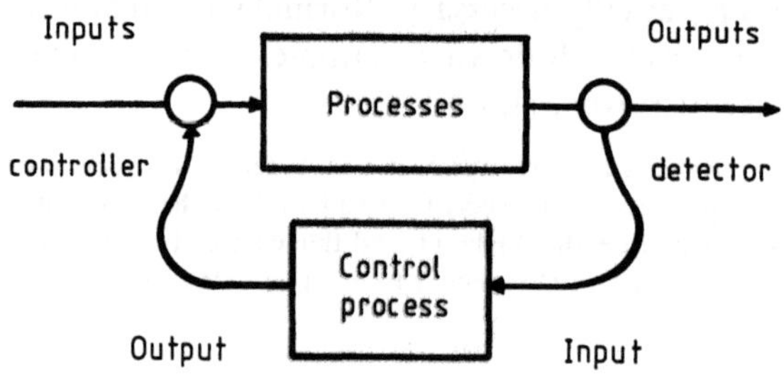

Illustration 4.4. The decision making and action taking sequence

A most important concept that will reappear several times under different guises in this book is the control loop.

The concept of the activity system has already been established. Almost every activity effects its own inputs, although the relationship is not often so direct as the control loop shown above. The control loop is simply a special form of activity where the output product reacts directly on the inputs into the activity, and so immediately effects the output itself. Examples of this are legion: driving a car has several information inputs to the driver who can make appropriate changes to speed and direction. A business example would be the function of marketing research in altering the products of a business.

fairly uncomplicated by today's standards: "Should I run away from this sabre-tooth tiger?" or "Should I stay and be eaten by it?"—clearly our ancestors made the correct choice—but they display all the characteristics of any decision making situation. There are courses of action we have to choose from, and there are the corresponding results of those various choices.

However, just because we make a particular choice does not mean that a particular result must occur. Choosing to run away from the sabre-tooth tiger does not guarantee that we will not run straight into the open jaws of another one around the next rock, nor, for example, does choosing to have a barbecue guarantee good weather (O, that it were so!).

There may be a large number of potential outcomes, many of which we will be able to avoid should we want to, but rarely are we able to guarantee the result of a particular choice that we make.

These and other points concerning decision making are dealt with in Illustration 4.5.

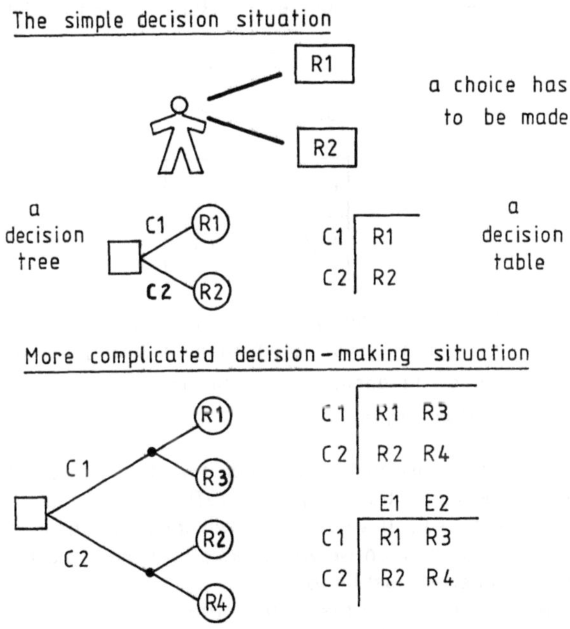

Illustration 4.5. Decision making

It is a characteristic of life that we are faced with choices, C_1 and C_2 in this case. Each possible course of action will lead to a reward of some kind, R_1 and R_2.

The initial drawing can be formalized into a tree or a table.

Generally, things are never so simple as a straight choice between R_1 and R_2.

We are not normally quite sure what will happen if we choose to do something. Suppose we choose to do C_1, then either we will get R_1 or we will get R_3, but we do not know which.

Similarly, if we choose to do C_2, then either we will get R_2 or R_4. As long as all of the rewards are nice, life is still not too difficult. However, suppose we want R_1 but certainly do not want R_3. Would it be better to choose C_1 and hope that we get R_1? Or would it be better to do C_2 and so definitely avoid R_3?

There are a variety of rules for helping us to decide which course of action to take, provided that the value of the rewards R_1 to R_4 can be expressed numerically. Although many things can be expressed in numerical terms, profit and loss, for example, not everything can. How would we feel about having to choose between C_1 and C_2 if R_1 represented a big profit while R_3 represented loss of life due to a dangerous production process? In this case putting a numeric value on R_3 means putting a financial value on life, something that many people find morally unacceptable.

The various potential rewards associated with a particular course of action are allocated to various states of the environment (E).

Generally, we do not know what the state of the environment will be. All we can do is guess how likely some particular state will be. These guesses are converted into estimations of probability of occurence. From this complete table the likely value of taking different courses of action can be calculated.

WEATHER IS:

	Good ?	Bad ?
FLY	£2000	£ 0
DRIVE	£1000	£ 1000

If the probability of bad weather is more than 50% (0·5) then it would make Financial sense to drive rather than fly

Example. Suppose that we are trying to decide whether to fly or drive from one city to another. The reason for travelling from A to B is to make a sale. If we get to B we will definitely make a sale. If we do not we will not. Additionally, if we get to B quickly enough, that is, fly, then we will be able to make two sales. So far the picture is clear, the answer must be to fly.

However, what if the weather may cause problems?

Now the first column corresponds to clear weather, the second to fog or snow or something that grounds the plane but does not stop the automobile. Clearly we would not choose to travel by plane if we knew in advance that the weather was going to ground the plane. We would drive instead. From these kind of considerations the financial value of information can be estimated so that we can determine how much we would be prepared to pay for more accurate information about future weather conditions, for example.

Information and Decision Making

Information connects with decision making because information tells us which and what decision making situation we are in. We use information to determine (i) what rewards, (ii) what environments, and (iii) what choices we are dealing with.

Although the diagrams of Illustration 4.5 may look complicated, they are only a very simple representation of the decision making process that we actually go through. In fact, the decision making model of Illustration 4.5 is most useful in showing us how little we know of our own decision making processes.

As a simple example of the difficulties that face us when we try to decide how we go about making decisions, how exactly do we measure the reward? It clearly is not simply a question of money: in many cases there will be no money involved. There are other factors involved as well.

Although the principles may be there, rarely is the decision making model of Illustration 4.5 formally invoked in making real decisions. The decision making model is only formally used in those situations where there is an important decision to be made, perhaps where a lot of money is involved, and the time and effort in establishing all the facts is justifiable. Examples of this situation would be deciding whether to launch a new product or whether to sink an oil-well test bore. Almost any book on business decision making will have a chapter dealing with this aspect of decisions.

Recognition of the Environment

For most of us most of the time, rather than trying to sort out what is the best choice we can make to deal with a somewhat uncertain environment, what we do is establish what the state of the environment is so that we can take the appropriate, predetermined, course of action.

This situation can still be represented by a decision making table, although it is somewhat modified, as can be seen in Illustration 4.6.

The modified decision table of Illustration 4.6 can also be represented as a set of written rules or procedures, perhaps as a procedure or instruction manual if there are enough rules (Illustration 4.7).

Program of Instructions

Once a firm rule exists, whether it is portrayed as a diagram or written as some text in a book, we are dealing with a situation where we are saying: *do this.* In general terms this is a program of instructions.

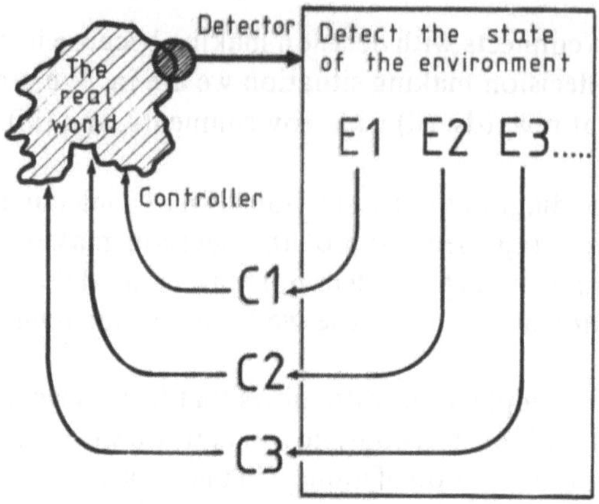

Illustration 4.6. Modified decision table

In many decision making situations we are not actually interested in discovering the best course of action. Rather we are concerned with finding out what the state of the environment is. Once we know the state of the environment, we then follow an already prescribed course of action.

Programmed Machines

Once it is possible to be certain about what is to be done, then it is possible to at least imagine having a machine take over the doing.

It is only the bounds of the knowledge and ingenuity of the designer and engineer that limits the extent to which a machine can carry out a task for us. It becomes possible, once we know what it is that we are trying to do, to build machines that will take over the whole of the decision making process from recognizing the state of the environment to implementing the correct action.

Two examples of such machines using noninformation technology are shown in Illustration 4.8.

Limitations of Machines

The rosy picture painted above of getting machines to take over tasks from us is severely limited by our technical inabilities, not to mention our poor understanding of what it is that we are actually trying to do.

Often in the real business world we are dealing with extreme uncertainty:

- we do not know what all the possible courses of action open to us are;
- we do not know what all the possible states of the environment are;

State of the environment

Are you now and have you always been a British subject ?	N	Y	Y	Y	Y	Y	Y	Y
Has your father always been / was he always a British subject ?		N	N	N	N	N	Y	Y
Is your father now a British subject ?		N	Y	Y	Y	Y		
Has your mother always been (disregarding loss of nationality due to marriage prior to 1.1.1945) a British subject ?			N	Y	Y	Y		
Are you a British citizen ?				N	N	Y	N	N
Do you undertake to become a British citizen ?					Y		N	Y
ELIGIBLE					X	X		X
NOT ELIGIBLE	X	X	X	X			X	

Allowed actions

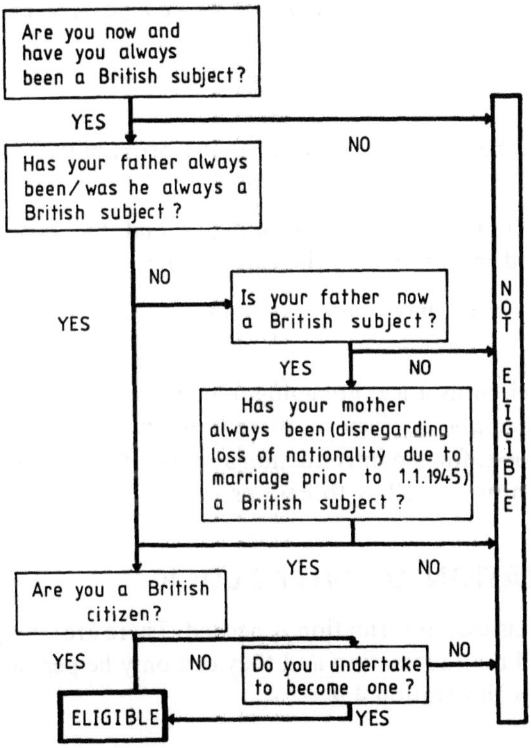

Illustration 4.7. The equivalence of procedure rules, diagrams, and tables

As an example of the different ways in which instructions can be presented, the following text describes the conditions under which a person may qualify for the British Civil Service.

(1) At all times since your birth you have been a British subject, and (2) each of your parents have always been, or (if dead) always was, a British subject, and (3) the Secretary of State is satisfied that you are so closely connected with the United Kingdom, taking into account such considerations as ancestry, upbringing and residence, that you may be properly appointed, and (4) you undertake to become a citizen of the United Kingdom and Colonies as soon as possible after your appointment if you are not already such a citizen. (5) If condition (2) is not satisfied, you may nevertheless be admitted to appointment, by special permission of the State, if (a) one of your parents has always been, or (if dead) always was, a British subject (see below), and (b) your father, if not always a British subject, is or was at death a British subject. (c) For the purpose of (5) (a) above, any period before January 1, 1945, during which your mother lost British nationality as a result of marriage to an alien, may be disregarded.

This text can be presented as a flow chart diagram or as a table as well as being presented simply as a piece of text for reading an analysis by an administrator.

All of these forms contain the same information presented in different ways. Which form of presentation is chosen depends on factors such as the educational level and cultural background of both the people responsible for drawing up and presenting the instructions and the people who are going to be carrying the instructions out.

- we do not have reliable values for the probability of occurrence of different states of the environment;

and because of our individual psychologies and the different technical processes involved in performing the calculations,

- we do not even have agreed values for the results of the various outcomes.

Clearly the circumstances are going to be more complex than the simple situations discussed above. Even so, there is plenty of scope, as we will see in the rest of this book, for the introduction and use of information technology to take over from us as well as to help us.

THE INFORMATION ACTIVITY BLOCK

To make decisions, information is needed. There are six operations that can be performed on information and they can only be performed in certain ways as shown in Illustration 4.9.

The Business as an Information System

From the fundamental relationships it is possible to see the outline of how an information system is built up and how the information processing

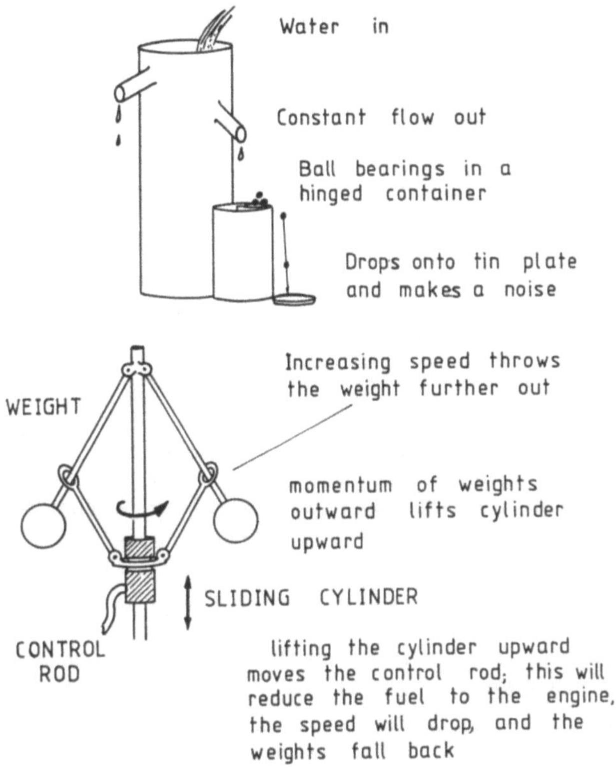

Illustration 4.8. Automatic machines

In the first example we have a single fixed objective—to be woken up at a certain time.

In the second example, the objective is to control the speed of a machine within certain limits. This second example shows the principle of the control loop in action.

activities of a business can be represented as an activity system diagram of the form shown in Illustration 4.10.

Information Processing Productivity

Since the information system is a system of activities, it is possible to think of the productivity of the system. Productivity is, of course, derived from measured values of effectiveness and efficiency, and so in concept it is easy to define the productivity of the information system. There are pitfalls, however.

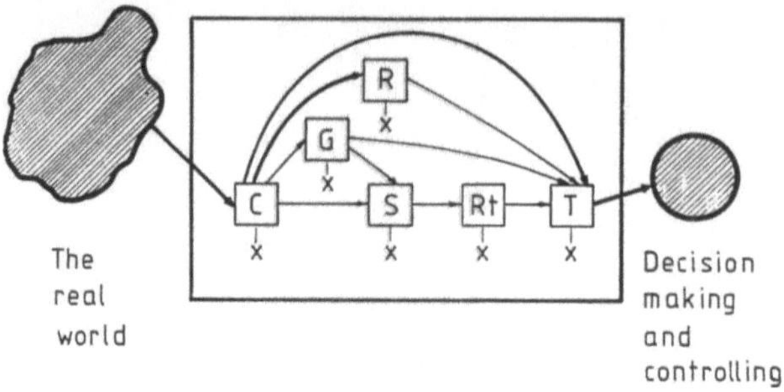

Illustration 4.9. Information operations

Information has first to be *captured* by the information processing activity. Once captured it may be (see also Illustrations 8.12 and 4.10)

(i) *transmitted*—a telecommunications link, for example;
(ii) *reproduced* and then *transmitted*—a print room operation;
(iii) *stored, retrieved,* and then *transmitted*—as in a file room; or
(iv) used for *generation* of further information.

Once new information has been generated it may in turn be transmitted, reproduced, and transmitted, or stored, retrieved, and then transmitted. And, of course, at any time it may simply be destroyed or lost!

This diagram shows the various possible sequences of activities that may be carried out on information.

Information Value

Although it is quite easy to determine most, if not all of the costs for an information system, it is often quite difficult to determine the value of the output.

> In order to determine efficiency we have to measure both the output from and the input to an activity. And these measurements have to be useful. For example it would be easy to measure the output of an artist in terms of the number of paintings produced, but although an easy measurement it might not be a very useful or meaningful measurement. At least if output was measured in terms of money we would have some idea of what other people think of the artist's worth, and then the efficiency of the artist could be determined using the monetary cost of the tubes of paint, canvases used, and all the other inputs used (Doswell, 1983).

While it is often difficult to determine efficiency, it is generally impossible to determine effectiveness except in hindsight when it is easy to see and measure how previous activities were ineffective and failed to achieve what they should have.

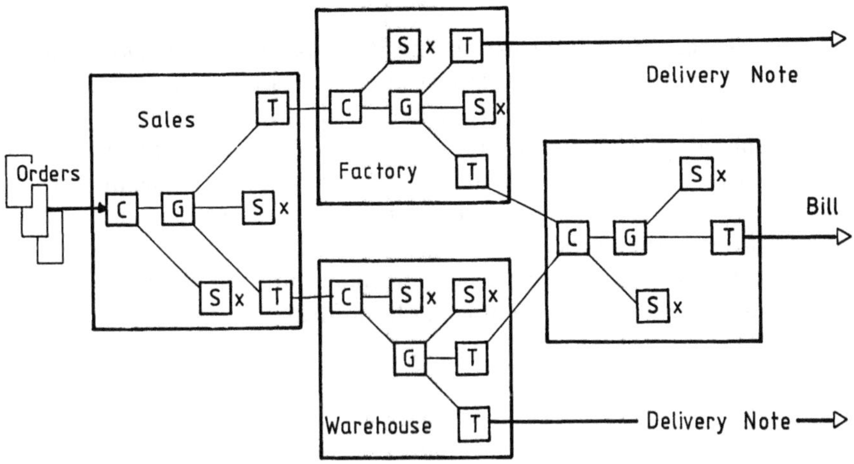

Illustration 4.10. A business as an information processing activity system

Here some key business activities—sales, warehousing, production, and accounts—are shown with an indication of the fundamental information activities that go on in these functions. The system is concerned with the transactions involved in processing a customer's order. In each of the activity areas the processing of information in terms of capture, generation, storage, and transmission is shown. The X indicates information destruction. The information processing is shown in broad overview rather than procedural detail.

Measurements of effectiveness that are not carried out in hindsight are personal guesses based, if anything, on what has been achieved elsewhere by others. Clearly, although this guess if well informed can be right, it can also be wildly wrong.

Operating Instructions and Information

Before leaving these ideas concerning the information block and information operations there is one final comment to make.

In Illustration 4.9 there are six basic information operations: capture, generation, storage, retrieval, reproduction, and transmission. These six operations are carried out on information. The operations are not part of the information itself. Think, for example, of a clerk filing some documents; the operation of filing is quite clearly carried out on some pieces of paper. The paper is the information, filing is the operation. It is particularly important to understand this distinction between operations and the information that they are carried out on when considering how computers work.

INFORMATION PRODUCTS AND SERVICES

The processing of information and the making of decisions is not just limited to the managerial and administrative processes of management information systems, data processing systems, and office automation. Decision making and information processing are often carried out by the actual product manufactured by the business, and in these cases information technology will directly affect the marketable outputs of the business as well as those processes used to produce the marketable outputs.

In the following pages we will consider how, in general, products, services, and processes can be affected by information technology.

Products

Any product that does something, reacts to, or interacts with its environment performs the activities of Illustration 4.9. If the activities of Illustration 4.9 are being performed, information is being processed and decisions are being made, so information technology can be used.

The main reasons for using information technology in products are:

Direct Cost Savings. The microelectronic devices of information technology can be very cheap compared to their mechanical equivalents.

Greater Reliability. Electronic devices do not have moving parts and so they will inherently be much more reliable than mechanical machines.

Ease of Maintenance. Even if the microelectronic product does develop a fault, maintenance can be much easier since the devices are simply replaced rather than repaired.

Updateability. Information technology devices can have great flexibility through virtue of their reprogrammability. Altering the instructions that they have to follow means that they can become a new product.

Physical Smallness. Microelectronic devices can be much smaller than their mechanical equivalents. This can mean that activities that previously were impossible because of size restrictions now become possible.

This list of benefits looks, and is, impressive. However, these benefits are not totally one-sided.

Cost Savings? Although microelectronic devices are inherently cheap, there can be considerable costs involved in developing a set of instructions that enable the product to react to its environment. Additionally there will be costs of developing and linking the various sensors that are needed in order to provide information about the product's environment, to the information processing equipment (Illustration 4.11).

Reliability? Although they do not contain moving parts and so will not

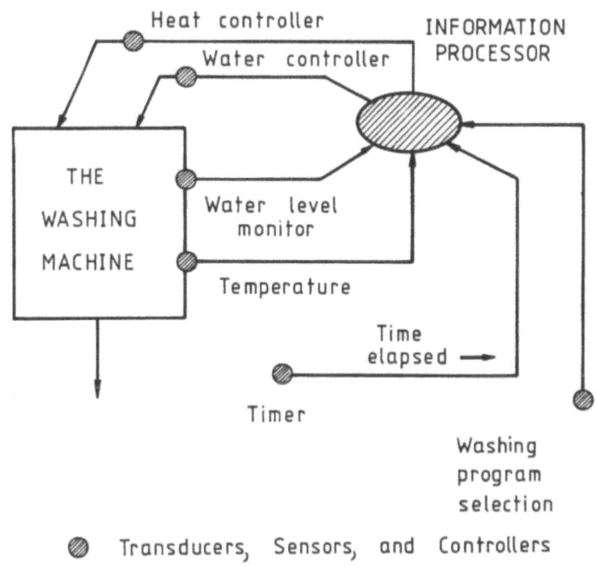

Illustration 4.11. The washing machine control loop

As far as information processing is concerned, a washing machine is a device for which information concerning water level, water temperature, and motor speed are required.

These three factors are controlled by the washing instructions that have been previously selected by the human operator.

As shown, three controllers and three sensors are required. According to the information received from the sensors and from the rules supplied by the washing program the input controlling devices are operated. In order to make a practical washing machine, there are other items that are required: a motor to agitate the washing and control devices to direct the agitation of the washing machine paddle, for example.

wear out, microelectronic devices are not insensitive to their environment. Their biggest problem is in coping with electrical interference: static electricity caused by too dry an environment, "dirty" electrical supplies, and power failure are all problems that have to be contended with. For example, it is doubtful whether the new generation of microelectronic washing machines will be significantly more reliable than their predecessors.

Physical Smallness? Their smallness means that they are fragile and can be easily damaged physically unless protected, and, of course, the provision of physical protection means that much of the advantage of smallness may be lost.

The Lack of Revolution

The incorporation of microelectronic information technology into products has produced a few notable product changes—digital watches have replaced mechanical watches, electronic sales terminals have replaced mechanical cash tills, word processors have replaced typewriters, and multitune door chimes have replaced simple electric bells—but compared to the announced revolution this list (although not exhaustive) is perhaps somewhat disappointing. It is becoming increasingly apparent that as with all other change, the implementation of information technology is not having quite such a dramatic impact on the customer as was heralded.

What has happened is that many products that previously used electronic devices, such as electron tubes or transistors, have replaced these by microelectronic devices. Although externally the product is the same as it was, internally it is different, and for the business itself there are cost savings which can be used in a variety of ways.

Processes

Manufacturing activities are diverse, but there are some common elements in this diversity. Primarily, when carrying out any manufacturing activity, there is the need at all times to control. This control consists of ensuring that what has been achieved matches up with what was planned to be achieved in terms of:

(i) *Movement* of items for manufacture;
(ii) *Processing*—variables such as pressure and temperature, and operations such as cutting, grinding, mixing and assembling; and
(iii) *Inspecting* for quality.

There are three approaches to using information technology for carrying out and controlling movement, processing, and inspecting.

One approach is to equip the specialized processing machines that are used for cutting, drilling, shaping, and so on with "intelligence" so that they can operate by themselves, without the need for skilled human operators.

The second approach is to use intelligent general purpose, or universal, machines which add to the intelligence of the intelligent specialized machines an ability to perform a range of tasks rather than just one. These intelligent general purpose machines are known as robots.

The third approach is to leave the manufacturing process essentially alone and to concentrate on installing information systems that can provide better control of the production processes.

Specialized Machines

The development of intelligent specialized machines has a long history. In France in the eighteenth century Jacquard produced a programmable loom that for all intents and purposes could operate by itself. The reason for wishing to develop such machines is, of course, because they are cheaper to use than people. Machines are cheaper because they work longer hours, are more reliable, do not require pay increases or promotions or suffer from any of the other drawbacks that people often exhibit.

In order to have intelligent machines it is necessary to have, besides some way of processing information, some way of controlling actions. Although it is not impossible to have intelligent machines without using electronic computers, it is far easier to use computers. So although intelligent machines have been in existence for hundreds, even thousands of years, it was not until the 1950s and the introduction of electronic computers that manufacturing processes really started to develop with the advent of numerically controlled machine tools.

A numerically controlled machine consists of a tool that carries out the actual manufacturing process and a controller which controls the tool. The instructions that the controller uses are prepared by production engineers who have determined what sequence of machining operations are required (Illustration 4.12).

What information technology now offers through the inherent advantages of microelectronics combined with increasingly more sophisticated sensing devices, is better and more affordable numerically controlled machines.

Robots

A robotic approach to manufacturing processes is predicated upon the use of a machine that can mimic human motions, particularly movements of the arm and hand (Illustration 4.13).

This could in theory lead to a "universal" machine that could perform a range of tasks. By simply putting the correct tool into the robot's hand and providing a new set of instructions a new machine is created. In comparison the specialized machine has a limited single action. In practice, however, most applications of robots are to three specific areas: picking and placing, paint spraying, and spot welding. And a paint-spraying robot does not change into a pick-and-place robot.

Training Robots. Rather than write the complicated sets of instructions that will be needed to get the robot to perform its required actions, it is becoming increasingly common practice to use a human instructor to teach

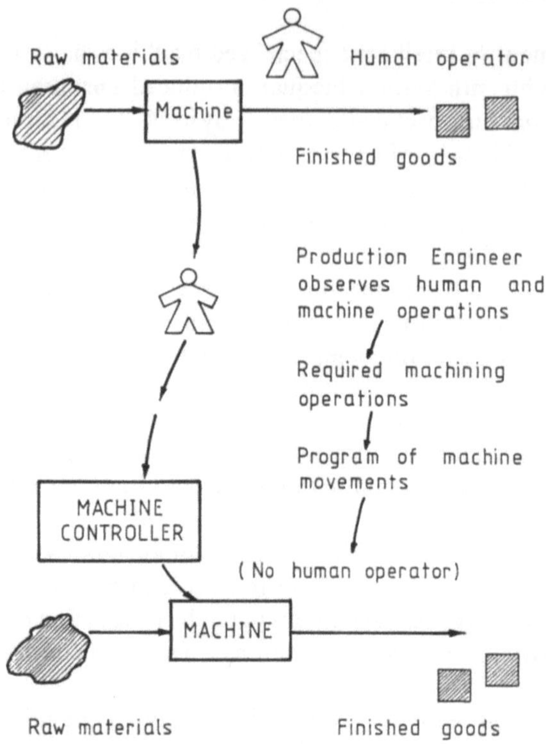

Illustration 4.12. The NC process

This exhibit shows diagrammatically the activities involved in replacing a human machine operator by a numerically controlled (NC) machine. In acquiring and using the machine there is quite clearly not just the cost of the machine to take into account but also the cost of studying and improving the current work in order to make it better before programming it for the NC machine.

Additionally, there are the human and societal costs involved in making people redundant from their work.

the robot the required actions. This teaching is achieved by allowing the human teacher to use the robot's tool to perform the job. As the robot's tool is linked to the robot's controlling computer, all the movements that the human instructor makes are recorded and translated into a program of instructions that the computer will be able to follow out automatically by itself.

Although the principles of using robots to carry out manufacturing operations are simple enough, that does not mean that the implementation is simple. The technical problems alone are enormous and the robot systems

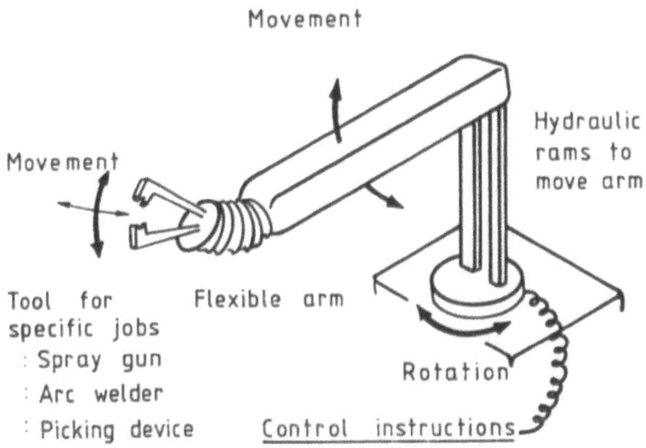

Illustration 4.13. A typical industrial robot

The typical industrial robot looks rather like a human arm. Various joints are provided to allow movement. The standard Unimation robot has five arm joints. The controller is the information processor that provides the movement and operation instructions. By changing tools, the robot can in theory change jobs. However, robots are usually installed on the basis of carrying out a few simple and limited operations rather than on the basis of their inherent flexibility.

that have come into fruition in the early 1980s are generally the results of work started in the mid-1970s.

Production Control Systems

The third approach to manufacturing processes is to point out that there are enormous costs and time delays involved in developing automated production processes and to suggest that greater benefit could be obtained, for the time being at least, from simply improving the managerial control of the production process rather than attempting to improve the manufacturing process itself. Examples of specific problems that can be tackled using this approach are:

(i) *Production scheduling,* where the difficulty is in deciding what should be made when, given that there are conflicting requirements for simultaneous use of the same machine.

(ii) *Inventory control,* since typically one third of factory floor space is used for storage. There could be significant benefits accruing from controlling the amount of stock that is held.

Although the use of computers to provide production management information is in itself not new, it has been given impetus by developments in information technology. This impetus has arisen directly from the fact that it is now much easier to get the shop floor information that is necessary in order to be able to manage the production operation well. Computers and computer terminals can now be placed where they are needed on the shop floor either to enable production supervisors and operators to feed in the information through the computer keyboard where necessary or to allow, by the use of cameras or other input devices, the necessary information to be input directly (Illustration 4.14).

Services. Although in marketing terms all products provide a service to customers, we will distinguish between the physical products produced by a business and intangible services. Clearly those services that are concerned with providing information can be greatly affected by information technology, and indeed some have only become possible with the advent of microelectronics.

One way of categorizing business information services is to consider them in terms of: (i) transaction services: banking and ordering; and (ii) publishing services: electronic newspapers and books.

Transaction Services. This is an area in which information technology has really made a noticeable impact. In the private domain, transaction services are proving to be a useful way for manufacturers of mass produced items such as automobiles to communicate with their distributors. Using this method distributors can order product supplies directly, thereby eliminating or at least reducing the need for salespeople as well as reducing the cost of order processing. Additionally, businesses can offer a better service to their potential customers by finding out the location of a particular wanted item if they do not happen to have it in stock themselves.

As far as the general public is concerned transaction services mean better banking and better seat reservation.

As far as banks are concerned information technology enables them to offer a better service, in terms of the hours that banking facilities are available, and at the same time allows them to reduce their operating costs because much of the work that had previously to be done slowly and expensively by their employees is now performed either quickly by computer or for free by the customer instead.

Computerized reservation systems allow businesses that are selling a scarce service through a number of outlets, an airline, for example, to provide a better service to their customers by providing instant booking confirmation and to be much more flexible in handling bookings.

A refinement of the reservation system, which is invariably operated by an employee on behalf of the customer, is the do-it-yourself electronic

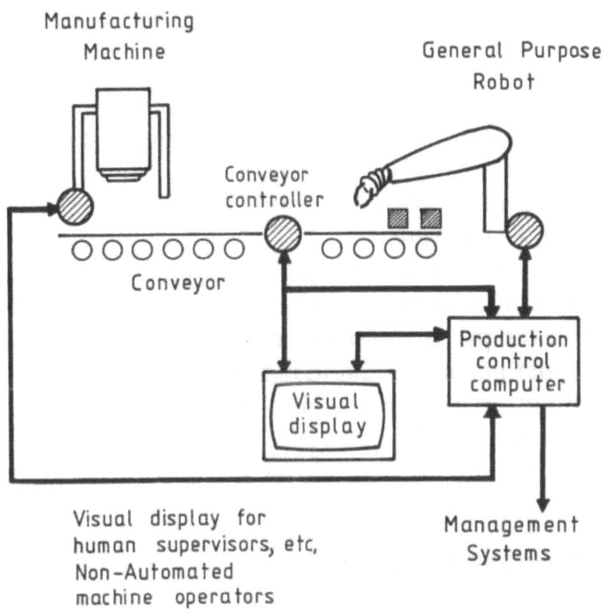

Illustration 4.14. Shopfloor information systems

Here are portrayed diagrammatically the range of information processing tools that could be deployed on the shop floor.

The manufacturing machine could be automatically controlled through a version of NC. The conveyor speed and distribution could be controlled automatically according to centrally stored production plans and schedules, or the information about output could be displayed onto a visual display device so that human workers and supervisors could make their own judgemental decisions. Packing and unloading of the conveyor could be carried out by general-purpose arm robots.

As well as allowing for computer or human control of the day-to-day running of the production operations, this system would also automatically generate all the information required for the general management information systems and for the activities of the sales, purchasing, and accounts departments.

shopping service—teleshopping. Here information technology is taking over the function of the mail-order catalogue, and so is merging into electronic publishing, but it is also combining this with the financial transaction of purchasing. Sitting at home using a telephone and a television set, the shopper can purchase items for delivery or later pick up without having to go to all the trouble of travelling to one, or possibly many, shops. This idea is still at the development stage.

Publishing Services. Electronic publishing proper is also an area of developing interest. The inherent advantages of electronic publishing are that the published information is much more up to date than is possible with the more traditional paper methods, and that the information is much more conveniently accessible. On the other hand, there are inherent disadvantages. Both a telecommunications link to the publishing computer (currently provided by a telephone line and modem) and a screen to display the information on (a television screen) are required. There are two types of electronic publishing: public and private.

Although there have been some successful public applications these have been limited to professional users where quick access to information is important, for example stock price information, and these uses really represent an updating of the traditional ticker-tape machine. The more general publishing services such as Prestel have failed to capture public imagination through a combination of excessive cost and limited scope of information available.

Business Information Systems

The final area of application of information technology is in the managerial and administrative information systems of the business itself where in recent years most publicity has concentrated on the paperless electronic office of tomorrow.

General Management and Electronic Offices. This area is in many ways the most interesting since in many ways it represents the last frontier of more or less unmechanized human activity. Offices and office tools have for all intents and purposes remained the same for the past 100 years. Certainly offices are extremely important because of the ever-rising costs of business information systems.

> Much clerical work, most of the work of such professionals as engineers and accountants, and some of the work of managers, consists of the application of specific factual knowledge gained through education and experience... If nearly all the data to which this knowledge is applied is available in a computer data base, it is possible to write computer programs to aid or replace the efforts of the human knowledge worker... (Vyssotsky, 1980)

So for the really routine operations in general the reason for getting a person to do a payroll calculation, for example, is not because a computer cannot do it, it is because using a certain set of financial and economic arguments it does not appear to be worthwhile to get a computer to do it. Similar arguments apply to other routine systems: sales orders and accounting, for example.

However, as Vyssotsky goes on to indicate:

> ...trying to write such programs brings one rapidly around to the viewpoint succinctly stated by C. West Churchman, that "it is no easy matter to make the computer behave as a clerk would." (Vyssotsky, 1980)

It can be difficult to get the right instructions together for even fairly routine operations. These difficulties became particularly apparent with the appearance from the 1960s onward of management information systems.

Management Information Systems. Management information systems (MISs) were intended to provide managers with all the information they needed to run their business:

> The assumption is made that computer systems will benefit the management of the enterprise primarily by providing more historical or projected data and by supplying data of greater accuracy in a more timely fashion directly to the line manager for use in managing. But the problem of creating a good management information system is not solved by providing more data to the manager more quickly and accurately. Rather, the chief problem seems to me to lie in the difficulty of designing systems that will let managers at various levels get the answers they need in a world that feels no compulsion to mold itself to the design of anybody's computer system. (Vyssotsky, 1980)

To a significant extent MISs have failed. Information technology has not been able to meet the needs of managers:

> Most management information systems have two major weaknesses. Firstly, computing power has outstripped information systems analysis techniques, particularly where small- or medium-sized companies are concerned. Even a small minicomputer has more than enough power to produce a plethora of unwanted reports. The second weakness is associated with the inability to input external information into an MIS and correlate this with internally generated information ...the majority rely on the manager himself interpreting an increasing volume of internal information in the context of his own appreciation of the external situation. (White and Marajian, 1982)

Applications. It is important to realize that the failure of MISs does not stem from an inability to build machines to carry out the tasks that we want performed.

It is not surprising, however, that given the relative failure of MISs, which stems fundamentally from our inability to understand what it is that we are trying to do with information, that information technology applied to business systems has over the past few years taken on a piecemeal pragmatic approach.

Particular applications are being dealt with one at a time. Since the most routine applications have already been dealt with, that means that the ones remaining are more difficult to handle.

Identification of General Areas. One approach is to look at the overall time and cost allocations of a business's information systems in the hope of identifying particular activities that consume large amounts of resources. This way the overall picture of a typical business's information systems can be portrayed as in Illustration 4.15.

Major activities such as typing can be identified as being potentially worthwhile improving. This potentiality can be confirmed or denied using standard accounting conventions that normally show that the introduction of

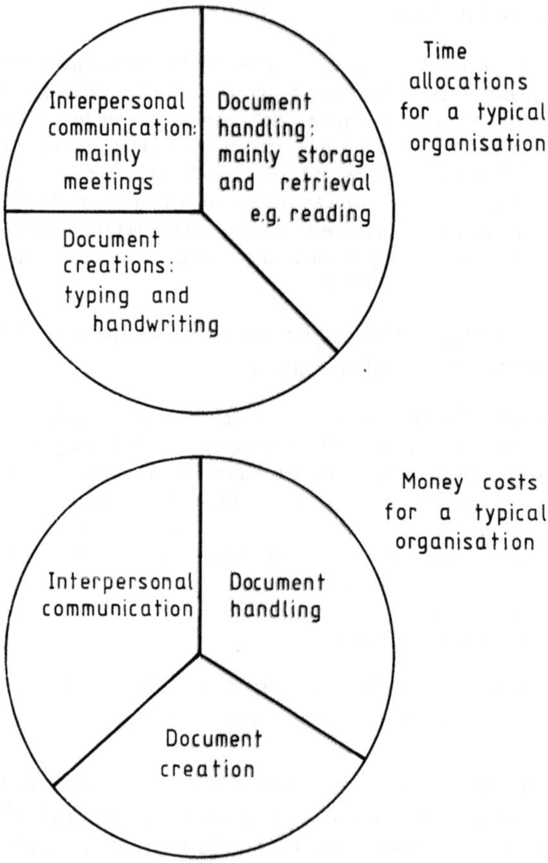

Illustration 4.15. The time and money allocations for a typical business

Aggregation of the total time, and hence cost, spent on general information processing activities results in the typical kind of picture shown here [for details of this kind of approach, see Doswell (1983)].

Notice that because it is mainly expensively paid people who take part in interpersonal communication, interpersonal communication takes up a far larger proportion of financial costs than its time allocation would suggest.

word processing is a cost benefit while other applications such as improved conferencing facilities are, at present costs, only marginal [see Part IV of Doswell (1983) for an outline of this approach].

Specific Jobs. The alternative to the global approach is to look at specific managerial activities and seek ways of improving them.

The most notable success of this approach has been the burgeoning of Spreadsheet programs which since their inception in 1980 have proven to be a tremendously popular development. We should note, however, that this approach is different from anything seen before in that we are now dealing with the development of a computer program, an idea, or a set of instructions, rather than with the development of a piece of equipment.

Success and Failure

The introduction of information technology into business administrative systems has so far been a decided mixture of success and failure. The success has been concentrated around those applications that are very specific, while the failure has stemmed from an inability to understand that while business information systems generally need to be flexible, technology requires a degree of inflexibility. The purpose of technology is to formalize activities and processes. By this process of formalization and routinization, benefits in terms of increased efficiency, effectiveness, and productivity can be achieved.

Formalization. For an example, let us assume you wish to talk with someone. A technologically based answer to this need is to provide you with a telephone. Now the use of the telephone undoubtedly improves efficiency of conversation and makes possible communication between individuals which previously was not possible, but it does also introduce attendant formalization and the disadvantages that formalization has. Quite obviously you can only talk with those people who also have a telephone. You need to know where they are so that you can telephone them. They need to be near that telephone, and it has to be working and not in use, and so on. Additionally, the conversation has to become, even if only to a slight extent, formalized: you probably give your name and or telephone number when you are starting a conversation just in order to establish that you are the person for whom the telephone call is intended, and so on. Technology is biased towards the introduction of formality and will achieve the best results where formality is introducible.

The second source of failure stems directly from technological limitations. The success of any technological development is increased as it becomes easier to use. Equipment that is any way unreasonably difficult to operate, such as word processors which require complex codes to achieve simple operations, will simply not be successful.

SUMMARY

What Is Information?

Information is signs. This may not sound correct grammatically, but it is true. Information processing is sign processing.

Decisions

We, or our machines, process information in order to make decisions. We make decisions by determining what our environment is and then choosing one of the various courses of action open to us. The decisions that we have to make range from simple ones corresponding to identifying what state our environment is in—Is it hot or is it cold? Did the customer ask for a burger or a waffle?—to those situations where we are not even sure what it is that we are trying to decide—Are we trying to decide whether we should be doing what we are currently doing, or are we trying to decide how efficiently we should be doing what we are currently doing?

Decisions and Rules

In the simple cases of decision making it is possible to write down specific rules outlining what to do. These rules may be given to a person to follow out or to a machine.

Information technology is based on these two factors:

(i) the provision of a set of rules for a machine to follow; and
(ii) the provision of a suitable machine to follow the rules.

Use of Information Machines

Information technology machines can be used in one of three ways:

(i) as the products, or the providers of the services sold by a business to its customers;
(ii) in the processes used to produce those products and services; and
(iii) in the information systems that make up the organizational structure of the business itself.

The machines may be word processors or other office computer equipment where the processing of information is apparent; the machines may be production devices; or the machines may be domestic appliances such as washing machines or stoves. In all of these cases, information about the environment is being processed.

DISCUSSION QUESTIONS

1. What implications do the relative powers of transient informal and permanent formal signs have for the design of information systems? [Compare the relative powers of a transient informal sign (such as a smile) and a more permanent formal sign (such as a memo)].

2. How could the idea of quantifying the value of information be developed in theory to determine the value of a business information system? (See Illustration 4.5.) What practical problems could you foresee in such a course of action?

III

INFORMATION TECHNOLOGY

"...(Darius) called a meeting of the Ionian commanders and showed them a long leather strap in which he had tied sixty knots. Men of Ionia he said... I want you to take this strap, and every day undo one of the knots, beginning with the day on which you see me start my march against the Scythians. Should I fail to return before all the knots have given out, you are at liberty to sail home..." Herodotus iv, 98, translated by Selincourt.

SUMMARY: A brief review of conventional information technology, followed by a description of how computers work and communicate.

5

TRADITIONAL TECHNOLOGY

INTRODUCTION

The face of information processing has been transformed by the development of cheap computers, and in the next chapter we will look at the principles of their operation. However, to understand and appreciate the effects of the new information technology, we will first deal with the more conventional and traditional ways that are used for processing information. So this chapter is concerned with the more traditional information technology of paper.

The Purpose of Technology

The concept behind any technology is that by using artifacts we can help ourselves to perform some task either more *cheaply* by using fewer resources, whether those resources are raw materials, people, machines, time, or money, or *better* by producing a better output or product, or even by producing something that simply was not possible before.

Basis of Information Technology

The basis of information technology is the use of signs. Any sign will do so long as all the users are agreed on the meaning of the sign. Examples of signs that have been and are being used include smoke signal clouds, flashes of light from heliographs, semaphore arm positions, and rope knots (Illustration 5.1).

In no way does the tool that is being used to generate or handle the sign understand the sign. The fire does not understand the smoke any more than the computer understands the commands that it is given.

Essential Features

Whatever form the technology takes it must display the following three essential features: some way of allowing information to be put in and

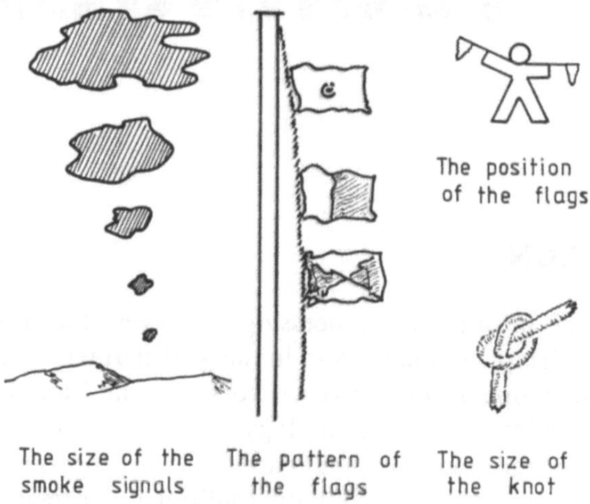

Illustration 5.1. Information and signals

Anything that can be varied can be used as a signal to convey information. Popular mythology has American Indians signaling by the use of smoke clouds, where the size and perhaps the color of the clouds can be varied by the adroit manipulation of a blanket.

Certainly well into this century all ship-to-ship messages were carried out by the use of flags where the sequence and patterns of the flags was used to transmit messages. Care has to be taken since they can be flown upside down unintentionally with unintended meaning. The British Union Jack, for example, if flown upside down (which is very easy to do) means that a ship is in danger, which may not be the message meant.

Flags can also be used, as in semaphore, where rather than the patterns on the flags it is the positions that they are held at that indicates the message.

As a final example, knots can be used to convey information. The Aztecs used knots tied in leather thongs as a means of transmitting information. Notice how this method depends on the physical transfer of the message itself. Unfortunately for us, the meaning of these knot messages is still unknown.

manipulated; some way to allow the storage and retrieval of stored information; and some way to output information.

There is, for example, no point in having a technology that enables us to put information in and have it stored but from which we can get no reply.

Stability of Technology

In addition, there is a fundamental need of the technology to be able to provide dimensional and spatial stability for recorded information. Having in some way generated information, we require that the record we make does not change or deteriorate excessively with the passage of time or as a result of physical movement.

Cost and Ease

Finally, besides offering permanency and stability, any information technology employed in business has also to have ease of use especially annotating and updating, and low cost, both capital and running.

HUMAN INFORMATION TECHNOLOGY

There are two ways for humans to communicate information to one another, by writing or by talking.

Writing

For formal purposes, where it is desired to keep a record of what has occurred, written information is used.

As far as written information for human purposes is concerned the essential storage and display requirements resulted in the initial use of massive items such as stones. While offering stability these methods suffered from lack of portability.

Portability was introduced by the use of materials such as clay tablets and papyrus. Unfortunately, although portable and fairly convenient to use, these media are not physically rugged and either deteriorate or can be damaged relatively easily. It was only with the advent of paper that a material was found that combined the required properties with relative cheapness.

Paper and Machines

Since the invention of paper a variety of machines have been developed to assist people in the creation, storage, and dissemination of written information. These machines in themselves, however, were not capable of processing information. They were simply tools that enabled people to carry out their work better in some way.

Training in the Use of Paper

Paper has been the obvious medium for handling information for some four or five hundred years. Paper has become so much part of our life that we tend to think that it always has been there, although, of course, it has not. On the other hand for each of us paper has always been available—we grow up with paper. We are taught before and at school how to handle paper-based information technology: how to operate books, how to record onto paper, how to retrieve information from paper systems. We each have some 10 to 20 years of formal education in the use of paper-based systems. No wonder paper appears to be such a natural technology!

The Good and Bad Points of Paper

Even with all its good points (Illustration 5.2) paper has weaknesses. These weaknesses are most clearly seen in the organizational effects resulting from the use of paper. A major effect of paper has been the setting up of expert functions. This development was necessary simply because it is not possible for an individual to cope with all the information of a business. Not only is business expertise in particular forms of information processing technique such as accounting required; additional bureaucratic structures are needed in order to cope with the amount of information coming in. Each level of the

Illustration 5.2. The good points of paper

Paper:

- is permanent under a wide range of conditions of temperature and moisture;
- is easy to use and does not rely on a power supply;
- is cheap;
- is available; and
- accommodates a wide range of character sizes and colors.

organizational structure has its own competence limit beyond which information is passed on to the next level for processing there.

Besides these organizational problems there are other technical difficulties. Paper has a low storage density so that in order to store a large amount of information, a lot of paper has to be used. Also the machines that use paper are passive or unintelligent. By this we mean that the symbols contained on the paper only have an effect upon humans. Putting the sheet of paper shown in Illustration 5.3 into a photocopier would not result in the photocopier switching itself off. The photocopier cannot respond to the information it is processing. Both these problems—low storage density and passivity—have been faced and dealt with from the 1880s onward.

Microforms

To overcome the low storage density of paper, microforms were developed. Microforms are photographic miniaturizations of paper-based information. Generally these small images are put onto photographic film,

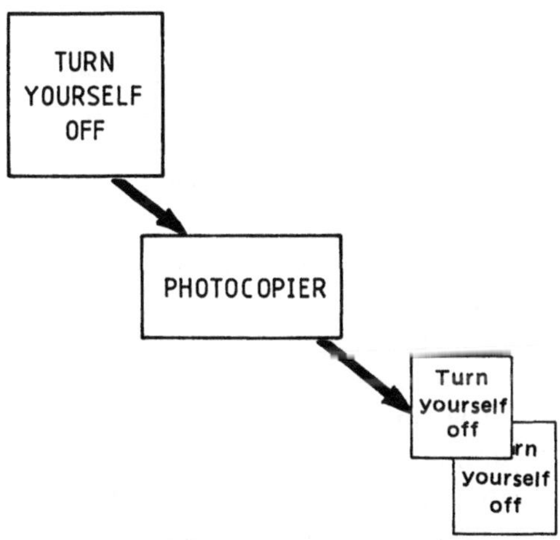

Illustration 5.3. "Turn yourself off"

Inserting a piece of paper with the instructions "Turn yourself off" will not affect the photocopier.

The photocopier does not comprehend the instruction. This is one of the great weaknesses of paper-based information. Except in special circumstances, using an OCR machine, for example, there is no way that symbols on paper can directly affect the operation of the machine.

although there are the microopaques that consist of microimages on translucent paper, which are not, however, in general use.

Microforms come in six categories:

Film. Generally 100- or 200- ft lengths of 16- or 35-mm wide photographic film. The difference between microfilm and ordinary film is that the photographic emulsion of the microfilm is of a much smaller, finer grain, which means that a much higher-quality and better image resolution can be achieved so that the orginal can be more faithfully copied (this corresponds to the communication idea of having a higher signal bandwidth).

The contrast range is reduced so that images show up much more definitely as being either black or white.

The film does not have any sprocket holes in it.

Cassette. Rather than leaving the film on an open reel it can be packaged into a cassette (or more rarely now, a **cartridge.** A cassette has both unwind and take-up spools, while a cartridge has only one unwind spool) for much easier handling and material protection. With a cassette, as for an audio cassette, the film can be left in any location and does not have to be rewound after use as is the case for open-reel or cartridge formats.

Microsheets. Distinct from reeled film, the film can come in sheet form either as fiche, jacket, or card.

Microfiche. Microfiche is simply a large sheet of film (generally A6 size) with from 60 or more images photographed onto it. Sixty images on an A6 sheet corresponds to a linear reduction of the order of 18 times. Greater numbers of images can be put onto a fiche by using greater linear reductions, but clearly the greater the degree of linear reduction, the better the optical system that is used to photograph the images and represent them on a microfilm reading screen has to be.

Microjackets. A microform jacket consists of individual microform images being placed within a protective plastic envelope. Jackets contain fewer images than fiche but can contain different-sized images mixed together and provide a way for maintaining updatable microform files.

Aperture Cards. The final version of microform is the aperture card which is a standard computer-punched card with a slot or aperture of some kind cut into it into which either a single- or multiple-film frame can be mounted. The rest of the card can hold eye-legible writing or punched-hole information for card sorting, selecting, and retrieval.

The various microform versions are illustrated and described in Illustration 5.4.

Microform Cameras

Microforms were developed as a convenient way of copying something that already existed on paper. The image on the paper original is transferred to

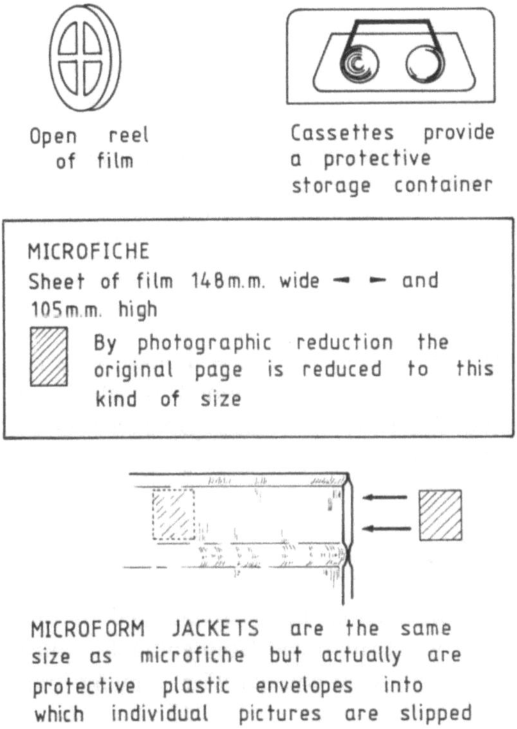

Illustration 5.4. Microform formats

Open film reel. Usually 100 or 200 feet long, the film has to be completely rewound after use. It is a slow method of getting at information used for archival storage where the information is unlikely to be wanted again.

Cassettes provide a protective unit for the film and also allow film to be left unwound in any position for easy reference later on.

Microfiche. Microfiche is a small sheet of film, 148 mm wide and 105 mm high, and it has a number of photographic images of paper sheets stored on it. Standard reductions are from 20 to 60 times giving anything from 50 to a few hundred pages on a sheet of film.

Microform jackets are the same physical size as microfiche but are made from two sheets of plastic stuck together. Channels are made in the jacket and individual photographs can be slipped in. Microjackets contain fewer images than the same-sized fiche, but can hold different sizes of photographs mixed together. Additionally, jackets can be used to build up a file of information since new information can be added to an individual jacket from time to time.

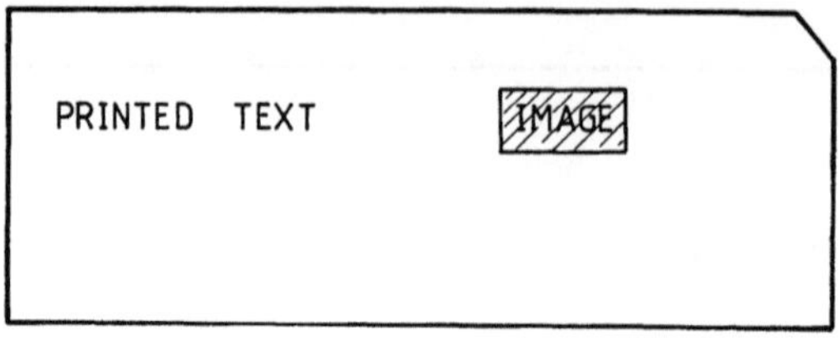

The *aperture card* uses a standard punched card with one or more big slots onto which pictures are glued. In this way printed information can be stored on the card and easily read. Aperture cards are usually used for engineering drawings and plans.

film using a photographic camera that will either be a rotary or planetary camera designed for handling paper originals or which may these days be a televisionlike camera designed for recording images produced by a computer on a CRT screen (Illustration 5.5).

Microform Copying

Copies of the film original may be obtained by diazo (ammonia) or vesicular (heat) developing treatment from contact duplication; the original film is placed in direct physical contact with copying film.

Microform Display

In all cases some form of microform display mechanism is required as the miniaturized images are not eye-legible otherwise. The display devices should contain light sources and an optical system capable of enlarging the microimages a suitable number of times. They may be able to cope with a number of different format arrangements. If the devices can produce suitably enlarged paper copies they are reader–printers while they may alternatively provide only viewing facilities, readers, or printing facilities, enlarger–printers.

The Usefulness of Microform

The fundamental idea behind microform is that of image reduction and subsequent enlargement. However, from this basic feature springs other useful properties relating to file integrity and information access.

Because a lot of information can be put together into a small area it becomes feasible to provide users with complete sets of information at their finger tips. A single fiche the size of a postcard can hold the contents of a complete book. This facility allows information workers to get at stored information much more conveniently since each person can have a complete set of business records conveniently on their desk.

Besides making life easier for those who actually use the information, an additional effect of this form of information storage is that it can easily result in a need for fewer people. There will then be less need for a clerical staff for information filing and retrieving.

Drawbacks of Microform

Microform suffers from several drawbacks: the need for optical devices to make the stored information legible is one obvious disadvantage. A second disadvantage is the inability to easily update microform information.

In addition to these, microform also suffers a drawback in common with paper: it is a passive medium used with passive machines. This can be overcome to an extent by coding the microform images so that retrieval can be speeded up.

Active Information

For stored information to be used by machines, the information has to be stored in some way that can operate the machine itself. Until nearly the end of the 19th century, the only way that stored information could be used to operate machines was by having punched holes that were used to operate levers (Illustration 5.6).

The Punched Card

This situation was changed by Hollereith's introduction of electro-mechanical punched-card machines. Where holes were punched into cards, electrical circuit contact could be made and the ensuing electric current used to operate motors and relays that could record the required information as appropriate. This approach was perfected in the period up until the 1950s with the punched card (Illustration 5.7) being the standard way for storing information.

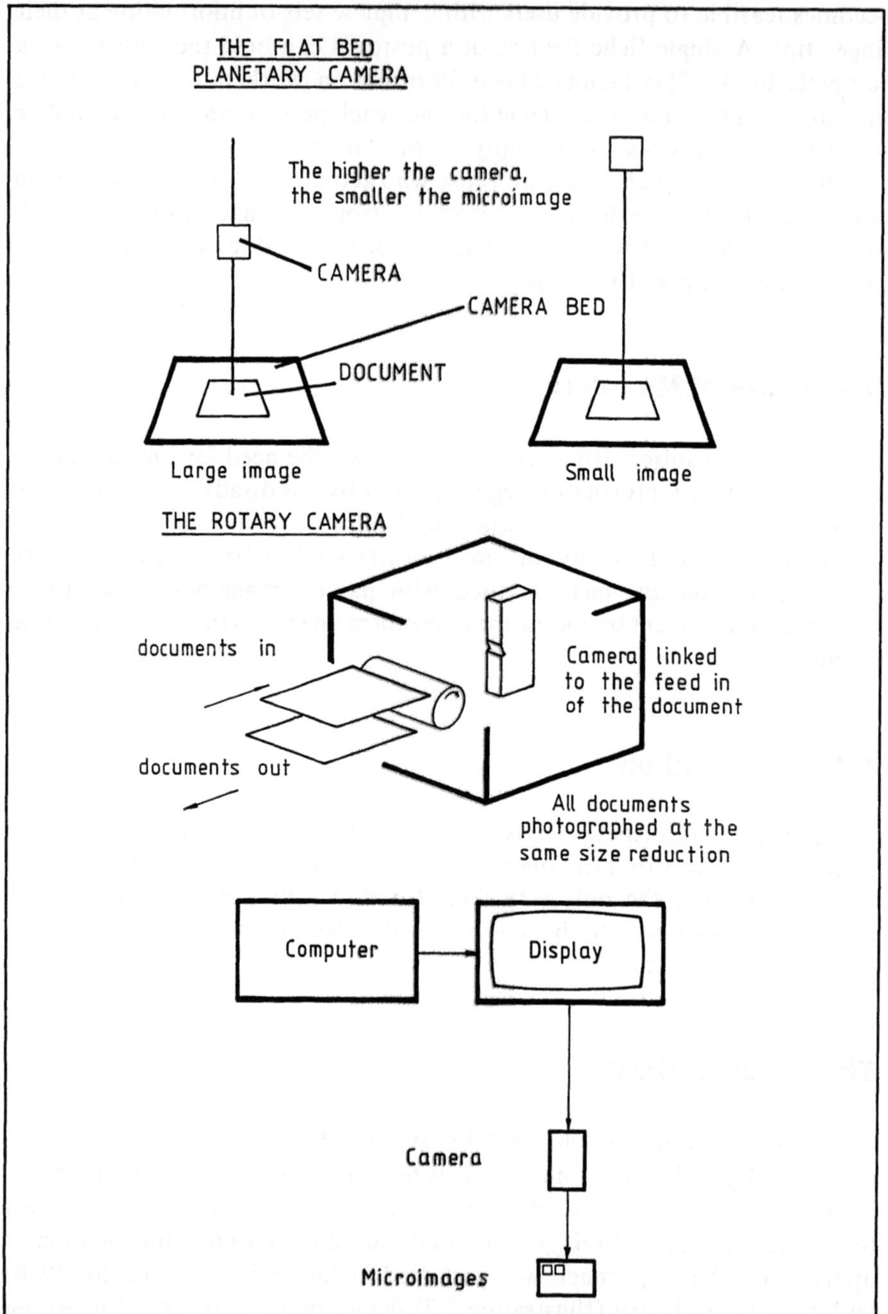
THE FLAT BED
PLANETARY CAMERA
The higher the camera,
the smaller the microimage
CAMERA
CAMERA BED
DOCUMENT
Large image
Small image
THE ROTARY CAMERA
documents in
documents out
Camera linked
to the feed in
of the document
All documents
photographed at the
same size reduction
Computer
Display
Camera
Microimages

Illustration 5.5. Microform camera arrangements

Microforms can be prepared either from paper originals or directly from computer output. If paper originals are being used, then a rotary camera will be used for photographing a continuous stream of identical documents. A planetary camera is used for individual documents where high-quality images are required, with maps and plans for example.

If the information being microformed is actually computer output, then rather than photographing the paper version, the computer output can be photographed directly. This process is known as COM (computer output microform).

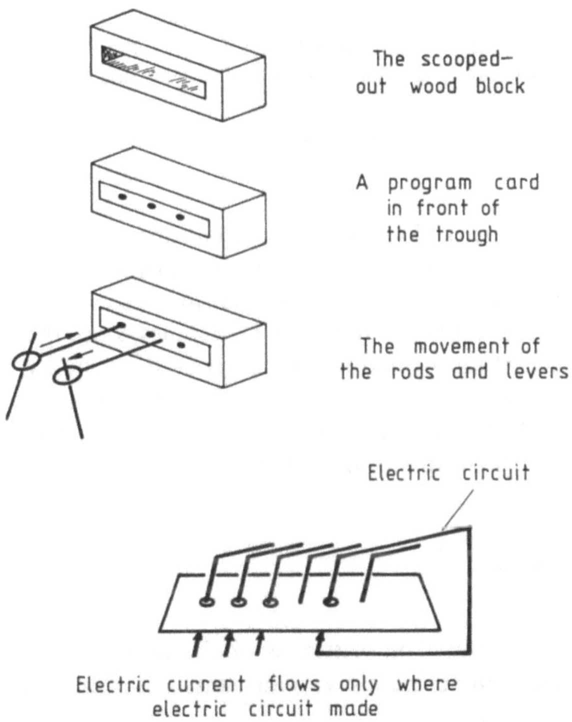

Illustration 5.6. Early information-operated machines

Jacquard's loom, an early, although not the first, example of a programmable weaving machine, used program cards to determine the pattern weaved. The motive power for the machine was provided by people.

The basic idea was to use a wooden block from which a trough had been scooped. In front of this block would then appear punched program cards, made from drilled-out slats of wood. Where the holes were drilled rods could move right into the block because of the scooped-out trough underneath. Where there were not holes the rods could not move. On the ends of the rods were loops around levers, so that movement of the rods pulled the levers back. The levers were attached to hooks that lifted up the weaving thread and so caused the required pattern to b^ made.

By the end of the 19th century, the mechanical movement of rods and levers was replaced by the making (switching on) and breaking (switching off) of ele^tri-cal circuits.

Hollereith's punched-card machine used metal brushes that made contact where holes were punched through cards, with an electrically conducting surface underneath the card. The resulting electric current was used to operate a mechanical counting, clocklike display.

The difference between Jacquard's loom and Hollereith's machine was in the use of mechanical rather than electrical technology. The description of the principles behind the mechanical loom should be enough to convince most readers of the inherently greater reliability available using electrical rather than mechanical technology.

Handling the Punched Card. The information stored in the punched card could be handled by sorters, collaters, and printers to carry out many information-processing activities. But even in these cases where punched paper tape or cards were used to operate machines, since the machines were electromechanical the information processing used was bulky, and by today's standards, slow and unreliable. Additionally, the amount of information processing that they could provide was limited particularly because of the limitations of information storage capacity.

Oral Information

We have concentrated on written, symbolic information. However, in life in general, let alone in business, a vast amount of information is conveyed by speech.

While in Roman times auditors were people who *listened* to business transactions, today they are people who check the legality of written records of transactions. The reason for the demise of spoken information as a means of carrying out formal information processing is because until very recently the only way to store spoken information was by the use of human hearing and

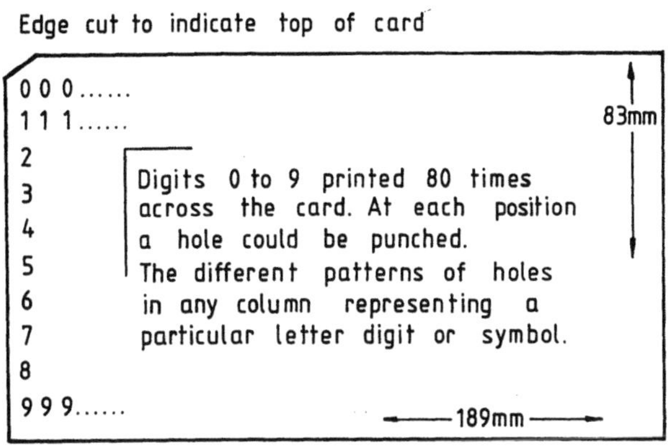

Illustration 5.7. The punched card

Pictured is a thin piece of card with one corner removed to indicate the top right-hand corner of the card. This card is shown from the back!

Small rectangular slots are punched into the card by operating a key punch, a typewriterlike machine, that punches different arrangements of holes corresponding to whichever key is pressed. By use of photoelectric cells, rather than the direct physical contact of Hollereith's original tabulator, electric currents can be generated that can be used to operate machines.

This development represents the use of paper as an active medium to control machines. However, neither cards nor the alternative of punched paper tape are particularly suitable for repeated use with machines. The paper tears and the cards bend and can easily get out of order.

Punched paper tape is still encountered in numerically controlled production machines that were developed before magnetic recording methods were fully developed.

memory both which arc notably fallible. Although from the 1950s on increasingly convenient methods of recording spoken information have been developed, our dependence on written information in business has reached such a state that rarely is it possible to use vocal rather than written information.

INFORMATION TECHNOLOGY PRODUCTS AND SERVICES

We are not only concerned with information processing carried out by people working *in* business but also with the information processing carried out by the products and services *of* business. And so we will complete this chapter by briefly looking at the traditional information technologies involved in business products.

Development of Information Processing Machines

Until the 1850s the underlying principle of all machinery was mechanical. Machines consisted of gears and levers that rotated and pushed. The gears and levers were activated by human, other animal, or inanimate sources of power such as wind, water, and steam. These machines had started from primitive ancestors that had been initially designed perhaps thousands, certainly hundreds, of years ago. What happened until the 1850s was a refinement of design and manufacturing.

Development of Electromechanical Technology

From the 1850s on there has been increasing use of electrical and electromechanical technology as opposed to the earlier purely mechanical technology. So in addition to gears and springs, relays were added as another method for processing information.

Even though the use of electrotechnology was increasing, skilled mechanical engineering skills were still required, as were vast amounts of materials, such as steel, and considerable amounts of energy to make and drive the resulting machines. And all the time because they were electromechanical and involved many moving parts the machines were liable to failure.

So information processing machines able to operate by themselves and able to follow sets of stored instructions, are not new and peculiar to our age, although the scale of operation in earlier machines was limited. The list of early information processing machines includes Jacquard's loom, Watt's governor, and da Vinci's automatic roasting machine.

Barriers to Intelligent Machines

The technical problems that delayed the availability of intelligent machines were a lack of sensors that could provide information about the environment in a form suitable for further processing, and a lack of suitable devices to process the information.

Even with the intelligent machines that did exist there were problems. Because the intelligent machines that could be built tended to be bulky, expensive, and unreliable, there was a lack of demand for such machines. In addition, the machines were clumsy. In short, people were better at many of the tasks than were the machines being built. It is only very recently that machine systems capable of a wide range of actions and reactions to their environment have become widely available.

Information Technology Services

Information services can be conveniently categorized for the moment as being either services linking individuals together, communication services, or as services providing individuals with access to stored information or information services.

Communications Prior to the 1840s

While in the period leading up to the 1850s the sophistication of machines had developed as greater engineering skills had been achieved, certainly as far as communication processes were concerned nothing had changed for thousands of years. If a message had to go a long way then quite simply someone took it—whether as writing on paper or as knots in a rope being hardly important.

Telecommunications

This situation was changed radically by the development first of telegraphy and then telephony. In a period of a few years it became possible, in theory, to communicate over long distances rapidly.

This theoretical possibility was, however, severely limited.

First, there was a lack of wiring linking telegraph coders and telephone handsets and, second, there was a lack of use. Faced with new means of communication it was not clear to people at first what they should want to communicate.

This situation has over the years changed until nowadays a measure of national economic development is the number of telephone sets installed. In the U.S.A. the figure is 65 telephone sets per 100 people; the European figure is approximately half of that.

The Nature of Information Services

Traditional information services are based on people, augmented by some machines: telephones, typewriters, and calculators.

The result of this is two-fold: First, a tendency for businesses providing information services to be small and localized so as to overcome problems associated with the distribution of information; second, a tendency for information to be old because of the considerable time it takes to gather it prior to distribution. These effects were eroded with the development of the telegraph, telephone, and broadcasting, but still have a considerable bearing on those information services such as newspapers which continue to rely on methods of physical distribution.

SUMMARY

Paper and Microforms

The traditional forms of information technology are based on paper.

Although it is very useful, paper does have drawbacks. The main disadvantage of paper is that it is bulky and that it cannot be conveniently used to *operate* machines.

Microform overcomes some of the problems of paper, but it also has drawbacks of its own.

The Future

The real requirement is for an information medium that can be used to operate information processing machines without any effort from human operators or users. The idea is not new, some information processing machines were designed thousands of years ago, but what has happened in the past 100 years or so is the development of a universal and convenient method for representing information—electronic pulses.

DISCUSSION QUESTIONS

1. Why has so much effort been directed toward changing oral information processing into textual processing? What are the drawbacks to formalized textual procedures?

6

PRINCIPLES OF NEW INFORMATION TECHNOLOGY

INTRODUCTION

The 19th century technology of electricity was to change the face of information processing rapidly. One of the first and certainly most dramatic of changes was in the sending of messages, and as we have seen by the 1850s electricity was being utilized to send messages from one place to another near the speed of light by telegraphy.

Babbage and Pierce: Mechanical and Electrical

By the 1880s, not long after Charles Babbage had died in England, an unhappy and dissatisfied man because of the failure of his mechanically based computer designs, Charles S. Pierce in the United States had designed simple electric circuits consisting of switches and light bulbs that could represent ideas or concepts such as "and" and "or" (Illustration 6.1). These circuit designs form the basic principles used in today's digital electronic computer.

Rather than draw out the circuits in full as in Illustration 6.1 we will use the symbols of Illustration 6.2. By combining the symbols of Illustration 6.2 we can construct complex circuits such as those of Illustration 6.3. The circuit of Illustration 6.3 adds and takes forward a carry digit if necessary.

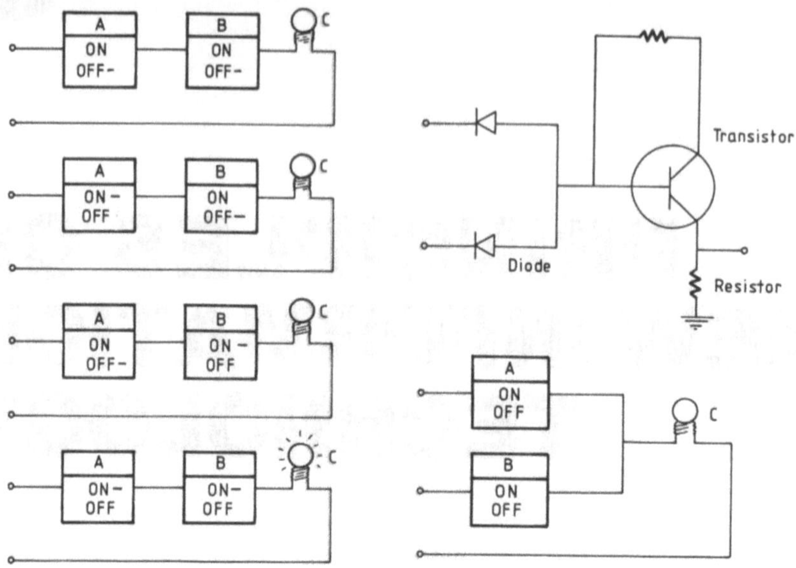

Illustration 6.1. AND/OR circuits

For the first circuit shown, the light only comes on when both switch A and switch B are switched on, so that this circuit performs the logical operation of AND.

Rather than using the terms of "on" and "off," we can instead write 0 (= off) and 1 (= on). The operation of the circuit can then be noted in a table rather than as a circuit diagram.

Switch A	Switch B	Light
0	0	0
1	0	0
0	1	0
1	1	1

C, the light, is only on (= 1) when both A is on (= 1) AND B is on (= 1). A slightly different arrangement of switches gives the OR circuit, which is shown both as a combination of diodes, transistors, and resistors, and as the arrangement of switches and light that we have been talking about.

The diode-transistor circuit shown here is called diode-transistor logic (DTL). There are other forms of logic: transistor-transistor (TTL or T^2L), for example. These different forms of logic circuit will all perform the same functions, but in different ways, and have different characteristics—voltages, cost of manufacture, and speed of operation.

It is easy to see that a large number of components (diodes, transistors, and resistors) are needed to build a computer, hence the requirement for miniaturization in order to achieve low-cost and physically small machines.

AND 

OR 

NOT 

Illustration 6.2. Logic, symbols, and tables

AND $C = A \cdot B$

A	B	C
0	0	0
1	0	0
0	1	0
1	1	1

Both A AND B have to be 1 before C becomes 1.

OR $C = A + B$

A	B	C
0	0	0
1	0	1
0	1	1
1	1	1

If either A or B is 1, then C becomes 1. Another useful circuit is NOT.

NOT $C = \overline{A}$

A	C
1	0
0	1

where C is the opposite of A.

The Importance of Addition

The adding circuit is important because once you can produce a device that will add, provided you work with some ingenuity, you have a device that can perform any of the four arithmetic functions. With an ability to perform these functions, we have a calculator.

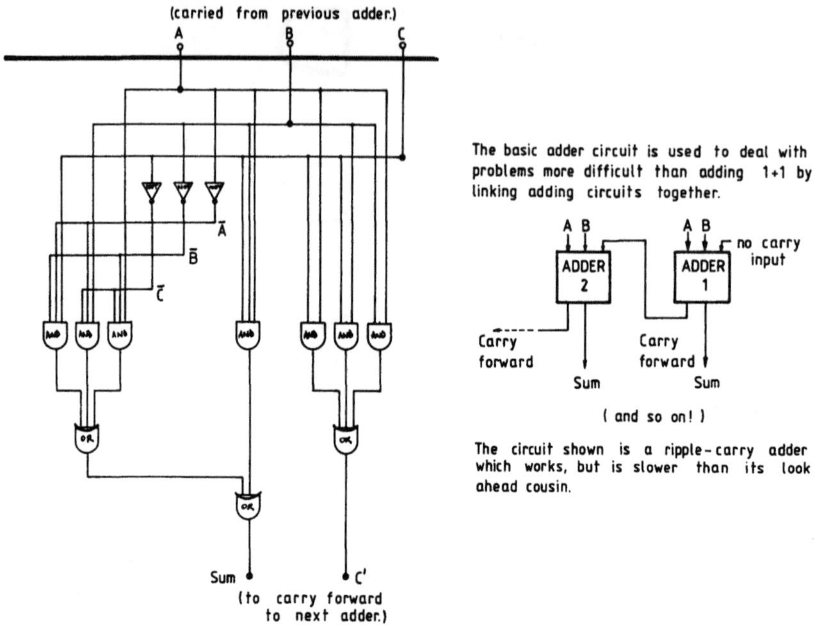

Illustration 6.3. An adding circuit

Illustrated is the symbolic design of the layout of an adding circuit. An adding circuit simply adds numbers together. The numbers will be expressed in terms of their binary, ASCII, values (see Illustration 6.7). To understand how the circuit works, imagine a set of values for the inputs A, B, and C, and then follow through the resultant outputs from the various logic units (or gates, as they are often called).

This circuit performs addition on 2 numbers consisting of 1 bit, that is, this circuit could perform a sum as complicated as adding together 1 + 1. Most current small computers use 8 bits to represent their numbers, and so their adding circuits will be more complex than that shown here. For each bit used in representing the number, one complete circuit like the one shown here would be necessary. And as shown, this could be dealt with by having a sequence of adders linked together. The one shown here is a ripple-carry adder, which carries forward rather like we do when we are adding. There is a faster arrangement known as a look-ahead adder.

Note that there are *thirteen* logic gates in the circuit shown here. These thirteen gates consist of transistors and other components such as resistors and capacitors. There could easily be a half-dozen different items in a logic gate. This means that some 80 items are necessary in order to be able to perform a simple addition using the circuit shown here. Imagine, or, if you want, calculate the number of items necessary to get the addition of two realistic numbers performed. That is why it is necessary to put a large number of items onto an individual wafer so that a machine will do something useful.

Concept to Reality

Although we have the conceptual foundations of a computer in Illustration 6.3, not until the 1940s was it possible to turn the concept into a reality.

The first serious attempts in the late 1930s to build the forerunners of today's computers were constructed from batteries, relays (which are large switches), and light bulbs. There are some clear disadvantages to this approach. The components being used are too large, too prone to break down, and too difficult to operate. But even so these machines were able to perform arithmetic operations far faster than could be done by any other means. In order to make the modern computer a reality, better components were required, and the most important better component required was a better switch.

SOLID SWITCHES

Vacuum-Tube Switches

Throughout the 1940s and early 1950s computers using vacuum-tube switches were developed for military and then business purposes. In the mid-1950s the IBM 704, the last of the vacuum-tube computers, occupied some 250 cu ft. Into that space today it would be possible to get some 250 desktop computers, all capable of operating much more quickly than the 704, and each costing a fraction of the price and being much more useful.

The demise of computers such as the 704 was brought about by the transistor.

The Transistor

A transistor is a switch; it can be either "on" or "off." The transistor is also a solid-state device, that is, it is made from one piece of material and contains no moving parts. These features combine to produce a solid-state switch that is physically small, mechanically reliable, cheap to run, and cheap to make. The essential operating features of a transistor are shown in Illustration 6.4.

Although transistors were a tremendous improvement on the vacuum tubes and mechanical relays they were replacing, they still required an immense amount of skilled individual labor to connect them into useful electronic circuits. The skilled labor was required because a transistor has three terminals, all of which have to be connected to other components or

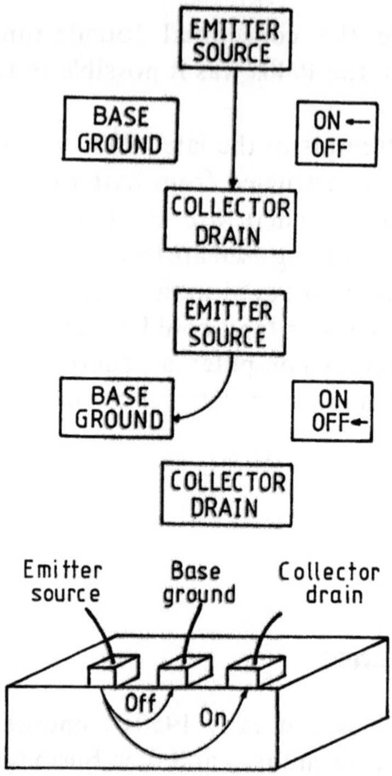

Illustration 6.4. The transistor

The switching function is achieved by using a base- or gate-controlling device that is switched on or off by the application of an electric signal of a few volts. Today, the gate, together with the emitters and collectors, is built into the flat slice of the microprocessor, which is known as a planar device. These devices can switch on and off very rapidly, millions of times per second, and are very reliable.

wires. The huge human effort required to wire the transistor circuits meant, of course, that computers were expensive. In addition, since thousands of individual transistors were being used to make up the computer, the computer still had to be relatively large.

However, since transistors are solid-state devices made from pieces of silicon by chemical and photographic processes, with the development of advanced photographic manufacturing processes it became possible to reduce the size of transistors and to place several together in one piece of material (Illustration 6.5).

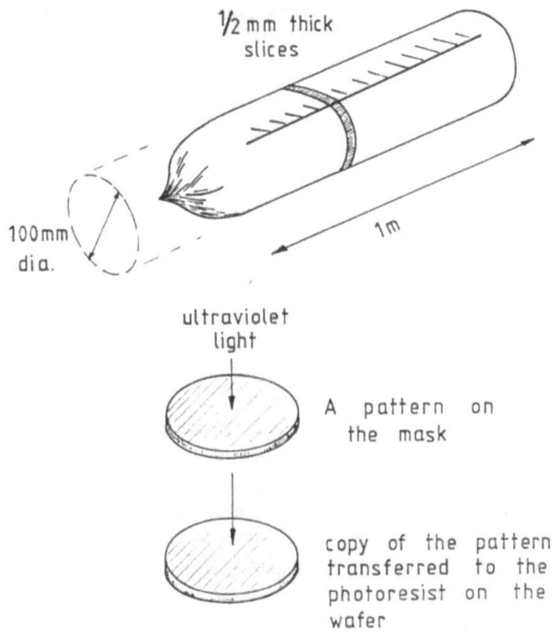

Illustration 6.5. Manufacture of the microprocessor

The manufacture of the microprocessor is a complicated process with perhaps 60 separate steps. Only the three basic steps are described below. Of these, steps 2 and 3 will be repeated with slight variations many times before the chip is tested and packaged.

The first step is to make the thin wafers, or slices, of pure silicon. Silicon is used because it combines appropriate mechanical and electrical properties. There are other materials, gallium, for example, that are better in some ways, but the better materials are also much more expensive.

The pure-silicon wafer, 99.99% pure, is made by slicing up a large lump of pure silicon 10 kg in weight, 1 m long, and 100 mm in diameter—produced by heating silicon to 1400°C. After cooling, the silicon boule, as the large lump is called, is sliced up into thin ½-mm slices with a diamond-edged saw. The slices are then polished to a mirrorlike finish. The boule has a flat surface so that even when it is sliced up in all further operations, the wafers can always be arrayed in the same direction.

The next step is pattern transfer. Insulating layers of silicon dioxide and nitride are put onto the wafers by heating them in steam at 1100°C and by using low-pressure deposition. Over this insulating layer is spread a light-sensitive photoresist chemical. This is done by putting a drop of photoresist onto the wafer, and then spinning it at high speed. Ultraviolet light is then shone onto the wafer through a mask. The mask pattern is therefore transferred to the photoresist on the wafer. The wafer is then washed with solvents and acids to wash away unwanted photoresist and to etch away unwanted parts of the wafer itself. In this way a chemically machined switch is constructed.

Finally, there is doping. The unprotected parts of the pure silicon wafer are exposed to special chemical impurities added to give the silicon the precise electrical properties that are wanted. These impurities are usually boron and phosphorus. The impurities may be added by implantation, that is, by bombarding the silicon with atoms, or by deposition, that is, by heating the silicon in the presence of the appropriate chemical.

Construction of the Switch. By repeating the basic steps of etching and doping, a complex structure of various layers can be built up. Because of their different electrical properties, different regions will act just like switches connecting up different circuits when electrical voltages are applied to them. There are a vast number of different arrangements of switches all with different advantages and disadvantages.

By using the photographic technique of shining ultraviolet light through a mask it is possible to achieve very small patterns. Because of this smallness, very clean working conditions are required. A dust particle would be big enough to destroy many circuits. Typically, a clean hospital operating theatre has 100 times the amount of dust that a microprocessor fabrication room has.

Although the manufacturing process is well-understood theoretically, in practice, because of such factors as the presence of dirt and faults in the materials, etc., production yields can be as low as 2 or 3% for complicated designs. For simple designs, the production yields can be nearly 100%.

Once all the wafer manufacturing processing has been completed, the circuits are tested electrically. Circuits that fail are marked with ink or are painted.

The wafer is then sliced into 5 mm × 5 mm chips. The marked failed chips are discarded, while the surviving good chips are mounted into individual plastic packages.

Development of Manufacturing Skills

With increased manufacturing sophistication, accumulated production experience, and increased use of the equipment, production capabilities have risen and unit production costs have fallen (Illustration 6.6).

Not only have the switches been miniaturized, but so also have the other necessary components such as resistors and capacitors. All of these devices can be put onto the same piece of silicon. This ability to combine many devices into what is effectively one device is called integration.

Since the mid-1950s we have moved from discrete (single-transistor) devices, through integrated devices (a few transistors on one piece of silicon), to large-scale and very large scale integration where hundreds of thousands of transistors, capacitors, and resistors can be constructed in a small area.

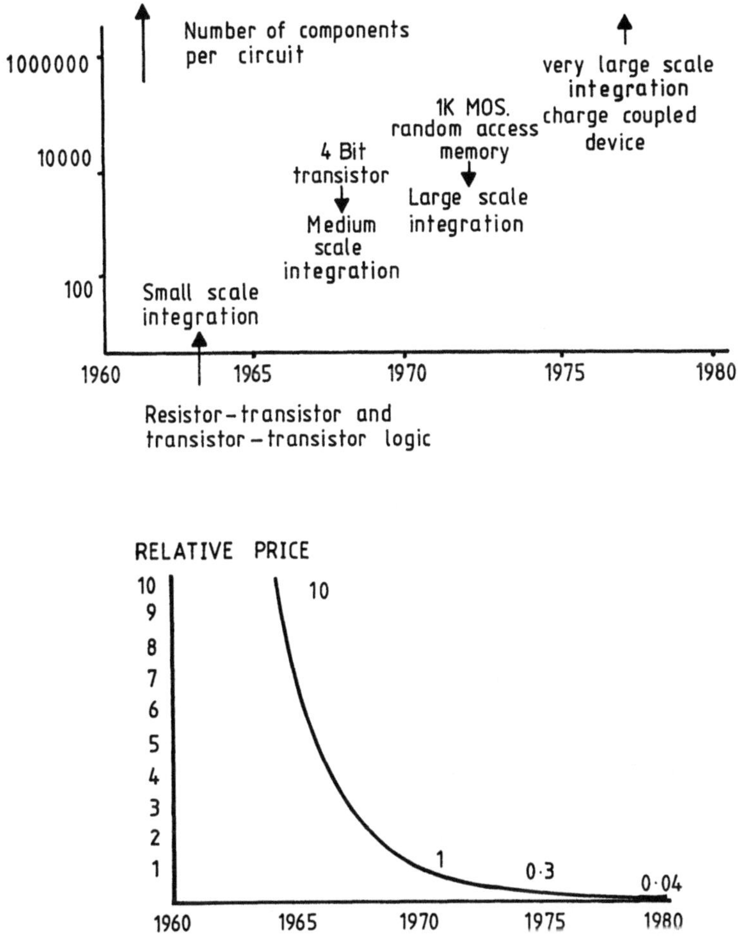

Illustration 6.6. Manufacturing performance

A single silicon chip will contain a few hundred processors. Each processor will contain many components. Since the 1960s the number of components per circuit has doubled every two years, which has also meant that the relative price of the devices has fallen since the cost of production is related to production of the wafer rather than to the number of circuits on the wafer.

Here manufacturing development is shown in terms of the number of components that can be put into a circuit and in terms of the relative price of these circuits. The price curve shown can only apply in those situations where there is mass production of a standard design which typifies many consumer products.

Future Manufacturing Technology

Inevitably there is an end to this progression. Since the manufacturing process is a photographic one, the number of switches and circuits that can be put onto one piece of silicon is determined by the quality of the optical systems being used and by the inherent properties of light. Light itself becomes too coarse a medium to carry out the manufacturing operations that are required: we end up in a situation where we are, in effect, trying to kill a housefly using a shotgun. Not daunted, experimental manufacturing projects using higher-energy electron beams are underway in an attempt to cram even more circuits into the same space.

COMPUTER OPERATION

Processing

Today's computer consists of an array of miniaturized electronic switches that are capable of being switched either on or off. How are these switches used to process information?

If we put the switches into groups, then we can have a code whereby each different arrangement of on and off is used to convey a particular meaning. This is precisely what is done in computers (Illustration 6.7).

We can store information, therefore, by arranging to have switches on or off as appropriate. Having found a way to store the information, the next need is to manipulate the stored information. This is done one simple step at a time.

Each individual item of stored information is moved out of the memory into a register, which is simply a temporary memory. Once in a register the information can be changed by the logic unit and then returned to the memory for restorage. The principles of this operation are shown in Illustration 6.8.

By applying some ingenuity it is possible to develop electronic circuits and instructions that can carry out any manipulation we want. So now the computer consists of banks of switches that store the information we are interested in and a logic unit consisting of circuits that carry out the manipulations, such as adding, that we require.

It is worthwhile at this stage to distinguish between the information that the computer works on and the information that forms the instructions that the computer follows. The instruction information is called a program.

Programming

Originally, that is, in the 1940s, the circuits of the logic unit had to be wired by human operators. So if we wanted to perform an addition, an adding circuit had to be wired. If we wanted to perform multiplication, then a

Illustration 6.7. The ASCII code

This table shows the ASCII 8-bit code for upper- and lowercase letters, digits, and some special symbols. If we are patient enough in looking at this table, various patterns will emerge. What differentiates the code between an uppercase and a lowercase letter, for example?

There are many other binary coding arrangements, most notably EBCDIC which is used by IBM.

A	10100001	N	10101110	a	11100001	n	11101110	0	01010000
B	10100010	O	10101111	b	11100010	o	11101111	1	01010001
C	10100011	P	10110000	c	11100011	p	11110000	2	01010010
D	10100100	Q	10110001	d	11100100	q	11110001	3	01010011
E	10100101	R	10110010	e	11100101	r	11110010	4	01010100
F	10100110	S	10110011	f	11100110	s	11110011	5	01010101
G	10100111	T	10110100	g	11100111	t	11110100	6	01010110
H	10101000	U	10110101	h	11101000	u	11110101	7	01010111
I	10101001	V	10110110	i	11101001	v	11110110	8	01011000
J	10101010	W	10110111	j	11101010	w	11110111	9	01011001
K	10101011	X	10111000	k	11101011	x	11111000	*	01001010
L	10101100	Y	10111001	l	11101100	y	11111001	+	01001011
M	10101101	Z	10111010	m	11101101	z	11111010	,	01001100

multiplication circuit had to be constructed. This obviously could be a slow and error-prone business. After all, even something as straightforward as wiring a plug causes most people problems. Furthermore, each time a new problem had to be dealt with a new lot of wiring had to be undertaken.

Hard-wire programming was relatively quickly replaced by stored programming. In stored programming, instructions telling the computer what to do are stored within the computer itself. By following the instructions that have been fed in, the computer sets itself up into a suitable configuration to perform whatever function is required. Throughout the 1950s and early 1960s the way in which the stored instruction were provided was refined so that instead of having to input sequences of fairly meaningless code the instructions could be input in a form quite similar to English. Since the mid-1960s a vast number of computer languages have been developed, each with its own particular strengths and weaknesses. A further, more recent, development has been the creation of computer programs, such as Last One, that simplify the process of writing computer programs by allowing the program writer to write a computer program without having to know anything about computer program languages at all. In Illustration 6.9, an attempt has been made to indicate the differences between the different types of programming now available.

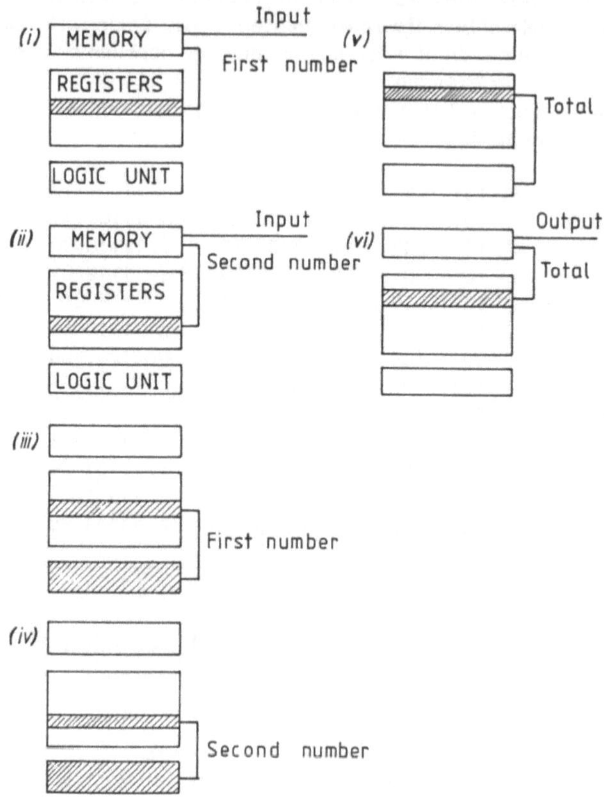

Illustration 6.8. Operation of a computer

The process of manipulation is carried out in elementary steps, and the detail of each step has to be present and correct. The microprocessor is powerful because the steps can be carried out very rapidly and repeatedly without error.

Instructions:

1. Get first number and store it.
2. Get second number and store it.
3. Put first number into the adder.
4. Put the second number into the adder.
5. Put the total in the register.
6. Transfer the total to the memory, and perhaps transmit the value to the outside world.

Illustration 6.9. Programming

The examples given here are not written in any specific computer language but in the *style* of the different levels of computer language.

Language	"Example" and comment.
High-level	"I want to add two numbers together and have the result displayed on the computer screen." This is how we would like to give instructions to computers. Unfortunately, this approach is not yet, and perhaps may never be, possible. A much more formal and restricted set of definitions has to be used.
High-level	"*Enter* firstvalue. *Enter* secondvalue. *Display* firstvalue + secondvalue." The italicized words and symbols have special significance since they are part of the computer language. In this case, *Enter* causes the computer to stop and wait for some information to be entered via the keyboard.
Low-level	"01 22 11 21 28 10." The instructions that the computer has to follow out are now specified in numeric detail and relate to the movement of information between the various registers (the temporary memories) that make up the computer. The high-level language above is built up by simply defining words such as *Enter* in terms of a whole series of these simple numeric instructions. Clearly it is easier for people to deal with the high-level language because it is easier to use—we do not have to worry about the operation of the machine—but it is slower because each of the high-level language instructions has to be translated into the low-level language instructions (which are themselves translated into the setting of switches).

Storage

So far we have discussed storage in terms of information and instructions being stored in the switches that make up the computer. There are, in fact, two ways of storing information in a form suitable for computers. One method uses an electric current, and the other uses the direction of a magnetic field, to indicate the presence or absence of a signal.

The principles of storage by recording values of electric current are described briefly in Illustration 6.10.

The alternative to semiconductor storage is magnetic storage (Illustration 6.11).

The methods of storing information in the computer itself may be supplemented by storage outside the computer, because, although slower, storage outside the computer is cheaper. Since such methods of external

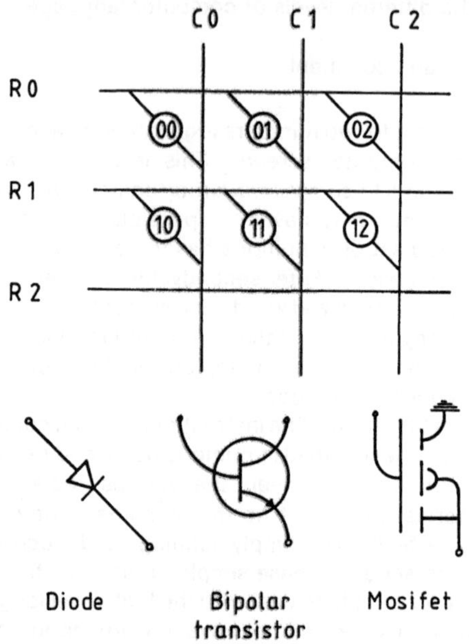

Illustration 6.10. Semiconductor storage

A semiconductor memory consists of an array of cells. One terminal of each cell is connected to a row wire, while the other terminal of each cell is connected to a column wire. In the diagram here only part of an array has been shown. Each cell has been given an address, 00, 01, etc. The cell address shows which row and which column the cell is attached to.

Each cell is capable of being either on or off. Since each cell can only be either on or off, the information stored in each cell is equivalent to either a 1 or 0. The value 1 or 0 is called a bit.

The address of the cell has got nothing to do with its contents; remember that each cell will only be either on, 1, or off, 0. The contents of the cell can be read by sending pulses down the appropriate row and column wires. So to read the contents of cell 11, pulses are sent down the row 1 and the column 1 wire.

The cell itself will be any device that can be either on or off. The cell could therefore be a diode, or a bipolar transistor, or anything else similar. The reasons for using a particular type of component will include cost, speed of operation, and convenience.

The storage can be either temporary or permanent. Read-only memory (ROM), is permanent. Permanent storage is achieved by disconnecting those cells that are to contain 0's (= off).

The disconnection is achieved by blowing a fuse.

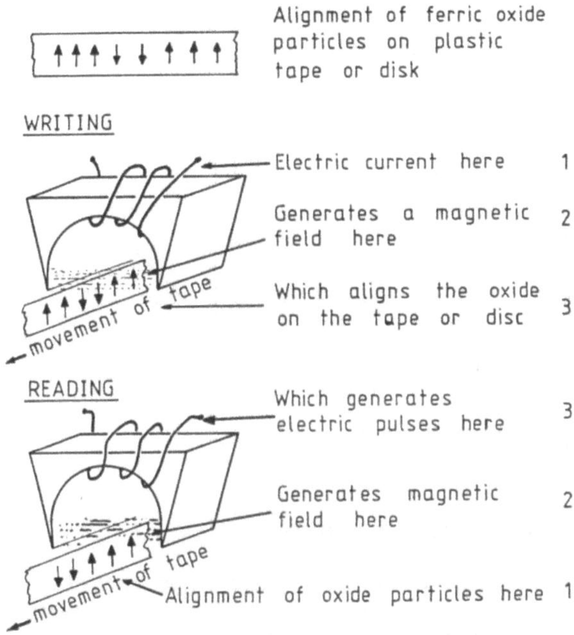

Illustration 6.11. Magnetic storage

Magnetic storage uses the magnetic effect of an electric current. The magnetic field aligns particles of ferric oxide which are stored on a plastic base of tape or disk. One direction is north, the other south. The magnetic tape or disk is then passed through a reader or writer.

It is not the actual alignment of the particles that matters; it is the change in the magnetic flux between the areas of different magnetization that generates the electric pulses.

storage tend to involve separate devices, they will be dealt with in the next chapter where we discuss information technology devices.

There are continuing developments in storage technology resulting in improved storage density, reliability, and costs. These developments are not necessarily based on the traditional forms of electromagnetic storage. As a guide to the arrangements, Illustration 6.12 shows the overall operating characteristics of standard storage methods currently available.

COMMUNICATION

Another aspect of new information technology is communication. The basic concept underpinning any form of signaling, which a study of semiotics

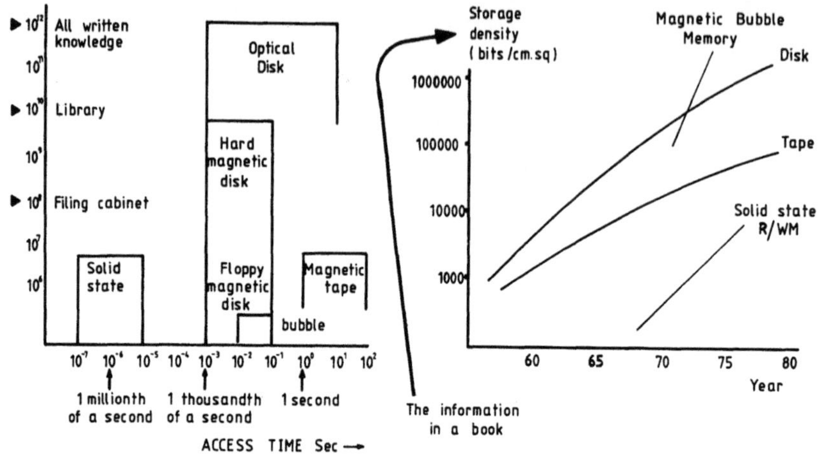

Illustration 6.12. Storage characteristics

This illustration shows how storage capacity, in terms of the number of bits/cm², has been increased by various technical developments over the past 20 years or so. It is apparently possible to just about get the contents of a book onto 1 cm² of disk or magnetic bubble memory! However, these figures should be treated with considerable caution since there are many factors working to reduce the actual achieved storage density and capacity of any particular medium. With disks, for example, we should always be careful to distinguish between unformatted storage capacity, which will be high, and formatted storage capacity, which might only be half the unformatted value.

In addition to storage density developments there have been developments in actual storage capacity and access time, the time it takes to get to a piece of information. The second illustration shows the typical kinds of storage capacities and access times available today. Again these figures should be treated with caution. Optical disks, for example, are only just becoming available for the ordinary user, and only one company was actually selling an optical disk storage system as of the autumn of 1983 and one year later optical storage is still much more talked about than used or available.

In terms of more familiar items such as a book, a filing cabinet, or a library, the equivalence of information in bits is rather speculative, but it is supplied to give a feel for the kind of potential available from digital methods. The interpretation given here has been based on the following calculation:

1 page = 250 words

1 word = 6 letters (or characters)

1 letter = 8 bits (using 7-bit ASCII coding with parity bit)

Therefore

1 page = 250 × 6 × 8 = 12,000 bits

1 book (at 250 pages) = 3 million bits

1 filing cabinet = 4 drawers each containing 2000 sheets of paper = 96 million bits

1 library = 300,000 books = 900 billion bits

All written knowledge = 30 million books (?) = 90 trillion bits

reveals communication to be concerned with, is the concept of change. Without change there is no communication. The symbols

AAAAAAAAAAAAAAAAAAAAAAAAAAAAAAAAAAA

do not, if taken by themselves, communicate very much simply because there is no change. Similarly, opening our mouths and saying "Ah" continuously and steadily does not convey very much meaning, no really useful information. The steadily spoken "Ah" can be represented diagrammatically as in Illustration 6.13. Quite where the loudness and frequency of the "Ah" would be depends on the characteristics of each particular voice. It is only when we start to vary the "Ah" that any information starts to get transmitted. It is this process of variation, achieved by opening and closing the mouth and changing the shape and size of the various resonating gaps of the body, that is represented in Illustration 6.14 by changes in pitch and loudness.

Telecommunication

So far we have concentrated on the humanly spoken word. However, the principle is exactly the same for electromagnetic, or more simply, electric waves.

Electromagnetic radiation covers a wide range of frequencies (Illustration 6.15), some of which are very familiar to us.

Modulation

We have already established that in order to communicate a message it is necessary to have something changing, or being modulated as the engineer would express the same idea. With any electric wave signal there are three distinct aspects that can be modulated: frequency, amplitude, or phase.

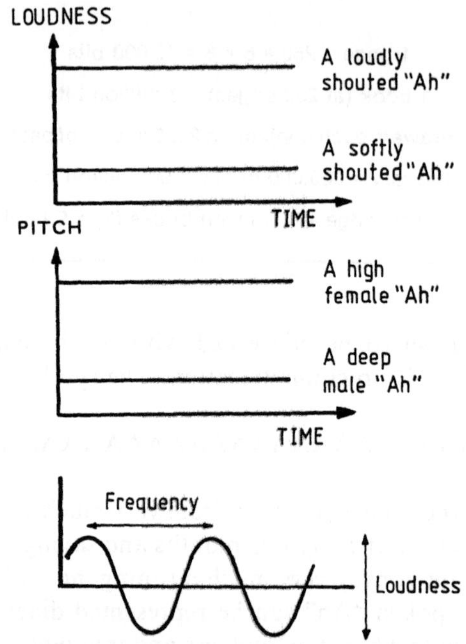

Illustration 6.13. Loudness and pitch

Here various properties of any wave are indicated. Of particular interest are the loudness, or amplitude, and the pitch, or frequency. Examples of sounds that are loud and soft and high- and low-pitched are shown.

Often it is useful to portray the two ideas of loudness and pitch in the same drawing. In the third illustration the amplitude is indicated by the height of the wave while the frequency is indicated by the distance between the tops of the wave.

Exactly what modulation of these three quantities does is shown in Illustration 6.16.

Amplitude modulation is the easiest to describe and so will be dealt with here. The other methods of modulation—frequency and phase—although dealing with different features of the wave, have many ideas in common with amplitude modulation.

Bandwidths

It is easy to see diagrammatically (Illustration 6.17) that the changing of the amplitude of a signal creates, in effect, a carrier frequency signal together

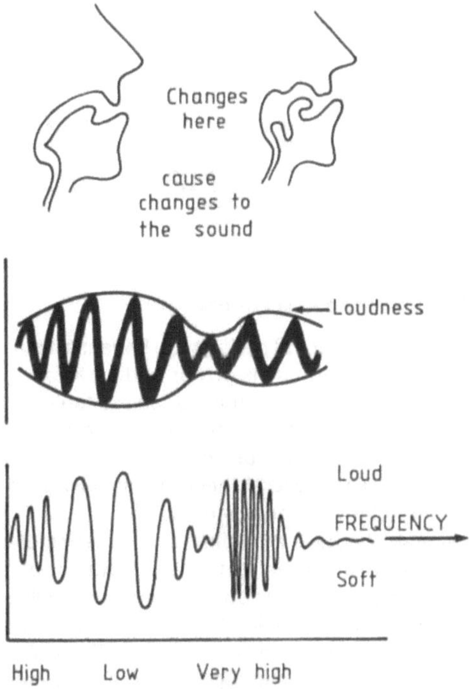

Illustration 6.14. Changes

If we think about human speech, then it is clear that changes in the mouth and other parts of the body change the sounds we make. These changes can be shown as modulations of both the amplitude and the frequency of our speech.

with a frequency band of modulating signals. The range of frequencies that the modulating signals create is called the signal bandwidth.

The greater the bandwidth of the device that carries the modulated signals the nearer to the original will be the received signal. A high-fidelity signal which is very much like the original signal—that is why it is called high-fidelity—occupies a large bandwidth. High-fidelity cassette tapes have a bandwidth of perhaps 20,000 Hz while lower-fidelity tapes have bandwidths of perhaps 10,000 Hz.

Unfortunately, the wider the bandwidth, and so the truer the signal, the more expensive it becomes to transmit the signal because more expensive components and higher-quality engineering are required.

The Telephone Link. As an example of a business communication system

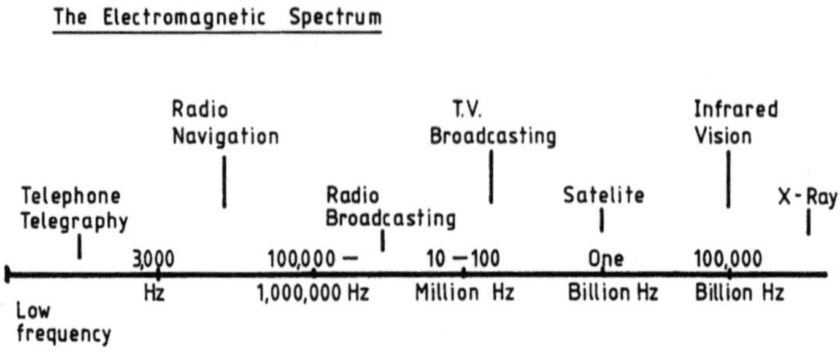

Illustration 6.15. Electromagnetic spectrum

All of these signals are electric. This is useful because it means that there is no fundamental difference between mains power and an X ray.

Suppose that the only form of communication available was writing on paper. The size of the message that could be sent would be determined primarily by the size of the sheet of paper that we were using. If paper was all of the same size, then in order to send a long message several sheets of paper would be needed, and this could obviously prove to be very inconvenient.

With electric signals we have a medium that in terms of message-carrying capability can be very small at one extreme—the frequency of mains electricity is 50 Hz—while it can be very large at the other—satellite signals operate at 1 billion Hz, for example, and lasers at 100 trillion Hz. The important fact is that the higher the frequency, the more messages can be carried (see Illustration 6.16 and 6.17). A laser beam can carry very many messages, and, as a tremendous bonus, the higher the frequency of the signal, the smaller is the physical size. It is almost as if the more writing we can get onto a piece of paper, the smaller it becomes! Because we are dealing with physically small signals, they become much easier to handle. A thin fiber carrying optical signals can carry very many more messages than a thick telephone cable.

we will look at the telephone network. The human voice extends over a frequency range from 10 to 5000 Hz. Telephone lines, however, only transmit signals over the range from 100 to 3000 Hz. The lower- and higher-frequency signals are simply not transmitted. This does not generally make a difference to the intelligibility of the received message. The only time that difficulties will occur is when we are trying to transmit something, such as the sound of a symphony orchestra, where the lack of signal bandwidth will become readily apparent—we simply will not hear certain instruments. The same kind of effect happens to human beings; as we grow older our ability to hear higher-frequency sounds erodes and we cannot hear as well.

Digital Telecommunications. The machines that we are interested in do not deal with continuous analogue waves. They deal with digital pulses. But digital pulses can be looked at as being built up by combinations of analogue waves (Illustration 6.18).

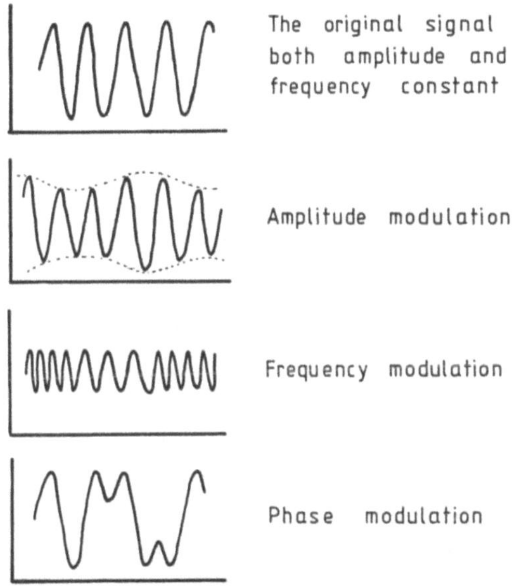

Illustration 6.16. Types of change

Modulation of electric signals is very much like modulation of speech, but there are differences. In particular, there is the possibility of phase modulation where neither the frequency nor the amplitude is modulated. Phase modulation, if applied to speech, gives a distorting effect sometimes heard on radios or seen on television when there is "good weather" interference (the kind of interference heard or seen during very good weather when stations not tuned into are received).

From Illustration 6.18 it can be seen that a digital pulse occupies a bandwidth of frequencies. Clearly the faster the pulses are sent, the quicker the information can be distributed. However, the faster the pulses are sent, the greater the operating frequency is, and so the higher the quality of the components and engineering required are, and thus the more expensive overall the whole operation becomes.

Guiding Structures. In order to get the electromagnetic radiation from one place to another, which is necessary for communication of information to occur, some transmission medium is required. Generally that medium will localize and direct the radiation from one location to another (the radiation will not always be localized and directed, it may be broadcasted). An obvious example of a localizing and directing medium is the metal wire used to supply electric power to our domestic and industrial tools and equipment, e.g., television sets, floor cleaners, washing machines, and computers.

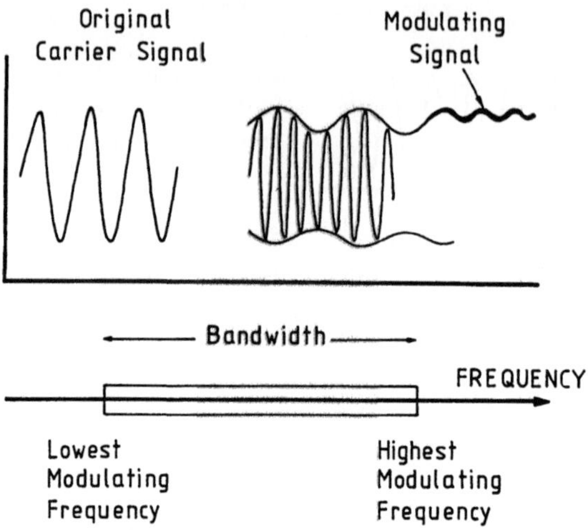

Illustration 6.17. Bandwidth

Modulation of the original carrier signal produces the kind of wave shape shown. The modulating signal has the effect of producing a set of signals over a range of frequencies, which is the signal bandwidth. If the communication channel being used has a bandwidth as wide, or wider, than the bandwidth of the modulating signals, then all is fine. If, however, the bandwidth of the channel is narrower than the bandwidth of the modulating signal, then some of the modulating signal will be lost, and distortion will occur. We come across this every day with the telephone system which has quite a narrow bandwidth, suitable for transmitting the human voice but not for playing a hi-fidelity record.

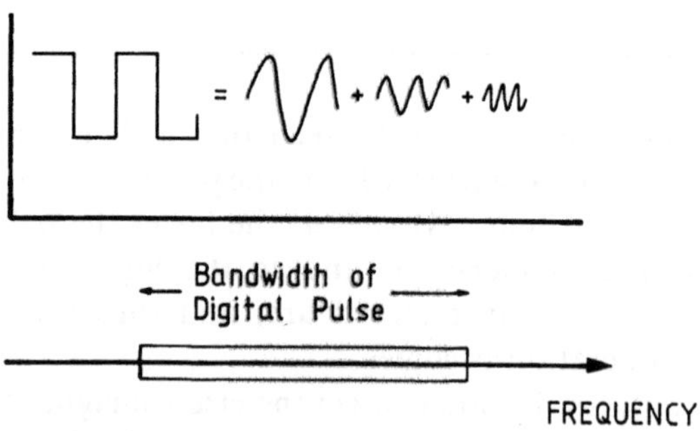

Illustration 6.18. Digital pulses

Digital pulses can be built up from a suitable series of "ordinary" waves, and because these ordinary waves each have their own particular and different frequencies, there is a bandwidth of the frequencies needed to make up the digital pulses. In fact, for a strictly perfect pulse, there is the requirement for an infinite bandwidth, but we can get away with something slightly less than perfect.

There are drawbacks to using metal wires. One major failing is that as the frequency of the electric signal (corresponding to the pitch of the human voice) increases, more and more of the energy of the electric signal is consumed by the wire itself. This is why a metal wire cannot be used to guide a light signal. The metal wire consumes the energy of the light wave so quickly that it is not possible to see anything. The rate at which the energy of the signal is consumed is measured by the attenuation coefficient. In order to transmit most of our information between machines we need high-frequency electric signals, although not usually so high a frequency as light. Metal wires are not particularly suitable, and so other methods of transmission have been devised. Examples of these other methods are shown in Illustration 6.19.

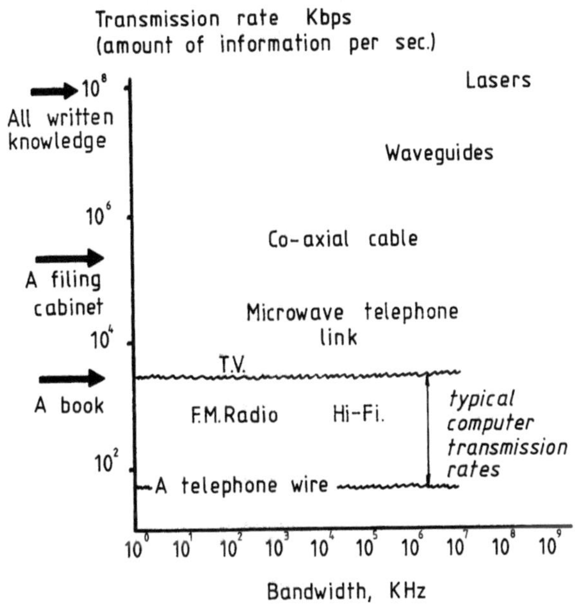

Illustration 6.19. Guiding structures

This illustration shows the possible transmission rates and bandwidths of various types of guiding structures. Low-bandwidth devices have low transmission rates. However, most of the channels shown here are more than adequate for dealing with communication between two computers.

To give an idea of the real meaning of the various transmission rates, typical values for a book, a filing cabinet and a library are shown along the upright axis. This is meant to indicate that, for example, the complete contents of a filing cabinet could be transmitted down a coaxial cable or the complete contents of a library could be transmitted along a laser beam communication link in 1 sec.

SUMMARY

The basis of the new information technology are small, fast, reliable switches. Production techniques have meant ever-falling costs for the popular microprocessors. Additionally, ever more powerful microprocessors have also been developed so that equipment that once was physically large is now small and convenient to use.

The principles of telecommunications are the same as they were 150 years ago: they enable machines that are linked by some form of guiding structure to exchange information.

DISCUSSION QUESTIONS

1. To what extent is change the essential characteristic of communication?
2. What are the relative drawbacks and advantages of digital as compared to analogue signaling techniques?

7

THE INFORMATION MACHINE

INTRODUCTION

The principles of information technology that have been described in the previous chapter will now be discussed as to how they apply to the specifics of TIM, the information machine. Although TIM is a computer it might aid understanding to use instead the name, "information machine." TIM consists of three separate parts: the processor, the store, and the communicator. Each of these three pieces will be discussed in turn.

THE PROCESSOR

The processor manipulates the information. It consists of many small switches together with other electrical components such as capacitors and resistors. The processor that will usually be of most concern to us is the microprocessor, a typical example of which is shown in Illustration 7.1.

The actual electronic circuits are hidden away from view inside the plastic encapsulation, which is what we normally see. Removing the encapsulation reveals the small (approximately 5 mm × 5 mm) rectangle of the highly polished and processed silicon chip.

Although it is possible to produce a useful information processing machine using only one or two processors, it is much more common to use many. If we were to open up the lid of a typical small business computer or word processor, we would find 10, 20, or perhaps 50 microprocessors, all soldered into position on their various circuit boards.

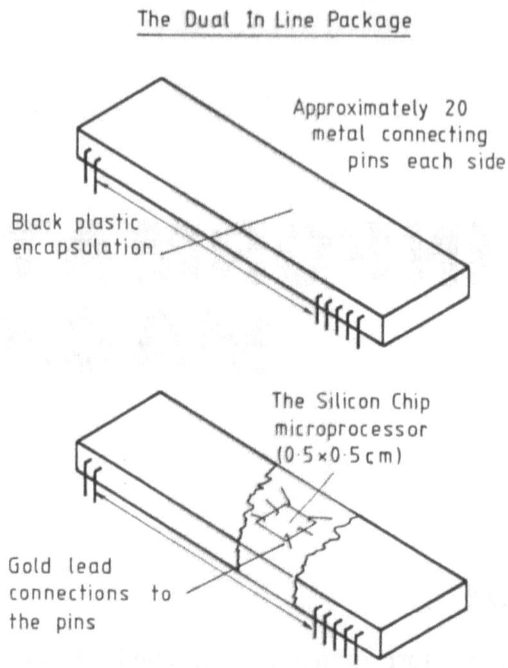

Illustration 7.1. The microprocessor

Although the microprocessor chip itself is very small, for practical purposes the chip has to be encased to protect it from physical damage. The most commonly encountered form of packaging is the "dual in line" shown here, which will have approximately 20 metal legs or pins on each side enabling it to be connected to the circuits of the computer. Inside the plastic packaging is the chip itself connected to the metal pins by gold wires.

Processor Word Length

The main distinction between processors is the word length, or number of bits, that the registers of the processor can handle. The longer the words, the greater the set of operations that can be easily performed. Hence, the more powerful the machine is. Typically, words are 4, 8, 16, or 32 bits in length.

Four-bit processors are used in simple applications such as car ignition systems, toys, and watches. They also normally have spare processing capacity so that, for example, in digital watches there are additional functions such as alarms and elapsed time indicators as well as simple time telling devices.

Eight-bit processors are used in process control equipment (used to control continuous manufacturing processes), video game machines, and most personal computers.

Sixteen-bit processors are used for the more sophisticated versions of the 8-bit applications as well as for making minicomputers.

Processor Programming

The processor is programmed by providing it with instructions that set the processor's switches by blowing fuses in the electronic circuitry. These instructions are set permanently in read-only memory, and once set they are unalterable unless devices such as EEPROMS are used (Illustration 7.2).

STORAGE

The first commercially available stored-program computer was the Ferranti Mark I which had a built-in memory capable of storing 10,240 bits (in the form of 256 words, each word being 40 bits). Today many of the smallest of

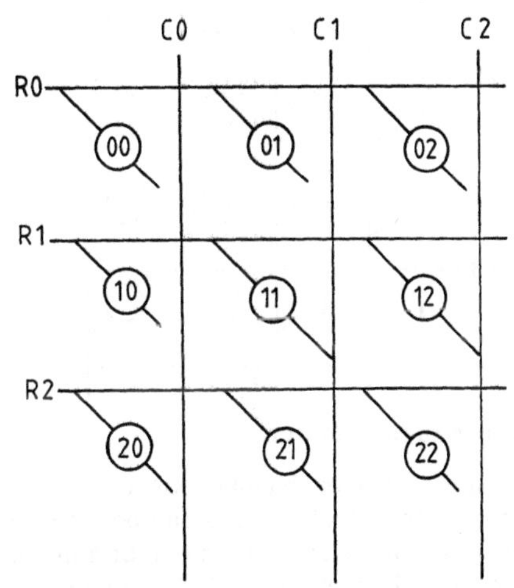

Illustration 7.2. Permanent programming

Bits of information are stored permanently by blowing fuses. Once its fuse has been blown, the cell is disconnected. Disconnected cells in the semiconductor array become permanently *off*, corresponding to 0. Here this is shown by being disconnected from the column wires.

personal computers will often have fifty times the amount of raw storage space provided by Ferranti.

The principles of information storage in semiconductor and magnetic memory have already been described. Generally speaking, semiconductor storage is used for a limited amount of fast-access memory, while magnetic storage is used for slower-access bulk storage. The primary reason for choosing the slower magnetic storage is because it is cheaper than semiconductor storage.

Semiconductor Storage

The amount of semiconductor storage that can be directly accessed by a processor is effectively limited by the word length that the processor uses, as shown in Illustration 7.3.

To look at, a microelectronic semiconductor storage device is the same as a microprocessor.

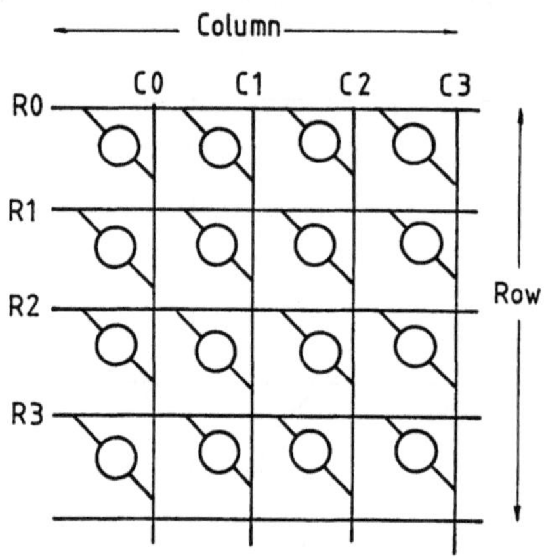

Illustration 7.3. Semiconductor storage

To operate a memory array, each cell needs to have a unique address, then the bit of information stored at that address can be retrieved at any time.

With a 4-bit processor any word is made up of a unique 4-bit combination ranging from 0000 to 1111. This gives ($2 \times 2 \times 2 \times 2 =$) 16 different combinations.

Using one word to identify the memory array's row address and a second word to identify the array's column address means that ($16 \times 16 =$) 256 different addresses are possible. So a 4-bit processor can have a 256-bit memory. By increasing the word length, much bigger memories can be used. An 8-bit processor, for example, can have 65,536 different addresses.

Magnetic Storage

Magnetic storage comes in the form of tape, which has become decreasingly important, or a disk, which has become increasingly important. Both these forms of magnetic storage suffer from the drawback that they rely on mechanical movement, and, as always, mechanical movement introduces decreasing reliability.

Magnetic Tape Storage. Tape is a slow method of storage. To locate stored information the magnetic tape has to be wound past the magnetic heads until the wanted information is found, and then the recorded information has to be transferred to the computer's memory. The first part of the operation is determined by the tape winding speed, the second part by the information transfer speed.

On mainframe computers tape lengths can be several thousand feet, and so it is clear that even with high tape-winding speeds it could take quite long periods of time to find some wanted information. At the other end of the range, personal computers use cassette tapes. For these it will usually take only a minute or so to locate the required information.

Having physically moved the tape to a suitable position it is the rate of transfer of information that then becomes important. For mainframe computers information transfer will be conducted at high speeds, perhaps 200,000 bits/sec. For personal computers information transfer rates are more likely to be a few hundred bits per second.

Magnetic disk. Disks offer very fast access, of the order of a few seconds. But the disk drive units are mechanically sensitive since they rely on the use of high disk speeds and narrow gaps between the magnetic head and the disk surface.

To give some illustration of the potential problem we face, for some disk systems even a particle of cigarette smoke is big enough to stop or even damage the disk drive mechanism. The problem is caused by the smoke getting trapped between the disk and the magnetic heads, thus "crashing" the system.

Floppy Disks. The first disk devices appeared in the mid-1950s, and the first floppy disk drive in 1971. A floppy disk is a thin disk of magnetic recording material enclosed in a square protective cover. The covering envelope protects the disk surface from damage by human physical contact, and the disk is never removed from the envelope. A slot is cut in the protective cover to allow the magnetic heads either to record onto the disk or to read from the disk. Information is stored on the disk in much the same way as information is stored on a gramophone record, in tracks, except that the tracks on a magnetic disk are concentric and do not spiral into the center of the disk. Illustration 7.4 shows the essential features of a typical floppy disk.

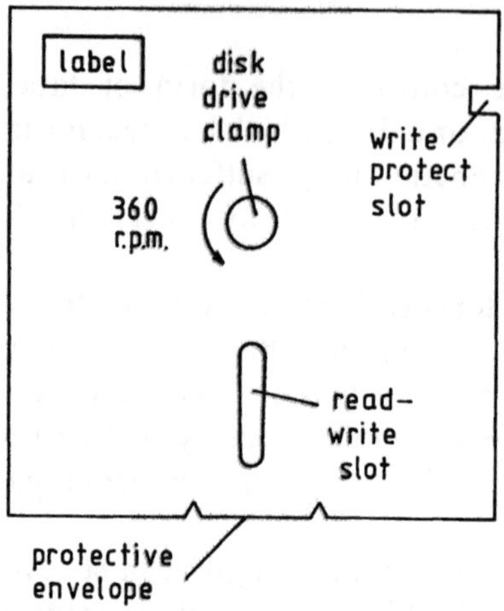

Illustration 7.4. Floppy magnetic disk

A floppy magnetic disk is a disk of flexible plastic like material with a magnetic coating. For the purposes of mechanical protection, the disk is enclosed in a protective envelope, and the magnetic contents of the disk are read by a sensing device scanning the exposed read-write slot. The disk is rotated inside the envelope by the disk drive and the disk may contain the equivalent of up to hundreds of pages of text depending upon the quality of the magnetic coating process and the diameter of the disk (bigger disks will tend to be able to store more information).

Disk Storage Density. Clearly, if both sides of the disk are used to store information (double-sided disks), then more information will be stored than if only one disk side was used. Additionally, more information can be stored by getting more tracks onto the disk. One approach is to make the disks bigger; the other is to make the recording tracks narrower.

As far as disk size is concerned, disks come in a range of sizes: 14, 12, 8, 5, and 3 in. diameter all being popular. Of these various sizes there is growing emphasis on the smaller sizes because, although tending to offer less storage capacity, they are much easier to handle.

The number of tracks that can be put onto a disk depends primarily on the track width. The narrower a track is, the less space it will occupy, and so the greater the number of tracks that can be recorded. The thinner the track coating is and the closer the magnetic head can get to the disk surface, the greater the amount of information that can be stored in a given area. The information storage capacity per area can be expressed in terms of bits/cm^2. Current storage densities are around 500,000 bits/cm^2—giving a storage capacity equivalent to 40 pages/cm^2! This information density is not actually achieved because of the need to have spaces between the tracks and the need to record on the disk itself information indicating what information is recorded on the disk, etc. Effective recording densities are in the region of 1 page/cm^2.

In addition to developing techniques for using thinner coatings and narrower head gaps, it is also possible to develop the recording material itself. In mid-1983 Eastman Kodak announced a 10-Mbyte 5-in. floppy disk which would provide approximately ten times the amount of storage currently available.

Floppy disk sizes have been standardized for some years on 8- and 5-in. Traditionally, 8-in. disks have been used in the more office-oriented equipment such as word processors, while the smaller 5-in. disks have been used in small personal computers. However, since disk size is one of the factors determining final equipment size, there is pressure for using smaller-sized disks, and so the 8-in. disk is considered by many to be obsolescent. Because of this pressure there are now, in addition to the 5-in. mini-floppy disk, a number of disk systems using disks of smaller diameters, around 3 in.

Hard Disks. The alternative magnetic rotating surface memory, which is another way of saying magnetic disk, is the hard or rigid disk. The reason for the existence of the hard disk is simply that as disk diameters increase, the disks droop if they are made from flexible material. In all other respects the hard disk works essentially on the same principles as the floppy disk.

Hard disks are usually connected today with the word Winchester. A Winchester disk is simply a disk based on a design produced by IBM, in 1973. The Winchester disk differs from previous designs in that it comes in its own sealed container which protects the disk from any dirt in the surrounding atmosphere. Additionally, the magnetic head actually rests on the disk when it is not moving and flies off when in motion; also, the disk is lubricated with oil. Winchester disks come in a variety of shapes and sizes. Illustration 7.5 describes hard disk devices.

Other Storage Devices

The three most popular candidates for successful future use as storage devices are: EEPROMS, optical disks, and bubble memories.

EEPROMs. EEPROMS are Electrically Erasable Programmable Read-Only Memories. They are semiconductor memories in which information can be stored permanently until it is required to alter the memory contents. Application of an electric signal, sent, for example, along a telephone line, alters the memory content. This form of storage offers a practical, updatable, but nonvolatile, memory.

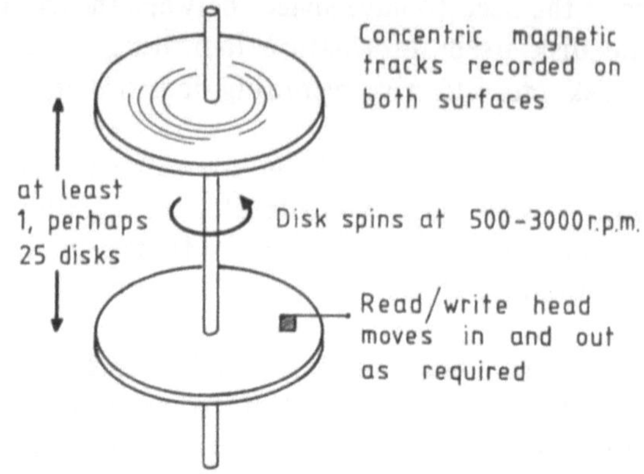

Illustration 7.5. Hard disk devices

Cartridge: a single magnetic disk in a plastic case. The whole arrangement looks rather like an oversize, 14-in-diameter tape measure.

Pack: Two or more, perhaps 26, disks in one container. One of the disks may be removable.

Both cartridges and packs can be put into and removed from the disk drive unit.

Optical Disks. Optical disks use a laser to apply a beam of light to a disk in order to store and retrieve information. There are different ways in which the laser beam is actually used. For example, it may be used to physically burn a sequence of small pits into the disk surface in order to build up the appropriate code sequences.

Whatever technology makes up the underlying concept the basic principle is that because the laser beam is so narrow, typically 1/1000 mm wide, high information storage densities can be achieved, currently 15–20 pages/cm^2. To give an idea of the effect that this has, a single 12-in.-diam. optical disk would be able to store at least 1000 Mbytes of binary information. If that idea seems remote, it may be helpful to think in terms of a 50,000 page book, or 200 typically sized paperbacks.

Although optical disk systems are well-established as a concept, it should be noted that as of mid-1983, although there were several companies working on the concept, only one company, NEC, actually had a complete optical storage system available. As we will see below when discussing magnetic bubble memories, sometimes a technological development does not always come to pass as expected. Current optical disk systems are expensive, around $15,000 for the optical disk drive itself, but experience shows that prices will fall quite rapidly and sharply with popularity, and they do offer a comprehensive way of dealing easily with large amounts of information.

Optical disks are currently available only in a write-then-read mode. The information that is already stored cannot be altered; however, erasable optical disks are being researched and may become available within the next five years.

Magnetic Bubble Memories. Magnetic bubble memories are magnetic memory devices that unlike tape or disks do not involve the use of any moving mechanical components. Superficially, the bubble memory device looks rather like a microprocessor (Illustration 7.6).

As well as offering potentially superior technical performance compared to other magnetic devices because they do not involve any moving parts and they are physically much smaller, magnetic bubble memories can also store reasonably large amounts of information, about half the amount of a standard floppy disk or 15 times as much as an on-line semiconductor memory device.

However, the cost of bubble memory storage is somewhere around ten times as much as other more conventional storage, and so bubble storage use is limited to specialized applications where rugged, nonvolatile, but reusable memory, is required.

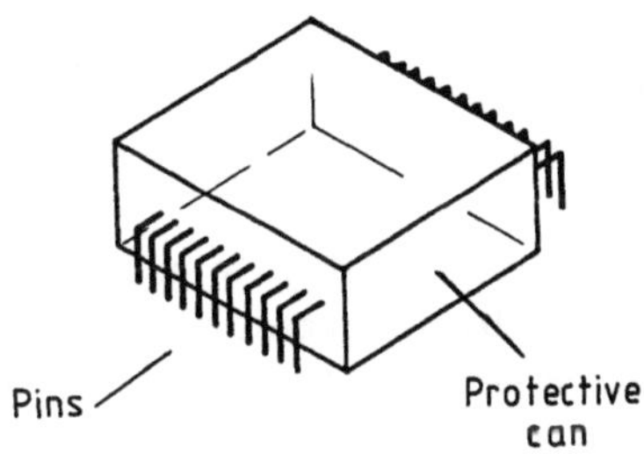

Illustration 7.6. Magnetic bubble memory device

Inside the can are flat permanent magnets, and beneath them are sets of coils. The coils are used to reduce or increase the strength of the magnetic fields and so increase or decrease the size of magnetized areas. Information is stored by an area of particular magnetization, called a bubble. The bubble can be moved around, and so the stored information can be circulated through a magnetic circuit. The result of this is a physically small device with characteristics similar to those of a magnetic disk but without the need for a disk drive unit.

The main advantages of the magnetic bubble memory are that (i) there are no moving parts; and (ii) it offers storage capacities and access times similar or better to those of a magnetic disk. It has one major disadvantage, however, it is more expensive to make than a disk.

COMMUNICATION DEVICES

Having described the devices that are used to manipulate and store information, it is now necessary to consider the last function: the communication of information. Communication can occur either between people and information machines or simply between information machines.

Communication from people to machines is not necessarily the same as communication from machines to people. We will deal first of all with communication from people to machine.

People-Machine Communication

In recent years a complete area of expertise has grown up around the study of the design of human–machine interfaces. Some sensible guidelines have been drawn up, and it has become commonly accepted that any device used by people should be easy to use and follow natural rules; for example, press the "right" control to move right and the "left" control to move left.

The reasons why communication between people and machines does not follow such sensible rules as these is because of a combination of the machine builder/designer either not knowing or not bothering to implement sensible practices and technological development not being advanced enough.

In fact, almost every artifact that exists manages to exhibit bad design to a greater or lesser degree. There are well-known examples of designs that do not seem to follow any rules for helping people. Why, for example, is the standard typewriter keyboard laid out the way it is? For reasons of ease of use by humans or for some other reason?

Currently, the most common way to achieve communication from person to machine is, in fact, by the operation of a typewriterlike keyboard, usually connected to a screen in order to provide a visual feedback display to show which keys have been pressed.

There are other input methods that either use modified keyboards of some kind or which depart radically from the keyboard method of control by using speech control. These will be considered in their turn.

Keyboard Control

The function of the keyboard is to transmit a signal to the rest of the equipment. The method by which the correct electronic signal is generated when a particular key is pressed varies somewhat between designs of keyboard and is not of great importance here. The point to note is that when a key is pressed a signal is generated and transmitted to the processor.

The simplest keyboard now generally available consists of about 15 keys, enabling the digits from 0 to 9 to be input together with some additional information such as the decimal point and arithmetic operators.

Even with something as simple as a numeric keypad there are different ways of arranging the layout of the keys (Illustration 7.7). Moving onto more complex arrangements, the typewriter keyboard is the dominant method for touch inputting information from humans to machines. This keyboard is also a particularly good example of poor design. Bailey (1982) summarizes the work carried out by others, all of whom show that there are a variety of improvements that could be made. In spite of these potential improvements, improved keyboards do not on the whole appear to offer any significant gains as far as speed, accuracy, or comfort are concerned (except apparently for Klockenberg's split-board arrangement for alleviating shoulder tension).

Although there is uniformity of design with English-language keyboards, generally following the QWERTY arrangement, there can be considerable variation within that standard (Illustration 7.8).

Number of Keys. Probably the most obvious variation is the number of keys on the keyboard. The number has to be limited if a reasonable input speed is to be achieved, otherwise there will be too many key positions for the operator to memorize.

If, however, it is desired to include *control* functions on a keyboard as well as character inputs, then either there has to be a number of extra control keys or some keys have to be able to perform several different functions, or both. On the whole it seems that a larger number of keys is preferred to multi-function keys (Illustration 7.9).

The use of special-function keys can be made easier by grouping and coloring to help identify them, and by separating critical but different function keys to reduce the risk of pressing the wrong key by accident—for example, by ensuring that the delete key is not next to the execute or insert key.

Illustration 7.7. Alternative keypad layouts

```
1 2 3        7 8 9
4 5 6        4 5 6
7 8 9        1 2 3
  0            0
```

There is some evidence to suggest that the left-hand arrangement is less prone to operator error than the right-hand layout (Bailey, 1982).

Illustration 7.8. QWERTY keyboard layout

The standard letter layout for the English language keyboard is

QWERTYUIOP
ASDFGHJKL
ZXCVBNM

There is considerable variation with respect to the other keys of a standard typewriterlike keyboard, however. For example, immediately above the letters are usually the digits 1 to 0. These will also usually have special symbols associated with them. What these special symbols are and how they are arranged will vary from machine to machine. The symbols on the digit keys for five different keyboards close to hand when writing this were, for example:

	Digit key									
Keyboard	1	2	3	4	5	6	7	8	9	0
Wang OIS	!	@	#	$	%	£	&	*	(	)
Spectrum	!	@	#	$	%	&	‘	(	)	_
Newbury terminal	!	“	#	$	%	&	‘	(	)	0
Commodore	!	“	#	$	%	&	‘	(	)	0
Olympia	*	“	/	@	£	_	&	‘	(	)

The various differences between them could obviously cause some confusion.

Modified Keyboards

The full-size, full-movement keyboard is the easiest to use but can make the equipment bulky and expensive. Because of these constraints, a variety of other design approaches have been tried out with varying degrees of success so that keyboards now come in a variety of engineering designs from the full-size, full-movement keyboard normally associated with a typewriter, through a range of reduced-size and reduced-movement keyboards, to touch-sensitive keyboards. In addition, there are a variety of devices that are modified keyboards in that they require people to push, press, or point something which is not, however, a full-bodied keyboard:

The Mouse. The mouse is a device that when rolled around on any work surface allows an operator to control the equipment. It is connected to a computer screen to show the operator what operation is being carried out (Illustration 7.10).

This device, introduced by Xerox and then used more notably by Apple, does away with a need for control key position knowledge since both the

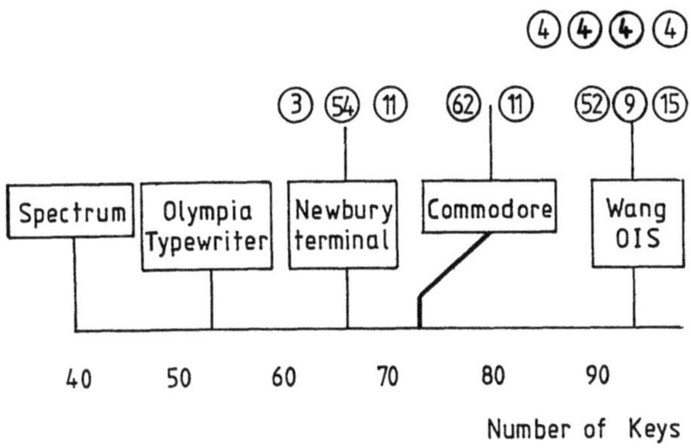

Illustration 7.9. Example keyboard key counts

Spectrum:	40. In one cluster, although some keys may perform up to five different functions.
Olympia typewriter:	54. In one cluster.
Newbury terminal:	68. In three clusters. Four light up.
3 11 54	
CBM 2001:	73. In two clusters. Four blue. Six red. Eleven gold.
53 20	
CBM 8032:	73. In two clusters.
62 11	
Wang OIS:	93. In eight clusters.
4 4 4 4 1 52 9 15	

operations available and those being carried out can be displayed on the screen. The screen display, therefore, acts as a varying keyboard, allowing the operator to concentrate only on those keys that are relevant at any given time.

Touch-Sensitive Screens. The other version of a screen-based modified keyboard is the touch-sensitive screen. By bonding invisible electrodes onto the glass panel of a screen and using computer programs that display the appropriate instructions, it is possible for the operator to control operations by pointing to whatever course of action is required wherever it is displayed on the screen. The signal generated by touching the screen is used as the input control instruction.

Handwritten Input

There are other techniques for carrying out communication between people and machines that rely on the use of handwriting. Since this process of communication is not carried out on ordinary sheets of paper but relies

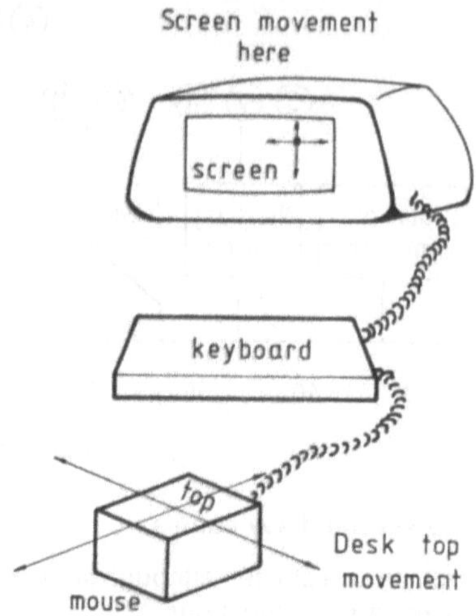

Illustration 7.10. The mouse

The mouse is a simplified keyboard. At the present time, however, no one is really sure whether the mouse is a very good idea or just a gimmick.

The concept behind the mouse is to relieve the computer operator from many tedious keyboard activities. By moving the mouse, which is simply a hand-sized box containing a ball bearing, the cursor on the screen is moved in an identical fashion. Pressing down a button on the mouse will result in the activity, over which the screen cursor rests being carried out.

instead on the use of tablelike devices, this can also be considered as the use of a modified keyboard. Such devices are not used widely because of their limitations. They are of use, however, in special circumstances such as inputting warehouse inventory data—which tends to be solely numeric and therefore easy to handle—directly to a computer-based information storage system.

Voice Input

The drawback to inputting information by touch is that it is, for humans, a limited and artificial way of communicating. In order to send messages of any length, many keys have to be pressed, which not only means that the process is slow because of the limited speed of keyboard operation, but also means that errors will occur that will either have to be corrected or that, if not detected and righted, may well cause operating problems later on.

The most natural way for people to communicate is by speech, although speech is only natural because of a long process of evolution for human beings in general, and several years of learning for each of us individually. It seems obvious then that machines should be built that can respond to spoken information.

Since physically speech is transmitted as variations in air pressure, it would seem easy to use a transducer that could detect air pressure variations and transform them into electronic signals which could then be processed. The general principle involved in speech input recognition therefore is to use a microphone (the transducer) to generate an electronic signal corresponding to the original sound-wave air pressure variations, and then match this signal against stored patterns of signals. The best stored-pattern match is then taken as being what was said.

Sampled Speech

The storage of speech patterns is carried out digitally, but when applied to continuous speech this takes up a considerable amount of storage capacity. Simplification is achieved by dealing with samples taken from isolated words rather than trying to deal with the whole of continuous speech. Using a sampling approach on isolated words it is possible to have speech recognition devices for small computers at a very low cost (£50). As an example of the difficulties of trying to deal with continuous speech, an experimental IBM system using a very powerful computer which can recognize a vocabulary of 1000 spoken words takes approximately one minute per word to analyze normal continuous speech.

The Sampling of Speech. There are two physical characteristics of speech (and their variation with time) that can be analyzed: frequency and intensity (Illustration 7.11).

Samples of the speech formants, e.g., the air pressure–frequency patterns, are stored and compared for voice control purposes. By the use of a fairly simple computer program, the spoken key words that will be recognized by the computer can then be arranged into menus to enable, in theory at least, quite powerful voice-controlled editing facilities to be developed (Illustration 7.12).

Communication from Machine to Person

The most common way for a machine to communicate the results of its labors is by some form of display of symbols on a screen or a page of paper. Of these two approaches reading words printed onto paper is still the most efficient way of absorbing information for people.

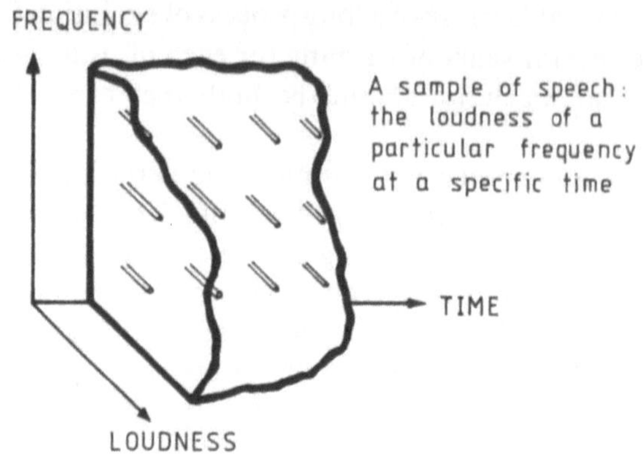

Illustration 7.11. The sampling of speech

As we have seen, any wave can be described in terms of its frequency and amplitude. Here these two parameters are used together with the way in which they vary with time. The sample of speech that is taken is represented as a tube. Because every spoken word will be different the height of the samples will necessarily vary from word to word, so there ought to be only a small chance of different words being confused with one another.

Paper

The prime advantage of paper is that it provides a permanent record of the results. In addition, paper is a familiar medium. We have grown up with it and know how to use it, and many machines and tools and much effort have been expended in developing ways to handle it.

Printing onto paper is achieved either by hitting the paper with some relatively solid physical object, which is known as impact printing, or by using some significantly less substantial object such as a beam of electrons or a jet of ink, which is known as nonimpact printing.

Impact Printing

Various impact printer arrangements are shown in Illustration 7.13.

Typewriters. The most obvious impact printer is the conventional typewriter. Typewriters have been developed over the years so that the totally fixed typing basket arrangement, which was slow and could not accommodate changes of type style, has been replaced in electric typewriters by some form of removable head, usually known as a golfball. Golfballs, or similar devices, speed up the printing process and are more reliable since they use far fewer mechanical components.

Golfballs and Daisy Wheels. The golfball is still a fairly complex mechanism and requires movement in three directions—raising, tilting, and spinning—in order to get the appropriate fully preformed character into the correct position for impacting the paper. So further developments have been undertaken that have yielded a variety of mechanisms based on the same idea but which are somewhat easier and faster to operate.

The advantages of devices such as daisy wheels and thimbles are that they only move in one direction, they spin, and being much lighter than other solid devices they can move faster.

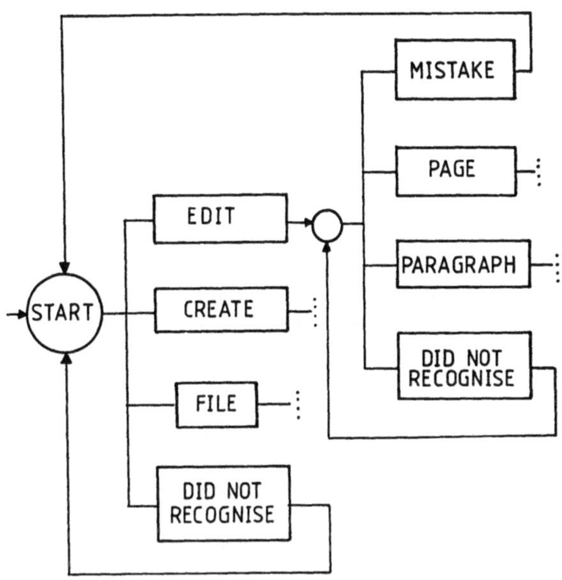

Illustration 7.12. A possible word recognition menu

At stage 1 only a few words will be recognized. It is suggested that these words might be: Edit, Create, and File. Any word not recognized will cause the computer to ask for a repetition of the word.

At the next level down the words following on from Edit might be Mistake, Page, or Paragraph. Here Mistake indicates that the speaker realizes that he or she chose the wrong word—Edit, in this case—and wishes to go back up one level.

By this branching approach many different words can be recognized without the need for a very sophisticated speech recognition device or program to identify between many different words simultaneously.

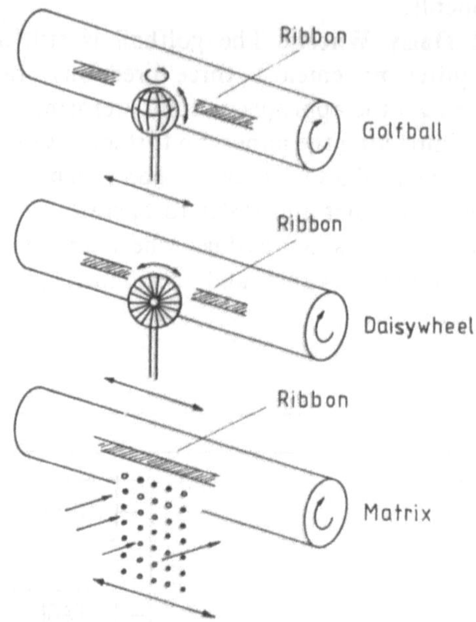

Illustration 7.13. Impact printers

In this illustration the principles of three different impact printers are shown.

The golfball printer uses a golfballlike printing head. The ball moves in three directions as shown, and this, together with its relative weight, means that it is a relatively slow device.

The daisy wheel printer has the characters to be printed on the end of each stem of the daisy wheel. The motion of the daisy wheel is simpler, and the wheel weighs less, so faster printing can be achieved. Additionally, because the device is mechanically simpler, it is more reliable.

The third version of impact printing is the matrix printer. Here, instead of having preformed characters as with the golfball and daisy wheel, the characters are built up from an array, or matrix, of needles. Different combinations of needles hit the paper to produce different characters. The bigger, or denser, the matrix is the higher the quality of the characters printed. Since this device is even simpler and less complex, it can be even faster and more reliable.

The fastest of these devices achieves an actual output speed of perhaps 200 words/min (15 characters/sec); the rated speeds are much higher but fail to take into account such details as the need to change paper which are encountered when actually using the devices in real life.

Changing Print Styles. With all preformed printing devices there is a limitation in that only the characters on the printing head can be used. This can only be overcome either by the manual changing of one printing head for another (although clearly the delays introduced by the changing process slow down the output printing speed and also means that an operator is required to be present to change the wheel) or by the use of automatic daisy wheel changing, using a double-headed daisywheel printer (although obviously only two different print styles can be accommodated by this approach).

In the late 1970s and early 1980s the daisy wheel printer scored well by offering a unique combination of quality, speed, and relatively low cost. Now, however, all these attributes are under attack by other printer designs. Perhaps, in the long term, the most important consideration will be simply that of cost. The daisy wheel-type of printer is still a relatively complex mechanical device, and, whereas in the mid-1970s the cost of a daisy wheel printer represented perhaps only 20% of the total cost of an information processing unit, by the mid-1980s it is possible that the declining costs of other components will mean that the daisy wheel printer will represent more on the order of 60% of the total system cost.

Further Speed Increases. At a rate of 200 words/min it takes only a minute or two to produce a standard-page-sized letter (European and American standard sizes are different but not significantly so as far as the discussion of output speed is concerned). Speed increases are obviously desirable if much text is to be produced, but naturally a price of some kind has to be paid, and generally speaking that price is one of quality.

Line Printers. Line printers, while still using fully preformed characters, set up whole lines of printing at a time, thus eliminating the delays involved in printing one character, moving to the next printing position, selecting the next character, and then printing that. However, a significant quality loss occurs.

Matrix. The matrix printer offers an alternative not by using fully preformed characters but by allowing characters to be set up by selecting which out of a matrix of needles will hit the paper. The quality of the final printout is determined by the matrix size. The bigger the matrix dimensions the higher the quality, so that a 7×9 matrix offers higher quality than one that is 5×7, but it is not of letter quality. Improvements to quality can be achieved by using multipass printing where each line is printed over more than once so that the characters are filled in and/or by using even bigger matrices, 20×30, for example.

Nonimpact Printing

The alternative to impact printing is nonimpact printing. Essentially a nonmechanical printing method is used. The inherent advantages of this approach are that there is greater speed, less noise, more reliability, and greater flexibility and adaptability in print styles. There are currently three methods of nonimpact printing.

Electrothermal. Electrothermal printing achieves print on paper by using an electric arc to burn off the top layer from specially coated paper. These printers are cheap to acquire, but they use expensive special paper, are slow in operation, and produce fairly poor-quality output.

Inkjets. In inkjet printers the ink is fired in jets through holes in a metal plate with the direction of the ink being controlled by the strength of electric fields controlled either by a microprocessor or, in the big systems, by a complete computer. Because there is no fixed-form font, in theory any shape of character can be formed and printed. In addition, printing speeds can be quite high because of the lack of any massive mechanical moving parts.

In the past, however, inkjet printers have suffered from an embarrassing lack of reliability, mainly connected with the difficulties of designing an ink that does not dry too rapidly and clogs up the ink jet holes or, alternatively, is not too runny and smears the paper it is squirted onto. Recently announced developments include an ink that only dries when in contact with paper which could, if true, eliminate many of the previous printing problems.

Lasers. Laser printers are based on the ideas behind the typical Xerographic plain-paper copying process. A beam of electrons from a laser is used to spray an electrostatic charge onto a moving belt. The charge is then transferred by contact and pressure to a sheet of paper, and carbon particles stick wherever the electrostatic charge is. The carbon is fused onto the paper by heating to produce the final printed image.

Using laser-based printers, speeds can be achieved such as those achieved by a paper copier (a printing speed of one sheet of paper per second, which can be easily achieved by a plain-paper photocopier, is equivalent to 1000–2000 words/min).

The initial laser printer designs were quite clearly intended for systems with massive outputs of paper since the machines cost upward of £250,000. However, technological developments have meant that laser printers are now becoming available from £10,000. Slightly more sophisticated and expensive printers from around £20,000, which can handle any of 30 print fonts in 10, 12, or 15 pitch, are now available. Microprocessor-controlled laser printers can achieve outputs of around 10 pages/min (50 words/sec) while the more powerful computer-controlled printers can achieve a speed of around 200 pages/min.

The quality of print, measured in terms of the number of printing lines per inch of paper, is good, in the range of 200–400 lines/in. As a guide for comparison, half-tone picture reproduction, used for producing photographs in newspapers and magazines, of an acceptable quality, is just about possible at 400 lines/in, while facsimile uses perhaps 40 lines/in.

Centralization of Printing

With the machines being so expensive, printing obviously tends to become a centralized operation because of the high capital cost. With centralization of operations it becomes more important to have a reliable printing device, and although figures relating to reliability are difficult to obtain, it would seem that 95% is not untypical, giving a working mean time between failures of 100,000 pages of output.

The three main contenders for general business use are the matrix, daisy wheel, and inkjet printers. These are further compared in Illustration 7.14.

Nonpaper Displays

The advantage of a paper display is its relative permanence, but this can also be a disadvantage. Among the major reasons for not wanting a permanent display is expense. As we have seen, printers can quite easily cost as much as the rest of the system itself—and reliability—of all parts of the system, the printer is most likely to be prone to fail. In addition, it could well be that permanent records on paper are not actually required so that the production of print onto paper is a waste of time and effort.

Illustration 7.14. Printer factors

Factor	Matrix	Daisy wheel	Inkjet
Reliability	7	7	4
Speed	8	4	5
Quality	4-7	8	5
Price	6	6	6
Noise	4	5	10
Output freedom[a]	7	3	6
Multiprinting	7	7	0

[a]Output freedom is the ability to produce color and graphics and to change print style.

Summary: The matrix printer is currently of low quality, although this is being improved by introducing multipass printing and higher-density matrices.

The matrix printer is noisy, but it is fast and versatile.

The daisy wheel printer, although producing a high-quality output, is fairly inflexible in output and is noisy.

The inkjet printer is extremely versatile and is noiseless, but it cannot produce multiple copies (except by reprinting, which reduces output speed), and it suffers from a reputation of being too expensive, unreliable, and of low quality.

Even if a permanent record is thought to be required, the storage of paper in some form of paper-filing system can create enormous organizational problems (typically, for organizations using paper-based records, some 10% of employee time is spent in finding and filing pieces of paper (Doswell, 1983)).

For all of the above reasons, transitory screen displays are a useful addition for providing information. There are three major screen display methods at the present time, although only one of these, the cathode-ray tube, is common. The other two methods—plasma screens and liquid crystal displays—seem unlikely to ever become widely popular, although they have useful niches to fill.

Cathode-Ray Tubes

The cathode-ray tube (CRT) is the same device as is used in a television set. Although there is a wide range of possible display colors and sizes to choose from, the most popular formats are green on black or black on white, 25 lines of text, 40 or 80 characters/line, displayed on a 10- or 11-in (28 cm) screen.

The character dimensions shown on the screen vary from one system to another but are typically between 3.5 and 4 mm wide and 4 to 8 mm high. The characters themselves are not solid but are built up from a matrix of bright spots with the possible matrix typically consisting of an array of 5×7 bright spots. The bright spots are caused by visible light being emitted from a screen of phosphor, with the chemical and physical characteristics of the phosphor determining the display color and permanence.

The cathode-ray tube is essentially a large glass envelope containing an electron gun at one end and a phosphor screen at the other. The glass bulb is pumped out to low pressures to form a vacuum. The electrons from the high-voltage electron gun are directed onto the appropriate part of the phosphor screen by sets of deflecting plates where they hit the phosphor, which then emits light that is received by the human eye. The screen size is determined by the technical difficulties connected with the construction of large robust glass tubes containing a vacuum.

Drawbacks to and Concerns about CRTs

The first displays used in the mid-1950s were, by current standards, appalling devices, but they were not used in the way that we use screens today. Even with 30 years of development, there are still three areas of serious misgiving concerning screen displays:

Size. The first is the size of the CRT; it is big, mostly long, occupying, typically, quite a large volume. The size is caused by the length of the tube itself, and although this aspect has been under investigation since the early 1960s it is not until recently that the first viable "flat" CRTs have been developed as a commercial proposition.

Flat screens are based on the idea of bending or folding the electron beam that is used to excite the phosphor screen. In the two flat screens likely to be most readily available the beam is simply bent through a right angle (Illustration 7.15). The importance of flat-screen displays lies in the increased future viability of portable desktop information processing equipment.

Health Hazards. The second difficulty is the potential health hazards. CRTs use high-energy electron beams, and these beams on impacting the phosphor screen must inevitably generate some x-ray radiation. X-ray radiation is simply a particular kind of high-energy radiation which is capable of penetrating the human body. It is known that in excessive quantities X rays can cause damage to the body.

No research yet conducted has shown the existence of any radiation danger. In the late 1970s federal legislation in the United States concerning screen use and design was rejected although there is always the future possibility that some individual states may introduce legislation.

Display Quality. The third problem is the quality of the screen display. One aspect of this quality is the resolution of the screen. Only relatively poor-

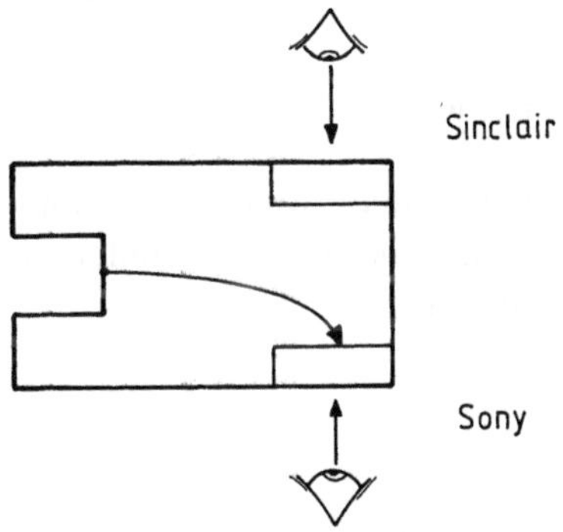

Illustration 7.15. CRT screens

For flat-screen devices viewing can be carried out either *on*, as with the Sinclair version, or *through* the phosphor screen, as with the Sony version. The advantage of the Sinclair arrangement is that it should provide a much brighter display with lower power consumption.

quality displays are available using the matrix arrangement, although this situation is now changing as higher-resolution graphic display screens are becoming available such as the ICL Perq, the Xerox Star, and the relatively low-priced Apple Lisa.

Another aspect of screen display quality is that case studies, particularly of those situations where screen-based word processing equipment has been installed, reveal a consistent theme of reports of increased eyestrain, backaches, and headaches. It is difficult, of course, with these kinds of reports to distinguish real from imagined increases—clearly the way that the question is put can have a significant effect on the response given—and in any case eyestrain and backaches are both fairly common complaints of office workers and result more from the methods of working, e.g., long periods of working at a terminal, than from anything about the terminal itself.

Reports from opthalmic associations suggest that the real problem has more to do with latent but undetected eye defects rather than the equipment itself. It is now commonly accepted that there is a normal but unreported eye defect rate of 30%.

Lighting. In spite of these three areas of concern, screen design is increasingly of a reasonable standard and in practice there are more important effects due to the lighting arrangements used. Display devices are stuck onto desks of the wrong height, making it difficult to operate the equipment without getting tired; they are placed against windows so that the operator cannot see the screen properly because of the excessive background illumination levels and with unsuitable overhead lighting arranged so as to cause glare and shadow problems.

Other Forms of Display

The remaining screen display methods do not require the use of such high-energy electron beams and so immediately overcome some of the potential health hazard problems.

Plasma

Plasma screens consist of a honeycomb arrangement with each cell containing neon gas. Arrays of wires are fixed into the glass sheets that form the ends of the neon gas cells, and these wires are used to switch individual cells on or off. The cells will stay on until switched off, and so do not need the continuous (50 or 60 times/sec) rebombardment that is required for the phosphor screen of the cathode-ray-tube display. On the whole, plasma screens seem to be less hazardous, smaller in size, and less power-consuming than CRT displays, but they are also more expensive and therefore are not used except in those circumstances where large-area displays, for which they are particularly useful, are required.

Liquid Crystal

Liquid crystal displays (LCDs) reflect rather than generate light. LCDs can be extremely small, and they consume minute amounts of power (that is why they are so popular as time display devices in watches), but they are

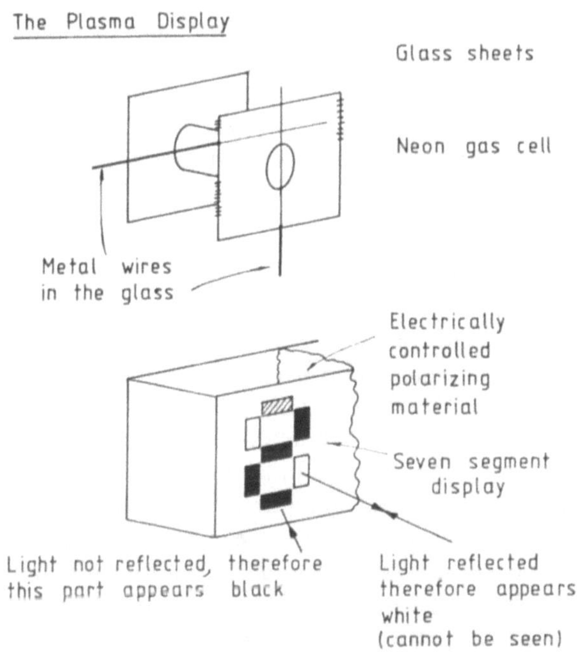

Illustration 7.16. Other screen displays

The plasma display uses a honeycomb arrangement of cells filled with neon gas. Once activated, by the appropriate wires being switched on—just as for the semiconductor memory array—the cells will stay on until switched off. Normally, semiconductor devices, such as transistor switches, have to be refreshed, that is, reswitched on, every 1/50 sec.

The LC display uses the polarizing properties of liquid crystal material. Because of this, the display relies on ambient lighting rather than on the excitation of phosphor or neon.

relatively slow. Currently, LCDs have found a particular use as display devices for portable computers (of the briefcase-size variety), but whether this role will survive the development of the new flat-screen CRT displays remains to be seen.

Voice Output

The third display method when communicating with people is to use voice output.

There are three different techniques that are currently used to provide computer voice output. Each approach offers a different compromise between cost, quality of sound, and ease of use. Since speech is an even more transitory form of output than screen display, the use of speech is limited to special applications where it is necessary to get users to attend quickly rather than to attend to massive amounts of detail. An example of the use of voice output is a warning and alert system where the computer system can, for example, be programmed to telephone and speak an appropriate message to a human recipient.

Machine-to-Machine Communication

Machines have to be able to communicate with one another as well as with people. As far as machine-to-machine communication is concerned, there are two categories to consider: those communications that are between similar types of machine, e.g., computer-to-computer, and those between dissimilar devices, e.g., computer to other machines.

For computer-to-computer communication, any difficulty that occurs will be concerned with ensuring that the meaning of the electronic signal that is sent is not mistranslated. With communication from a computer to another machine, the problem is usually to find some way of changing the electronic signal into mechanical motion. This kind of translation is achieved by a transducer.

Computer-to-Computer Communication

We will start dealing with computer-to-computer communication by considering the problems that face people when they wish to communicate with one another.

Let us suppose that we wish to communicate with someone else by talking. It is no good just opening our mouth and varying the pitch and loudness of our voice. In order to actually communicate something meaningful to someone else we have to ensure that the person we are talking to can hear us. We have to make sure that they are not deaf or busy listening to someone else, that they can understand the language we are using, and that they know the meaning of the words we are using.

Normally we carry out all of the above activities automatically, so we do not realize we are doing it. We only become aware of the above rules when faced with unusual situations, e.g., a foreigner who cannot speak our language, a layman when we are talking about a technical problem, or a child.

However, when dealing with intercomputer communication, all of the above communication rules have to be incorporated into the machine's communication facilities.

Interfaces and Protocols. The rules of communication for computers are incorporated into specifications of what signals should be provided and the format of the data being communicated. These rules are used to define interfaces and protocols. Interfaces are, in this situation, the physical connections that link machines together.

Quite clearly, there can be no communication between two machines unless they are connected by some form of communication link, and if this link is, for example, a cable and plug, then the plug must fit into the machine's socket. There are two popular standard sets of rules governing interfaces, RS232 and Centronics. The RS232 interface specification was drawn up by an American institute and is the basis of the European V24 interface specification. The Centronics interface is that of an American computer printer manufacturing company, and since it is such a big supplier the standards that it has set have been followed by many other printer and computer manufacturer companies.

But as we have seen from discussing the problems of communication between people, choosing an appropriate physical link is only just thc beginning. Whilc the rules governing the physical links between two machines are defined by EIA (Electronics Industry Association) and CCITT (International Telegraph and Telephone Consultative Committee) specifications, the way that any particular computer handles the information is an internal matter. And so in order for two machines to communicate, not only must they use the same plugs, sockets, and voltages, but the signals travelling from one to another must mean the same thing to each machine. This situation is taken care of by a protocol. Two machines, if they are to communicate successfully, must use the same protocol in order for the information being communicated to mean the same thing. There are some very popular protocols, many of them set by IBM because of its size.

A complete definition of communication, therefore, describes the communication between two machines in terms of both the physical connection and the meaning of the signals.

In Illustration 7.17 some further details concerning examples of telecommunication specifications are provided.

Substandards. A typical interface for communication between two machines would be the CCITT V24 or its equivalent, the EIA RS 232-C. These standards are, however, not completely unalterable! Because there are subsets of these standards, it is possible for a supplier to claim, for example, that a machine has an RS 232 interface but that it is impossible to use the interface to communicate with another machine which also has an RS 232 interface.

In Illustration 7.18 the minimum signals required for three types of communication link using the V24 protocol are given to indicate the potential complexity that can be faced.

The Physical Link. In setting up a communication link between two machines the engineering aspects of the link have to be given a considerable amount of thought. The simplest way to link machines together is to use a piece of cable and two plugs and plug the machines together. This approach may be quite satisfactory for distances of up to a few hundred meters—or perhaps it may not since any distance greater than a few meters can cause problems—but it certainly will not work for long distances.

The next step is to insert a signal amplifier into the cable joining the two machines to ensure that the signal level is high enough to get to the machine at

Illustration 7.17. Telecommunication

For telecommunication to work there must be definition and specification of the electrical signals and communication links between machines. The specifications cover aspects from the physical arrangement—how many pins in the plug—to what the presence or absence of signals at each pin of the connector means, how the communication process is carried out, and how errors are detected and dealt with.

There are two sources of telecommunication specifications: (i) the European CCITT which issues V standards (V24, V28, etc.); and (ii) the American EIA which issues RS standards (RS 232-C, RS-422/3, etc.).

However, even with a particular specification, the RS 232-C, for example, there are likely to be substandards, so although a machine's links fit the RS standards they may only do so to an extent.

As an example, RS 232-C defines communication up to 50 ft at up to 20,000 bits/sec. Signaling is defined as NRZ (nonreturn zero), with a 0 bit represented by a voltage pulse between +3 and +25 V and a 1 bit represented by a voltage pulse between −3 and −25 V. The RS 232-C definition is also used as the base for the V24 and V28 standards.

Illustration 7.18. Substandards

This table shows various subsets of the V24/RS 232-C.

Signal name	Application
Protected ground Reference ground TXD; transmitted data RXD; received data RTS; request to send CTS; clear to send DSR; data set ready CD; carrier detect	This set of signals is the minimum needed for a private and permanent communications link using asynchronous transmission.
DTR; data terminal ready RI; ring indicator	These additional signals are needed for a dialed-up telephone link.
SQ; signal quality detector Receiver timing Data signal rate select Transmitter timing	These additional signals are needed in order to have synchronous communication.

the other end. This amplifier is called a line driver. Line drivers will work for distances of up to a few hundred meters, but for greater distances more complicated arrangements using modems are required.

Networks. The links that have been described so far are intended for linking one machine with another. However, in many circumstances just enabling two machines to communicate will not prove to be particularly useful. Having two telephones linked together is not, for example, particularly useful. In many cases indeed there may be a need for linking several machines, perhaps hundreds, together.

We should note that here we are talking about linking together many machines that can send information between one another. We are not just talking about having many machines linked to just one machine, as is the arrangement with a central computer and remote terminals.

The machines may be linked together like a telephone network where there is a central switch that can be used to connect any two machines together. Alternatively, the network may be arranged in a loop or a line with the transmitting machine sending out a message that is collected by the intended receiver.

All of these different approaches have both advantages and disadvantages. Companies that come from a telephone background prefer to use a telephonelike solution, companies that come from a computer background prefer a looplike arrangement, while still other companies, like Xerox, prefer a broadcasting approach.

For all of these approaches a problem that has to be contended with is that of how to enable different kinds of machines to communicate with one another. As we have seen, different machines tend to have different protocols, and so communication tends to be restricted to those machines that use the same protocol, but just because two machines come from the same manufacturer does not mean that they will be able to communicate with one another. Although intermachine communication capability is often claimed, it is rarely actually available. Certainly, attempting to arrange for intermachine communication is at present littered with pitfalls for the unwary.

Illustration 7.19 gives broad details concerning the physical link.

Suppliers' Protocols. As far as individual manufacturers and suppliers of equipment are concerned, there is not a particularly good reason for changing what they each individually think is the best engineering solution to a problem unless there is some other underlying motive, like extra profit, attached. Therefore, in the past the setting of protocol standards has generally been left to individual manufacturers. For instance, IBM, by virtue of its market dominance, has defined many protocols for its own use, thereby setting de facto standards that others have been obliged to follow.

Sharing of Resources. A final aspect of telecommunication is that of the possibility of sharing resources. By linking together information machines we can also link together the resources that they use. Initially this was used to share a single printer among several otherwise independent processors. This was done because printers are expensive and are only needed for a fraction of the time that they are available for. So the first step was to link several computers to one printer, thus allowing each computer a slice of the printer action, although, of course, there could be occasions where there was a line waiting.

The next step was to share both storage and processing power so that rather than having each input station with its own disk device and processor, these devices were also shared among the users.

If this design is followed through to its extreme, then we simply end up with the input devices being terminals with a central processing unit somewhere else—the same old data processing solution.

There is the potential, however, for installing some processing and storage power in the input stations themselves because of the physical smallness of the microelectronic devices, while having still more processing power and storage capacity centrally located. This approach is known as distributed processing and is illustrated in Illustration 7.20.

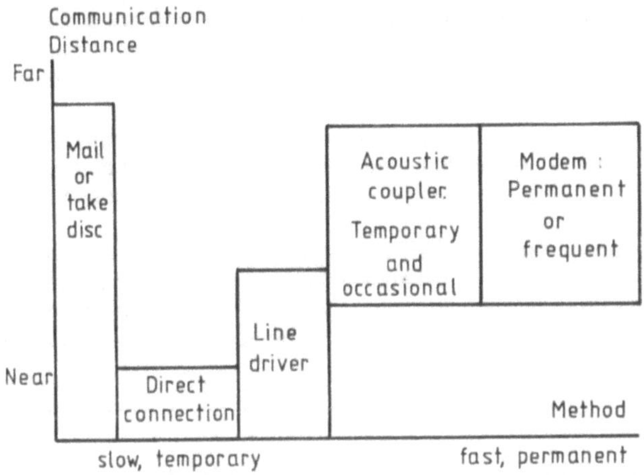

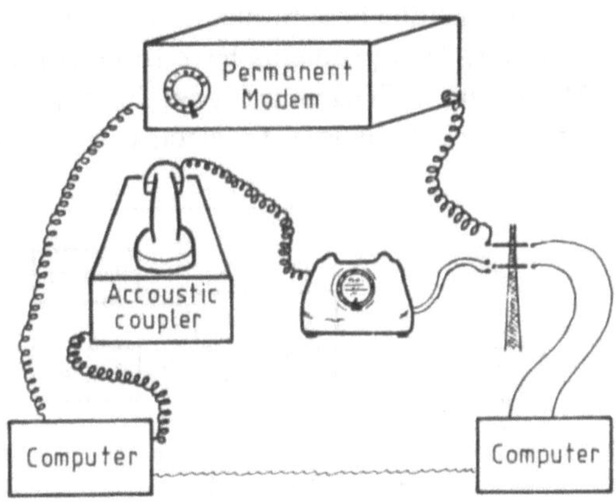

Illustration 7.19. Communication links

One way to achieve communication between two machines is to send the information recorded on a magnetic tape or disk. Provided that the two machines accept the same tape or disk, then communication can be achieved. This method, although it works, can be slow and expensive. There are better alternatives.

The first idea is to link the two machines together using a cable. This method is satisfactory for distances up to about 50 m, but it starts to fail after that as the signal begins to get distorted.

To overcome distortion a line driver—a signal amplifier—can be used. This enables signals to be transmitted up to 500 m.

For longer distances modems are required. A modem is a device that translates the digital pulses that a computer uses into the kinds of signals that a telephone line can handle. There are two types of modem, temporary or permanent.

The temporary modem is an acoustic coupler. The acoustic coupler is simply a box onto which a telephone can be placed as shown. The coupler translates the computer pulses into a more suitable telephone signal.

With an acoustic coupler, the receiving machine is simply dialed up on the telephone line, a connection made, and then the two computers are joined together by putting the telephone handset into the rubber moldings of the coupler.

A modem is similar to an acoustic coupler, but the connection can be permanent and the telephone handset does not have to be put into position since the sending computer is wired directly to the modem. The permanence of the connection means that faster transmission rates are possible than with the simpler coupler.

Computer-to-Noncomputer Communication

The other kind of machine communication is between a noncomputer machine and a computer. Two problems have to be contended with.

Mechanical Movement to Electronic Signal. First, we are concerned with conversion from machine movement to electric signals. The conversion

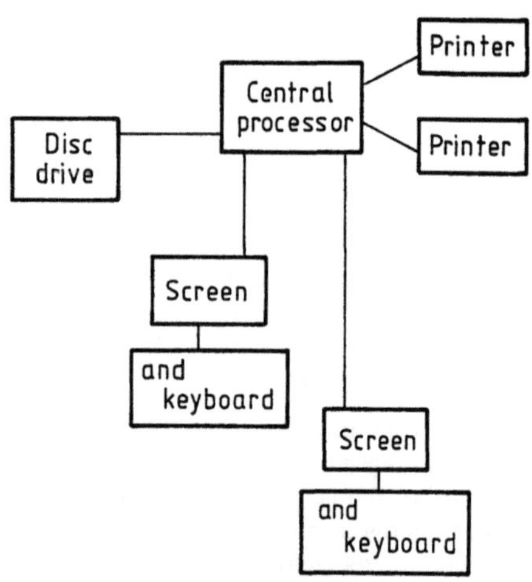

Illustration 7.20. Shared resource communication

A shared resource or distributed system uses a central processor with screens, keyboards, and printers attached as required. The advantage of this approach is that additional equipment can be obtained relatively cheaply, although the initial purchase of the central processor is expensive. By buying the storage capacity along with the processor, cost savings on relatively expensive storage equipment can be made.

process is carried out by a transducer which is simply a device that converts signals from one form to another.

There is no apparent theme to the way that mechanical movement is converted into an electric signal. Any physical property may be useful, such as the expansion of metals on heating. In many cases the transducer will be based on traditional mechanical principles, springs and levers, for example. There is a growing use of micromachining techniques that utilize the chemical etching processes described in Chapter 6 to make small mechanical devices so that not only is the information processor becoming smaller but so also is the machine that is being controlled.

Signal Suitability. The second problem is similar to that dealt with when considering communication between two computers. Having got an electronic signal from a mechanical movement, it has to be of the right form, size, and time duration in order to be processable.

Communication for Both Machines and People

There is one final grouping of communication methods, where the transfer of information is from an already existing label of some kind to the information machine. Here not only are we not concerned with providing information about machine movement but often we are also interested in making the information understandable to both humans and machines at the same time.

There are three techniques for achieving this: OCR, MICR, and bar coding.

Magnetic Ink Character Recognition. In magnetic ink character recognition (MICR) a restricted set of characters (Illustration 7.21) can be printed using magnetizable ink.

The MICR technique is used by banks where information about account

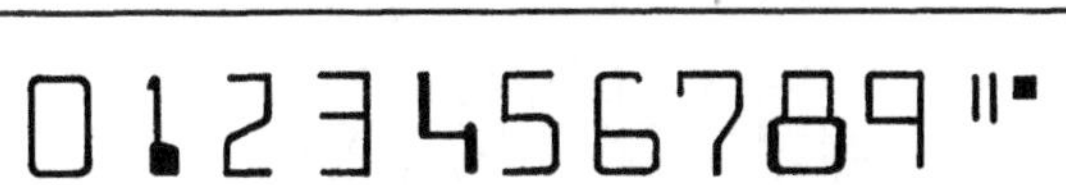

E 13 B Magnetic ink font

Illustration 7.21. MICR characters and recognition

MICR characters can be typed onto a document, if necessary. For reading, the MICR document is passed through a magnetic inducer which magnetizes the ink used in the printing process. The magnetized symbols are then passed through a scanner which generates different electronic signals depending on the magnetic field changes caused by the inducer.

number, check, and check amount is printed on the check. The MICR reader provides high-speed, 2000 checks/min, error-free reading.

Optical Character Recognition. Compared to MICR, optical character recognition (OCR) offers a complete alphabetic and numeric set. OCR can therefore be used to handle ordinary textual documents rather than the restricted information contained on checks. A simple OCR reader uses a matrix of photoelectric cells onto which the document's symbols can be projected. The resultant pattern of on and off cells can be compared to known patterns and can thereby be recognized (Illustration 7.22).

Originally OCRs could only accept the very stylized OCR A and B fonts. However, microprocessor developments have resulted in relatively cheap OCR machines being available that can handle several fonts, especially the popular typing fonts, and there is at least one machine that can be taught to recognize any set of characters. Even a stylized OCR font enables material to be easily readable by both humans and machines. It should be noted, however, that there are certain restrictions on document format for an OCR machine, particularly with respect to the number of lines of text per inch and the amount of margin around the document.

Bar Coding. Finally, there is bar coding. Bar coding is used with OCR equipment, but it uses a code that is not directly readable by humans, although the code value is usually printed in OCR-acceptable characters (Illustration 7.23).

The main advantages of bar coding are that (i) it is fast—even very simple bar code readers can work at twice the speed of the fastest keyboard operator—and (ii) it is convenient. Bar code labels can be attached to anything from groceries, through trees, to automobile components.

Illustration 7.22. Optical character recognition

OCR works by the reflection of light from the read paper onto a matrix, or array, of light-sensitive cells. Received patterns are compared to the library of stored patterns, and identical or close matches are recognized.

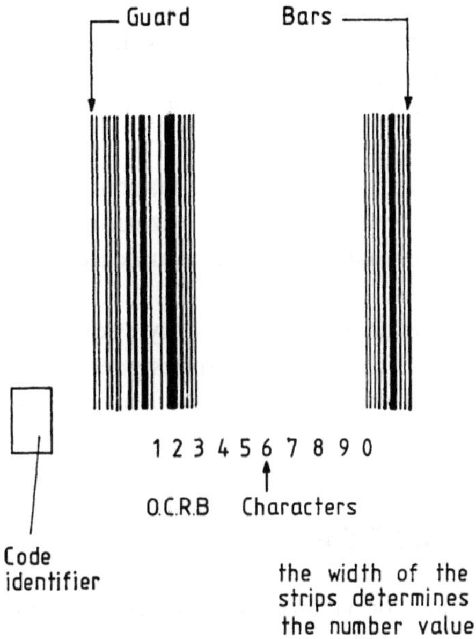

Illustration 7.23. Bar code

The black and white stripes of the bar code reflect different amounts of light from the laser beam which is shone onto the bar code label. The differing amounts of light are then translated into a sequence of electronic pulses for further computer processing.

Although bar coding is usually encountered in simple labeling applications, it can be used for other purposes. Some of the smaller Hewlett-Packard computers have bar coded versions of computer programs. In this way programs can be printed, in magazines, for example, and transferred directly into the computer without any need for human keying in.

SUMMARY

Internally, the information machine is a collection of microelectronic switches. Information is represented by electronic pulses which are recorded and stored on magnetic material and in semiconducting devices.

Communication between people, who do not normally use voltage pulses to represent information, and machines, which do, is achieved mainly by typewriterlike keyboards, TV-like screens, and printing onto paper. All of these devices suffer from various faults: bulkiness, mechanical failure, and expense.

Communication between machines is bedeviled by technical problems caused mainly by a lack of standardization. Slowly some of these technical problems are being overcome by the growth in the realization of a need for standardization and by the development of devices that can translate messages from the format suitable for one machine to the format suitable for another. However, this process of standardization is slow. And in the meantime the user trying to get machines to communicate with one another can face extraordinary difficulties.

In the end, the information machine only knows what it is told by people, and it is only as clever as the people who designed it and provided programs for it are. The information machine, therefore, is potentially as fallible as we are.

DISCUSSION QUESTIONS

1. Describe the ideal information storage medium. (Think in terms of the strengths and weaknesses of current media.)
2. Do you think that the effort being directed toward replacing the keyboard as a method of communication between people and machines is misplaced?
3. What are the reasons that have encouraged manufacturers to provide different and incompatible communication interfaces? What are the benefits of standardization (and who benefits)?

IV

BUSINESS INFORMATION TECHNOLOGY

"As we outfit ourselves with more sophisticated technological garb, nature seems to shrink in size and our own gait seems to stretch out over larger terrain." Jeremy Rifkin, The other half of the computer revolution, *Datamation,* May 1983.

SUMMARY: How information technology is being used in business, and how it is likely that it will be used. The effects of these uses.

8

APPLICATIONS

INTRODUCTION

In this chapter current and likely future applications for information technology are looked at. We will look at the application of information technology in four ways: as products, as services, in the production process, and in management information processes.

Overview

Before considering the four areas of application in detail we first consider information technology applications from a broad and general viewpoint.

As we said near the start of Chapter 2, information technology is concerned with the application of computers and telecommunication. Since both computers and telecommunication have been available since the 1950s, the general principles of application are well known, although no one knows the full extent to which information technology may be stretched in its application.

What has happened to information technology, especially since the 1970s, has been the increasing availability of convenient computing. What is now promising to change almost as radically is the easy availability of telecommunication between machines. The availability of convenient computing and telecommunication means that many things which were previously only conceptually possible have now become practicable.

Computer Aspects

Computers are becoming more powerful, more convenient to use, and yet cheaper. The ever increasing number of different transducers that can be attached to the computer either for taking in information about the outside world or for taking action to control the outside world, together with the fact that the way the computer operates is determined by an alterable program, means that, in theory at least, computers may be easily adapted to new and different applications.

There are three aspects of computers that are of interest in business applications of information technology: data processing, information storage, and control.

Data Processing. Although computers are popularly thought to excel as powerful calculators, data processing is not primarily concerned with complicated manipulations of massive numbers but rather with massive amounts of simple manipulations of numbers. The preparation of payrolls is a good example of data processing in action. There are some well-defined rules to apply to a few numbers which together with the operations of addition and subtraction and possibly multiplication and division detail simple information such as the number of hours worked and the wage rate.

It is important to realize that data processing is not limited to the administrative processes. Data processing is applicable in any situation where vast amounts of numeric data are processed according to a relatively few simple rules.

Information Storage and Retrieval (ISAR). The ability to handle vast amounts of data leads to the second application of computers—information storage and retrieval. Computer-based storage of information has some clear benefits compared to the more conventional forms of storage, but it also suffers from some clear disadvantages. First, we will look briefly at the benefits.

The benefits of computer-based information storage lie in the ability to search through and sort the stored information rapidly, no matter where it is.

It is not unusual for a standard computer-based system to be able to search for information when only a fairly hazy idea of what is wanted is available. This ability to handle information in situations where it is not quite clear as to what is wanted, together with the rapid access that is possible, can provide a very useful service to business functions such as inventory control.

The primary disadvantages of computerized ISAR are the dangers of over dependence on and an uncritical attitude toward computer-delivered information. A computer ISAR system is still dependent, generally, upon human operator input, and if a mistake of any kind gets through into the computer system, then mistaken information is recorded and becomes available. Human skepticism is necessary to ensure that erroneous information is not accepted as being true.

Control. The third application is control. Here the computer is being used primarily as a device to control the operation of other machines. The use of computer control is most highly visible in robotics where mechanical devices that can mimic a limited range of human actions are controlled by computer, enabling them to carry out, to a limited extent, construction activities such as paint spraying and arc welding. There are, however, a vast number of somewhat more mundane but still important control uses, including radar systems, process control, and numerically controlled machines, as the following extract shows:

> In the engineering industry individual parts, intended for later assembly, are made with machine-tools capable of working with high precision, at ever greater speeds, and with increasing versatility. Many new techniques have been introduced for forming materials into required shapes and for joining materials together. But the decisive advance has been the application of information technology to control the processes of fabrication. For example, the operation of a lathe can be controlled by information held on a magnetic tape. The appropriate cutting tools must be used and the workpiece fixed in position. The magnetic tape then directs the speed of the lathe, the path of the cutting tool, and so on. Whole sets of machine-tools can be controlled directly by a computer. A row of machine-tools, with automatic transfer stations to carry parts from one tool to the next, can be used to make complex artefacts, such as cylinder-blocks for automobiles, in large numbers. To make complex parts in smaller numbers arrays of cutting tools can be incorporated in versatile, numerically controlled machine-tool stations. (Hyman, 1980)

Telecommunication

The communication of information, between computers in particular, is the other face of information technology. No matter how powerful any single machine is, its power is increased dramatically when it can be linked up with other machines. The increase in its power is even more dramatic when the communication link between the machines can provide, if not instantaneous, at least very rapid transfer of information.

The use of telecommunication allows all the processing activities that have been described to be carried out at some other place. The need for this transfer of information may not be immediately apparent, but remember that information technology is intended to be of use to humans. It is people who want access to information. It can be far easier to use telecommunication to arrange for the transfer of information along telephone lines or microwave beams to where the people are, than to try to transport the people to where the information is.

Our increasing ability to transport information not only opens up the prospect of remote working, but also, through the use of value-added networks, opens up the prospect of enabling different types of machines to communicate easily with one another.

PRODUCTS

Superficially there are two distinct ways that information technology can be used in products: either as a replacement in an already existing product, which is substitution, or in an entirely new product, which is innovation.

In reality, it is sometimes difficult to decide which category a product falls into. While many products take an existing idea and do it differently, and sometimes better, a situation can be reached where the new version of an old product in fact becomes quite simply a new product. Personal computers, for example, probably fall into the new product rather than better-old-product category. But what about, for another example, the appearance of IDTs (intelligent display telephones)? IDTs combine with the standard telephone facility the ability to display telecommunicated text as well as the storage of frequently dialed telephone numbers. Are these new devices or are they simply better versions of things that have been around for a long time?

Substitution

The reason for using information technology devices as replacements in an already existing product is because it provides a better product. The better product is better for one or more of the following reasons: the product is cheaper to make; is more reliable in operation; has more functions; or has greater customer appeal.

Generally these reasons will get mixed up with one another. A product will not only be cheaper to make, but it will also become more reliable. And both of these developments will probably also result in greater customer appeal.

But it is possible to use the inclusion of information technology to increase customer appeal even though the product itself is neither cheaper, nor more reliable, nor more useful. It may just look better.

Existing Electronic Devices. The most obvious form of substitution is to use microelectronic information technology as a replacement for current mechanical or electromechanical devices. However, the initial greatest use of microelectronic devices was to replace the conventional electronic devices in already existing electronic-based products.

> The replacement of TTL circuitry and under-utilized minicomputers accounts for sixty to seventy percent of the current application of microcomputers. (Nichols, 1980)

This electronic substitution by microprocessors occurred because the suppliers of the electronic-based products already knew about electronics. These existing electronic users were able to accommodate developments in electronics far more easily than could businesses using nonelectronic technology.

Enhancement. Although making products cheaper and more reliable, microelectronics substitution has not taken place on just a one-for-one basis. Product enhancement often occurs simultaneously. This generally happens because it costs very little, if anything, more to add functions. The extra functions, i.e., enhancement, are achieved quite simply by writing the appropriate program of instructions for the microprocessor.

> The process of enhancement is most noticeable in the area of instrumentation, where increasingly sophisticated products are finding their way to market in growing numbers. For example, instrument manufacturers are finding it practical to add such features as remote control, programmability, improved readout and peripheral interfaces... (Nichols, 1980)

A common example of enhancement is television sets that can display channel number and time on the screen and allow remote color and tint control. These functions have been added while using microelectronics to provide better tuning and signal-processing circuits.

Telephone exchanges and telephones are also familiar products which have gained spectacularly from enhancement.

For computer-based telephone exchanges enhancement has been achieved by the addition of supervisory functions. Typical supervisory functions offered by modern telephone exchanges include: handset monitoring to establish where calls are made from, where to, when, and for how long. Use of this kind of facility is claimed to reduce business telephone bills by 15% typically; automatic call redirection enabling calls to be rerouted in cases where the handset user has moved temporarily to a new location.

Enhancement has produced the cordless telephone. Besides having all the extra functions typical since the introduction of microprocessors such as truncated dialing (enabling a user to dial a long telephone number while only actually dialing two digits) and automatic redialing (of engaged numbers), cordless telephones use local area broadcasting to enable users to move freely with their handsets anywhere within a few hundred meters of the base unit, which is plugged into the normal telephone socket.

Mechanical Devices. The use of microelectronics to replace existing mechanical devices is probably better known because of its greater visible impact. Mechanical devices are prime targets for replacement because they are inherently bulky, slow, and unreliable. Additionally, they are expensive to make and acquire because of the labor involved in assembling them.

The most obvious examples of this aspect of substitution are clocks and calculators. Although partially mechanical quartz analogue watches have a certain up-market status, for most people watches are digital electronic devices. Certainly all calculators are. This change over the past five to ten years has resulted in the nearly total elimination of two previously well-established but mechanical products.

However, although watches and calculators are outstanding examples of the effect that the successful introduction of microelectronics can have, there are a large number of mechanical and electromechanical products that have remained essentially unaltered. Perlowski (1980) summed up the domestic appliance sector not very long ago: "The appliance industry is still a metal-bending business, so it generally has been unaware of what is going on, or what is going to happen because of the microprocessor.... Nothing new has happened in washing machines or refrigerators for years." And today, often the greatest extent of electronics is in the use of one or two components such as thyristors rather than in the use of microprocessors. This situation highlights a major problem: It is difficult for an industry that has little or no experience with electronics to develop applications for microprocessors and then develop those applications into product reality. Without doubt, however, the appropriate use of microelectronics can prove to be very marketable. For example, in the United States the Amana Touchmatic microwave oven, which introduced the use of a microprocessor-controlled programmable timer to give accurate timings for cooking processors, picked up one-third of the microwave oven market in its second year. Clearly the provision of accurate programmable timing gave consumers a real benefit at an affordable price.

Innovation

We will classify innovative products into three groups: information technology devices themselves; devices in which the information technology devices are included; and, finally, software, the programs of instructions that make the products actually useful.

Information Technology Devices. Because of refinements in microelectronic manufacturing techniques, there is a continual development of information technology devices. These developments result in faster processors and larger capacity memories which when combined produce ever more powerful computers.

In addition to the ongoing development work, there are from time to time developments that make possible concepts that were previously only ideas. One device that held out that possibility was the magnetic bubble memory. However, as we have seen, MBMs have so far failed to achieve the impact once expected. Another device that currently holds out the promise of considerable potential is the EEPROM (electrically erasable programmable read-only memory).

Although what the EEPROM does is conceptually possible with existing microelectronic devices, the EEPROM provides a practical solution. The EEPROM is a read-only memory device. That is, once information is stored it cannot be changed—except, in the case of the EEPROM, the information can be changed!

The EEPROM acts rather like a solid-state magnetic disk. Information stored in it can be read and used but not changed except by intention. This arrangement could, for example, allow EEPROM-controlled machines to adjust their own performance as either the machine parts or the environment of the machine changes or deteriorates. EEPROM-controlled automobile ignition would allow for the eroding spark plug gap or partially blocked filter. Additionally, a diagnostic record of performance change could be made automatically to assist maintenance activities.

Other ways in which the EEPROM could be used are to enable remote sending and collecting of information by telecommunication. Monitoring devices such as electricity meters *could* be read and computers reprogrammed simply by being connected to a telephone line.

Information Technology Products. New products cannot, of course, be anticipated. All that we can do is look at recent new products and see if there are any clues as to the kinds of product areas that might develop. On this basis it is apparent that there are two new information technology products that have developed at an outstanding rate. These two products are the personal computer and the video games machine.

Personal Computers. The first personal computer firms like CBM, makers of the Pet, started to appear in the 1970s. Today there are a large number of personal computer companies and some of the companies, Apple, for example, are already appearing on the Fortune 500 list. Personal computers, and anything connected with them, such as personal computer magazines and books, are one clear example of rapid growth.

Video Games. Video games did exist prior to the recent developments in microelectronics but utilized conventional electronic circuitry. The use of conventional electronics limited the scope of the machines and so games machines have benefited significantly from the substitution–enhancement process. With the advent of microelectronics, solid-state cartridge machines capable of providing a vast range of games have been developed.

Although initially separate markets, in the last year or so the underlying conflict between personal computers and video games machines has come to the surface. The result of this has been that the video machine suppliers have been forced to move into the home computer market, with so far little sign of financial success. The video games machine is after all only a computer used for one particular purpose—playing games—but by modification it can be turned into a personal computer.

The target of both the video games machine and the personal computer is the individual user at home. It has been proved that the home user will buy a sophisticated electronic product provided that the price is not out of line with other similar consumer goods. And although low prices inevitably mean low profit margins, since the size of the domestic market is so enormous, there are significant profits to be made. However, how long these profits will be achieved and who they will be achieved by, with ever increasing competition as better/cheaper devices appear, is a matter for speculation. The market for personal computing is tough and turbulent. In any event "home information technology" has been established as a market.

One of the most interesting sectors in home information technology is the development of home robots. American-based Androbot has launched a series of machines which are essentially computers on wheels. Quite what the home user is supposed to do with the home robot is not quite clear—initial demonstrations involved a Topo getting a can of beer out of an intelligent Androfridge, reminiscent of the various intelligent machines in *The Hitchiker's Guide to the Galaxy*. But then quite what the home consumer does with a home computer is far from clear, and there is a lot of money to be made from home computers.

Intelligent Cards. Another new product that appears to have a bright future is the intelligent card. Plastic cards used as keys to gain entry into secure areas or devices or as the equivalent to money (decremental cards) are already well established. These cards use information stored on the magnetic stripe of the card which can be read by the machine they are fed into. Although generally fixed, the information can be altered as with the decremental cards. However, in all cases the card itself is simply a medium for carrying a piece of magnetizable storage space. There could be significant benefits from having intelligence, in the form of a microprocessor, built into the card itself. Intelligent cards would act rather like a diary or notebook, recording and processing stored information within themselves. One obvious application is as the electronic equivalent of a checkbook. Banks would benefit by not having to handle all the paper that normally goes along with a check transaction, shops would benefit by not having to have more expensive computer terminals to carry out financial transactions, and the card users would benefit by having a more secure and cheaper method for paying for items without having to use money.

Software. Just as for new physical products, it is not possible to predict what successful new software products will be. But it is important to recognize that the success of information technology equipment is primarily determined by the usefulness of the programs used to drive the machines.

Just as there is not much point in having a fast car if it cannot be driven anywhere, there is no point in having a powerful computer if there are no programs for it. Software products like Pong,® Space Invaders,® and PacMan® ensured the success of the Atari products they could be played upon. And, similarly, the initial availability of VisiCalc® for the Apple computer assisted the sales of Apple computers, and the ease of use of Wang word processing assisted the sales of Wang word processors. In each of these cases the fact of software success has been acknowledged by the software equivalents that have appeared for other machines.

Long-term successful software are programs that combine ease of use with effectiveness. Generally the development of a computer program is in two stages. The first is obtaining a program that works. The second is development of a working program into a program that is easy to use. The problem with software is not just identifying a need that can be met by a computer program, for example, a typing tutor, but in the development of suitable programs of instructions to enable the devices to work well as far as their human users are concerned.

User Friendliness. Because of the enormous amount of effort that can be involved in putting a program together, in the past users have on the whole been resigned to accepting programs that work rather than getting programs that work well. However, in the past few years a greater amount of attention has been paid to designing programs that are friendlier, or easier to use, than earlier programs. There has grown up an area of study, software ergonomics, to investigate and develop better programs, where the betterness is defined in terms of betterness as far as the user is concerned rather than in terms of the minimal use of computer memory. It is becoming increasingly accepted, for example, that it is preferable to use meaningful words rather than meaningless numeric strings as input instructions, and it is preferable to have error reports that explain in clear English why the program has gone wrong rather than to use unmemorizable numeric error codes.

Program Generators. As information technology becomes more pervasive, one likely area of development is in the construction of program generators. Program generators are programs that are used to help the human user create the necessary instructions to get the machine to do what is required.

As we have already seen there are various levels to the languages that the information machine can use, but even a fairly high-level language such as BASIC can present formidable difficulties to many people. In order to get to the state of really easy use of user-programmable information technology equipment, ever easier ways of providing the machine with its instructions will be required. Already, steps are being made in this direction with software such as The Last One which allows users to construct programs without necessarily knowing anything about computer programming at all.

Illustration 8.1 tells the story of two well-known information technology products.

SERVICES

Information technology services fall into three categories: communication, library, and transaction.

Communication services enable people to communicate with one another. Library services provide users with access to information. Transaction services enable people to carry out usually financial transactions such as buying goods.

Communication

The importance of communication can be seen by the extent to which communication services are often either controlled by the state or by an otherwise monopolistic supplier. Often this monopoly control is backed up by monopolistic union control as well. Communication services fall into two broad groupings: interpersonal vocal communications, such as the telephone, and symbolic communications, such as mail.

In the United States, mail services are provided by the Federal Government although telecommunication services are provided by private companies. The telecommunication service providers do not, however, compete so far as the individual telecommunication user is concerned. In Europe and the rest of the world generally, both the postal and telecommunication services are provided by the same government agency. There appears, however, to be a general move toward liberalization, allowing more than one supplier of communication services, although privately funded services such as Mercury in the United Kingdom have become stalled by the refusal of telecommunication workers to connect the Mercury system.

Vocal Communications. The essential feature of this kind of communication network is a physical link. The link in the past was inevitably a telephone line. However, in the past 25 years a variety of other links have become

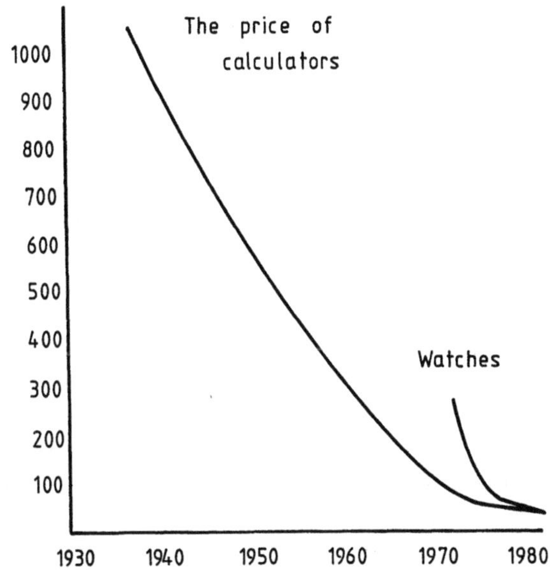

Illustration 8.1. The calculator and watch phenomena

Since the 1960s there has been an ever increasing use of microelectronic information technology in a variety of products. The two chosen here to demonstrate the effects of information technology are calculators and watches.

Calculators. The development of mechanical calculators had been going on since the 1600s when the French mathematician Pascal designed and built a simple mechanical adding machine (1647).

In 1935 a typical desk-top business calculator cost $1200, equivalent to the price of a car. By 1955 calculator prices had fallen to around $600, or a quarter the price of a car. Electronics started to be incorporated into calculators by the early 1960s, but it was not until the early 1970s that it was realized what could be achieved using microelectronic circuitry. In 1971 a typical calculator cost $100. By the next year the price had fallen to $50, the actual cost of production being around $15, and in 1983 a general purpose portable calculator cost around $5.

The calculator story is typical of the application of microelectronics—falling prices. Of course, the occurrence of falling prices is accompanied by the development of a mass market, as can be seen, for example, by the record of digital watches.

In 1973 there were about 1 million digital watches made, and a typical selling price was $250. By 1975 production was up to 3 million and price down to $150. The next year a digital watch could be bought for $20, and in 1977 the price was down to $10. Today, the cheapest digital watches sell for around $2, and a good digital watch retails at perhaps $10.

available, the most notable being the microwave beam. Using relatively low-frequency microwaves the equivalent of many telephone lines can be handled between microwave communication points. These kind of links are also used to set up communications between ground stations and satellites. The satellite acts in effect as a large mirror, enabling a communication link to be set up almost instantaneously over long distances.

The developments in international telecommunications, which hardly existed for the private individual before the 1950s, have been astounding, and some important features of it are shown in Illustration 8.2.

The voice communication services discussed here have, of course, also been enhanced by the development of communication products such as computer-operated exchanges and cordless telephones.

Mail Communications. Voice communication, although important, is not the only method available. Much business communication is carried out through letters and telexes, that is, by using the written word. Organized letter services have been available to the general public for one or two hundred years, although specialist courier services have been available for much longer. With the advent of telecommunication a much faster way of transmitting messages was available. It was used first in the telex system and then for facsimile transmission (Illustration 8.3).

Teletex and Electronic Mail. The development of smaller, in some cases even briefcase-sized screen-based computers and computer terminals has opened up the practical possibility of providing a telecommunication-based version of the traditional mail service. Since the mid-1970s the official term to describe this activity has been teletex, however in practice teletex is generally used to refer to a particular communications system offered by the postal/telecommunication authorities while the easier phrase, electronic mail, is used to describe private teletex arrangements, especially those occurring within an organization.

Teletex. Teletex can be seen as an up-to-date version of telex; however, "Teletex makes no sense if users regard it simply as a faster telex with upper- and lowercase characters. Its main virtue is not speed at all but its ability to be accessed from any of the organization's existing word or data processing units or direct from a local area network or computer store" (Riches, 1983).

While communication using teletex will be faster—approximately 30 times the speed of telex—and better—a full range of upper- and lowercase characters, together with full word processor editing facilities—the obvious application of teletex would be to overcome all the problems of incompatibility in intermachine communication while using the existing telecommunications network. On the other hand, this potential will be severely limited by the cost of the teletex equipment, since specifically designed teletex devices cost around twice as much as the older, more limited telex machines.

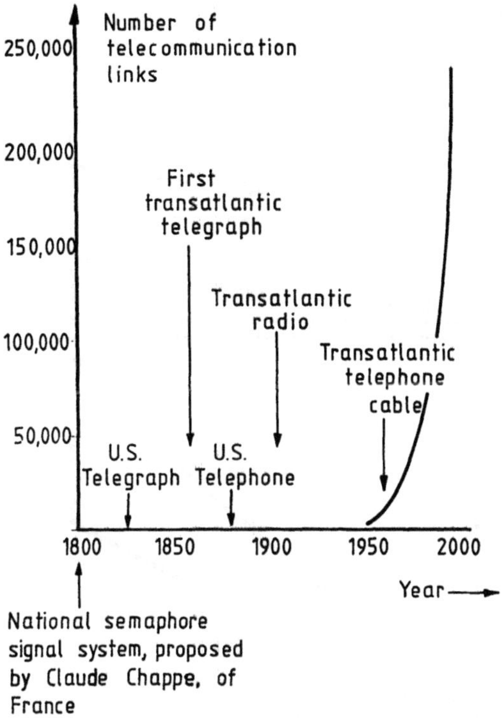

Illustration 8.2. Developments in telecommunication

Telecommunication, the long-distance communication of information, only really started in the sense that we understand it today just over 100 years ago. Less than 50 years before Samuel Morse's telegraph, Claude Chappe in France had been proposing a national semaphore network to enable messages to be flagged from one semaphore station to another.

Samuel Morse, United States, Telegraph. A link from Baltimore to Washington was established in the 1830s.

Transatlantic telegraph cable laid in 1858.

Alexander Bell, United States, Telephone. The first spoken telecommunication took place in 1876.

The first transatlantic radiotelephone communication was carried out by Marconi in 1901.

Commercial transatlantic radiotelephone, 1923. One channel, enabling one conversation between two people to be transmitted.

Transatlantic telephone cable, 1956. 36 channels. Estimated in 1957, 1000 international voice channels worldwide.

Telstar satellite, 1961. 50-MHz bandwidth (not used for telephone links).

Early Bird satellite, 1965. 240 telephone channels.

Estimated in 1972, 25,000 international voice channels worldwide.

First underwater lightwave cable, 1981. Lake Washington, Oregon.

Estimated in 1982, 250,000 international voice channels worldwide.

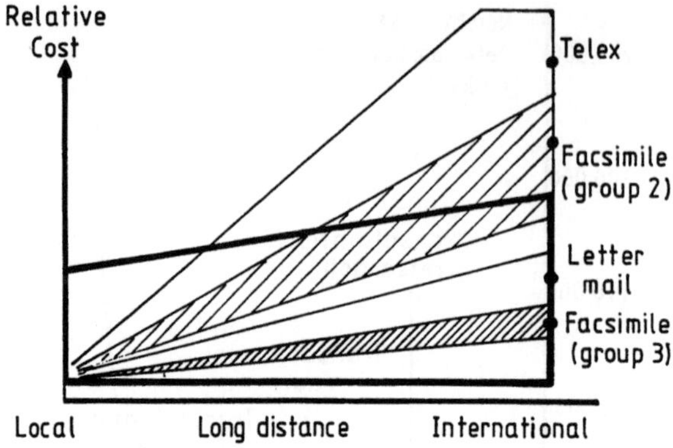

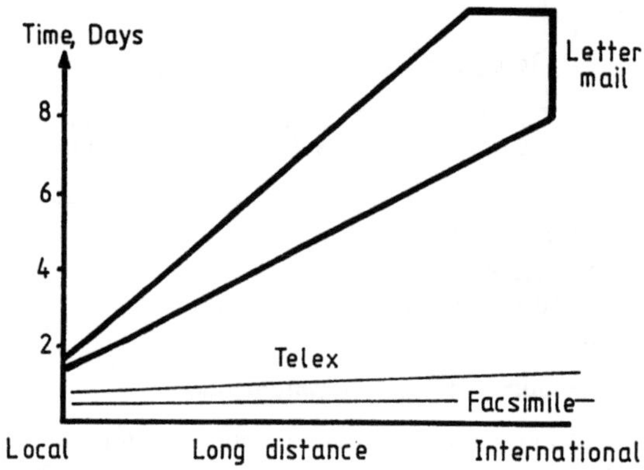

Illustration 8.3. Telex and facsimile

Telex stands for *tel*eprinter *ex*change; *t*eletypewriter *ex*change in the United States. The basic concept is to link teleprinters together in order to transmit typewritten messages, just as telephones are linked together for the transmission of spoken messages.

The telex service is by current standards rather primitive, offering transmission at only 50 bits/sec, equal to approximately 6 word/sec, and using only a limited set of characters: uppercase letters, the numbers 0–9, and fourteen other special symbols. There are some one million subscribers worldwide to telex with the Federal Republic of Germany easily being the biggest European user with over 100,000 telex installations.

An alternative to telex is facsimile. With facsimile services, already existing documents are used and telecommunicated. The easiest way to think of facsimile is as linked photocopiers. Because facsimile offers this kind of service, any kind of image can be transmitted rather than just the restricted character set of a particular terminal device.

Facsimile machines use a light beam to scan existing paper documents from which electronic pulses are generated corresponding to the black ink and white paper on the document. The electronic pulses are then transmitted along telephone lines to another, receiving, facsimile machine. Image quality is quite good, of the order of 4 scanning lines/mm of paper (100 scanning lines/in). A higher number of scans per inch of paper gives a higher-quality image but takes more time. In theory the likelihood of signal error, the dropping of pulses, or the insertion of unwanted additional ones, causing a significant but undetected error in the received message is negligible. Empirical research (Cawkell, 1983) shows that distortion due to noisy telephone lines can be a problem.

Facsimile is most popular in the United States. The practical use of facsimile is hindered by the existence of a variety of transmission standards which are only now being brought together. The standard facsimile arrangement is limited by the need to dial through and get a telephone connection with the receiving facsimile machine and with ensuring that the receiving machine is set for the same mode of operation as the sending machine. These and other similar limitations can be overcome to an extent by the use of automatic-dialing facsimile machines.

Comparative communication costs vary, of course, from one country to another and depend on government policy. However, as a guide, typical relative costs and times for different methods of mail communication are shown.

In any event, the overall plan for the development of teletex toward the 1990s includes the linking of teletex to the already existing telex network with its existing one-million subscribers (Illustration 8.4).

Electronic Mail. Electronic mail services have been in existence at least since ARPANET was set up in the 1960s. Electronic mail allows users to send text messages from their terminal via various switching computers to another user's terminal for screen display of messages. The details of any particular electronic mail system clearly depend on the equipment being used, but, in general, what electronic mail offers is: quicker transmission of information, when compared to conventional mail services; the use of existing telecommunication links; the ability to connect different types of terminals together through the "translation" services provided by the network computers; automatic acknowledgement of receipt of messages; and increasingly lower costs compared to conventional mail services.

Library Services

Information technology naturally offers library services. The foundation of library services, in this sense, is the use of computer-accessible stored information. This would, of course, suggest the use of big computers since only they have processors powerful enough to manipulate the stored information. And while this is to some extent true through the development of telecommunication smaller computers have a useful role to play, especially

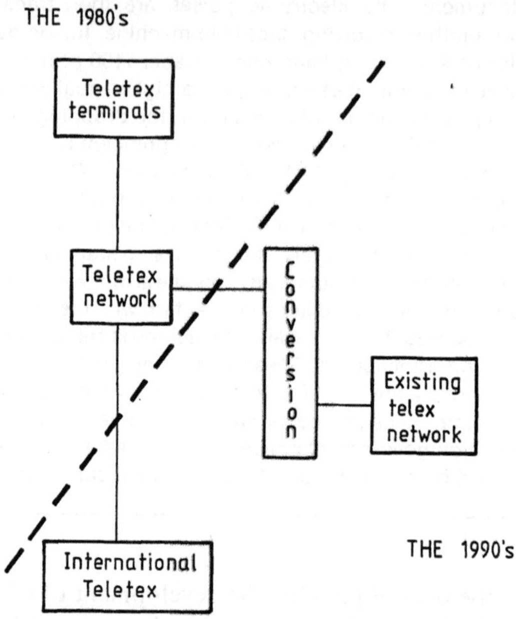

Illustration 8.4. The teletex plan

Teletex is already installed and working in some European countries, such as the Federal Republic of Germany and Sweden, for example, while others, France, Britain, and Canada either will or intend to start using teletex soon. Other countries, such as the U.S.A., have no plans as yet for introducing teletex. Once teletex is working in several countries, then the next obvious step is to introduce international teletex, perhaps toward the end of the 1980s. The plan for the 1990s includes the linking of the teletex network through a convertor to the existing national and international telex network.

since most businesses do not need to keep vast amounts of information for immediate access.

Computer-based library services take a variety of forms: ones that the user operates in order to extract information from; ones that broadcast information from which the user selects as needed; and ones that apply given facts about a situation to recommend what course of action to take using their own stored information.

Information Storage and Retrieval. Information storage and retrieval is the traditional aspect of computer library services. What developments in information technology have done is to increase the ease with which people can get at stored information.

An example of this kind of library services is the Rennes, France, teaching hospital. Here details of 2,000 diseases and their connections with 23,000 symptoms are available to French doctors through a computer network.

But the provision of information to the user does not depend upon having a central computer with remote access terminals as at Rennes. Using microelectronics a calculator-sized computer can store respectable amounts of information. In the United States the portable MD/SOS system contains information relating to potentially hazardous interactions between some 15,000 drugs.

Teletext and Viewdata. In addition to the more traditional ISAR library services there are other ways of enabling people to get at information. One such approach is to link a central computer to a simplified keyboard and television screen. There are two distinct approaches to information services: interactive and noninteractive. With noninteractive systems, the user receives information from a computer-based memory but cannot directly interact with the computer-stored information. The situation is rather like reading a book—although reading a book may change the opinions or perspective of the reader, the reader cannot change the book. In the second approach the user can interact with, even alter, the stored information.

Teletext. Noninteractive systems were pioneered in the United Kingdom and now labor under the generic title of teletext. Teletext operates through the auspices of television broadcasting companies which utilize their broadcasting transmitters to transmit information that is received and displayed upon slightly modified domestic television sets (Illustration 8.5).

Ceefax and Oracle, the two British national teletext services, publish general information such as news, weather, and program details. Obviously this kind of service could rival the more traditional forms of broadcasting provided by newspapers and magazines. The particular strength of teletext is that while newspaper information may be several hours old, and broadcasted information by the more conventional news program approach can be a few hours old, with the teletext the news can be just a few minutes old and is available at any time. On the other hand, the size of the television display limits the TV page to a fraction of the size of a newspaper page. Because of this limitation as well as the inconvenience of having to use a relatively bulky low-fidelity display device, text broadcasting by TV seems likely to be an interesting sideline rather than a major future development unless it is developed to the full extent possible.

This could be achieved by dedicating a broadcasting channel exclusively to teletext, which would enable much greater amounts of information, together with faster access rates, to be achieved. The current approach in the United Kingdom utilizes only 0.5% of the potential broadcasting time

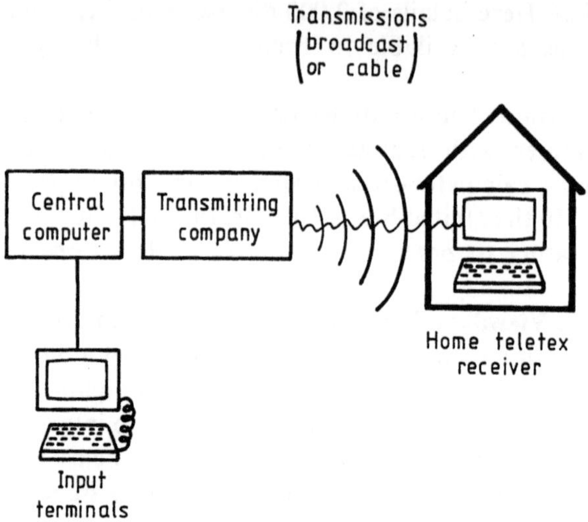

Illustration 8.5. Teletext

Information providers use input terminals, e.g., computers of some kind, to edit and arrange the information they wish to have displayed. The information is stored in the central computer and broadcast over the air or along cable to subscribers' homes.

available. Full use of a channel could enable perhaps 2000 pages to be transmitted with an access/update rate of about 1 sec. Essentially, instant access to thousands of pages of information could provide a service that people want.

Videotex and Viewdata. The interactive approach is officially called videotex, but this title seems unnecessarily confusing with other services such as teletex and teletext being available, and so the alternative title of viewdata will be used. Viewdata was developed deliberately to minimize the effect of any technical barriers experienced by users when coming into contact with interactive computer systems.

The ability to interact is provided by the use of a telephone line connected to the television set. The resultant service is similar to that provided by any other computing network but with the intended perceived difference of being easier to use. Much of the original ease of use comes from the provision of a simplified keyboard, with the original Prestel arrangement, for example, using only three control keys along with the ten numeric keys.

Viewdata can be either public or private. Private viewdata can be arranged using private computers or using a closed-off portion of the public computers.

Because it is interactive, viewdata allows users to carry out transactions as well as gain controlled access to information. The difference between the controlled access of viewdata compared with the access available with teletext is that with teletext the user has to wait for the particular wanted piece of information to be broadcasted, while with videotex the user can select which page to look at next.

The principles, range, and evolution of traditional ISAR and viewdata services are outlined in Illustration 8.6.

The Future for Public Viewdata. Among the questions needing to be asked about public viewdata are: should viewdata be offered using the TV/telephone arrangement or the personal computer/modem arrangement? Are people willing to pay for viewdata?

The greatest amount of experimental work is being carried out in France with electronic phone directories, video telephones, and smart-card systems, all either being set up for testing or actually being tried out. In early 1983 it was reported that there were some 40 experimental systems in use. This can be seen as an example of a country with a previously inadequate telecommunication system—"Half of France is waiting for a telephone. The other half is waiting for a dialing tone"—leapfrogging into a sophisticated system. Such great leaps forward do not always succeed, and the offering of information technology communication services has on the whole been greeted with a considerable degree of skepticism. Sigel (1983) concludes that

> Understanding the role of videotext services requires an understanding of how customers acquire information for business or personal use. Because this process is so complex, there can be no straightforward answers concerning the market for videotext. Nevertheless, the following general conclusions can be offered:
>
> 1. the business/professional market is far more promising in the near term than is the consumer market;
> 2. whether the market is business or consumer, the retrieval of specific facts is the most logical videotext application; and
> 3. videotext services may first appear in homes as a way for users to conduct shopping or banking; the purchase of information for its own sake should be a more limited activity.

Having established that business applications look to be more promising than general public services we will turn our attention to business applications next.

The Future for Private and Business Systems Viewdata. With respect to private viewdata systems, although there is already a healthy interest as indicated in Illustration 8.6 and a hopeful potential identified by Sigel, there is also a great deal of doubt. As one person has put it, "Viewdata is a solution,

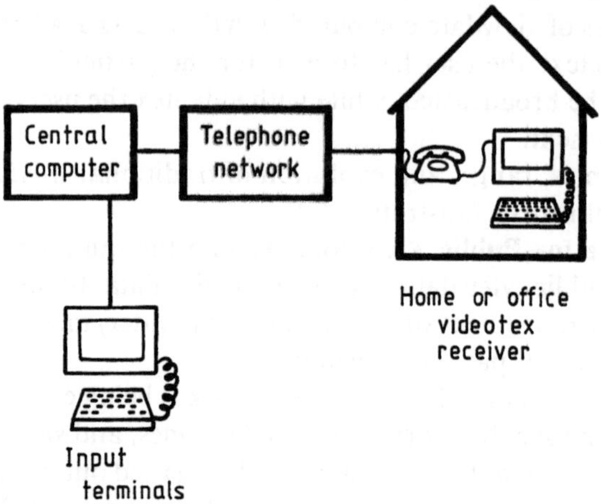

Illustration 8.6. Viewdata information systems

"Viewdata might be in its infancy, but there are several examples of working installations....

Typical applications are to establish communication links with home-based salesmen, service and maintenance engineers....

A number of organisations have also set up their own in-house systems. An industry which has found a ready use for viewdata is the travel and holiday business....

Previously, holiday reservations had to be made over the telephone. If lines were not engaged, then the person to be contacted was invariably unavailable. When the agent did get through, the transactions were usually protracted and expensive to conduct. Viewdata speeds up the whole operation and looks set to become the standard means of communicating with a travel operator's reservation system. The agent has access to timetables, weather forecasts and other travel information....

Motor manufacturers, too, have found that viewdata provides a practical means of providing up-to-date information on stock availability to its dealers. What previously could have involved a dealer in hours, even days, of work can now be carried out in minutes. Talbot is one of the car companies to have provided its dealers with a viewdata system. Now the job of tracing cars has been streamlined. Not only can one branch discover what the manufacturer's stock position is, it can now also find out about cars held through out the dealer network. Dealers also have the facility to communicate through VITAL (viewdata for Talbot) with others in the group. In this case, viewdata has scored over the computer. Computer printouts of stocks used to be distributed to dealers under the old regimen, but they would arrive days after despatch and already be out of date." (B.I.T., 1983)

Telecommunicated information services can range from systems for people to communicate computer-stored information to each other using telephones to full-blooded viewdata services:

At one end of the spectrum there is *Telemart.* Telemart links together people with items for sale and people who are looking to buy particular items. The initial Telemart service consists simply of a computer-based filing system onto which details of items for sale are recorded. People who wish to buy a particular item telephone their enquiry in, and the computer records are searched. Plans in the United Kingdom are for Telemart to use the national viewdata service to allow people to interact directly with the stored information rather than having to interact via Telemart staff.

At the next level of development is *Homefinder.* Details of two- to three-thousand properties are kept on a private section of Prestel. From this real-estate agents who subscribe to Homefinder can find out details of properties for their clients. In order to become a Homefinder user all that is required is a specially adapted television set and a telephone line.

At the next level up is *Artquest.* Artquest represents the traditional version of library services. Details of some half-million art items, paintings, etc., are recorded on a computer, and Artquest subscribers can interrogate this information base to determine whether particular items have been sold, how much they sold for, whether a certain size of painting was ever painted by a particular artist, and so on. Artquest subscribers have to have their own computer terminal.

Dealerscan is a private system owned by major European truck makers using the adapted television approach to provide truck dealers with details such as body type and body length for used trucks. This information can then be used to match customer demands with existing stock.

Viewdata for information gathering. Finally, in addition to using viewdata as an information provider, it can also be used as a friendlier and cheaper method of getting information from a number of sources. Baric uses a viewdata system, with up to 1,000 viewdata TV input sets feeding their input to one central computer, as a primary data input method for getting information relating to medical drug field testing. By using the keyboard as a method of input the problem of dealing with illegible handwriting is overcome, and because the questions are formatted, that is, the doctor is provided with the screen equivalent of a questionnaire, only the wanted information is gathered.

but we have to think of a problem. We can think of lots of uses, but no justification for them." (*Computing*, 1983b).

But it must be made clear that now we are thinking of business viewdata in terms of a method of distributing facts internally within a business. We are not considering, now, the business of distributing facts. The great advantage of viewdata-based fact distribution is that it can be far cheaper than using a computer network. The display device is an adapted television, the keyboard can be very simple, there is no requirement for dispersed long-term storage of information, and it can be far easier to use because of the familiarity of the TV screen as a method of display and the lack of a complicated keyboard to operate.

The concluding remarks on viewdata, both public and business, can be left to Sigel;

> ... if it is to be developed at all, videotext must flourish as an information service, not as a technology. Among the important questions, therefore, for those seeking to introduce videotext services are: what is the proper audience for these services; what type of information is best suited to electronic dissemination in general and videotext display in particular; and whether videotext can be used for transactions like shopping or banking. (Sigel, 1983).

Expert Systems. Much of what we call work is the application of factual knowledge. A human expert working in some particular area has access to a large amount of known facts together with a method for selecting those that are appropriate. Storing the information is an obvious computer application. Determining the rules used to extract the relevant information and to go on to reach a conclusion is a programming problem as well as a problem in understanding how we go about making decisions. The putting together of appropriate facts and rules about how to use them goes under the title of Expert Systems.

Expert systems can range from the application of well-known rules to very precisely defined situations, for example, decisions as to what kind of Social Security aid a potential client is eligible for, to the application of not very well-known rules, to ill-defined situations such as medical diagnosis.

Most current expert systems are in the medical diagnosis field. PUFF, pulmonary function disease diagnosis, for example, claims an 85% successful diagnosis rate, successful in the sense that the doctors do not decide that it has come up with the wrong answer!

The development of expert systems could obviously have far reaching repercussions on much work that is currently performed by information workers, especially the kind of work where judgement is needed to determine the likelihood of any particular outcome occurring. The application of a PUFF-like program in the legal field, for example, could obviously have significant effects upon lawyers.

Transactions

The third area of library services is transactions. Here we are using the word transaction in a restricted sense to indicate activities that result in the transfer of money from one account to another.

The telecommunication of information relating to the crediting and debiting of international bank accounts has been going on since 1977 through SWIFT, the Society for Worldwide Interbank Financial Telecommunication. Various national systems for the exchange of interbank transactions are also being developed. These developments show, if it was necessary, that financial transactions are no different from other information transmission activities. But transactions are not only limited to the obviously financial activities such as banking and brokerage. Already trials are under way for telemetering and teleshopping, see page 72.

Telemetering. Remote metering allows utilities such as electricity and gas suppliers to meter the usage of their product without having to have staff to call on consumers. The savings arising from eliminated house calls could, in total, be enormous since making an individual house call costs on the order of £1 in Britain, and some 40 million calls are made there alone each year.

However, in addition to enabling utilities to dispense with metering calls, the device provides enhanced services. More frequent billing of customers could lead to improved cash flow for the utilities, better peak demand forecasting, and demand management could stem from having the ability to instantly monitor individual demand and make rapid tariff changes.

The metering device also carries out the traditional functions of telling the consumer how much of the utility is being consumed, but in addition, through the use of microprocessor's programs, this information can be displayed in more meaningful terms as a cost figure since the metering is carried out by a special-purpose microprocessor device the size of a largish calculator which incorporates a display device. It is expected that this easy display of cost will lead to lower consumer demand and better demand management by the consumer.

Telemetering is not necessarily limited to households with telephones since the actual communication with the microprocessor meter could be achieved by mains-borne signals or by radio broadcasting as well as by dialing the telephone.

PRODUCTION PROCESSES

Earlier we split production into unit, batch, and mass. This is the typical way of analyzing the production function. However, now it will be convenient if we use other ways of characterizing operations methods.

First, we can simply distinguish between mass and other types of production:

> In both flow and mass production, which are appropriate to large-volume single products or a few standardized products, operations are continuous, follow a cost-efficient predetermined sequence, require specialized equipment, and are already heavily automated. By contrast, batch production, which applies to the manufacture of several different products each with relatively low volume and low standardization, is intermittent, follows no invariable sequence, requires general-purpose equipment, forces work to remain in process for considerably longer intervals, has higher unit costs—and is much less automated. (Gerwin, 1982)

While this splitting into two categories is a useful way of distinguishing the different kinds of operations, there is from an information processing viewpoint another useful categorization between manufacturing and assembly processing.

Manufacturing

In manufacturing, machines are used to cut, grind, drill, and press. These machines have in the past been operated by skilled work people, usually men, to produce the required outputs. The function of the operator is to position the raw material and actuate the machine tools, making adjustments as necessary to allow for material changes and machine wear.

Computerization of Control Activities. Rarely will a tool be powered directly by human muscle, and the operator's task is essentially an information processing one. Because of this use of the operator as an information processor there is a clear possibility of using computer information processing to control the machine.

> If the level of intelligence needed for a job is low enough, or the degree of discomfort is high enough, the chances are that a programmed machine can do it . . . as effectively as a human can. (Cunningham, 1983)

Defensive Use of Computerization. By using programmed computers we can achieve machines that are quite humanlike in their performance characteristics but which do not have the weaknesses that flesh is prey to. However, until recently, computers in operations have been used defensively.

> Much of computing in manufacturing industry has been defensive. Management has been concerned with systems for order processing and sales forecasting, for ordering materials and materials management. These applications have been all the more vital because lead times on the factory floor and on the factory floors of suppliers have been so long. They have defended companies from the shortcomings of their own production facilities. (Jenner, 1983)

This points out quite vividly the kind of effects first noted by Forester (1961). A computer-based simulation of an industrial system that used faster throughput of information showed that managers still had to do more or less the same kinds of things that they had to do before faster, computer-based information systems were installed.

Combine this approach with the constraints of accounting conventions, and the result is often an inappropriate crisis-driven management style:

> Fixated by the short run, managers have pursued all sorts of piecemeal efforts to hold down costs without stopping to map out systematic ways of organizing the factory floor for more efficiency. Too often production procedures in U.S. factories appear to be little more than accretions of ad hoc solutions to problems ranging from space shortages to union-dictated work rules. Managers focus obsessively on chipping away at direct labor costs rather than exploring better ways to organize the work force—or investigating the extent to which new technologies are making direct labor costs less important. (Bylinsky, 1983)

Offensive Use of Computers. When, in Forester's simulation, computers were used to reconstruct the systems information flow, it was found that the kinds of problems managers had to deal with changed and decreased in urgency. This approach can be characterized as the offensive use of the computer.

> Now there is a new philosophy. The philosophy of computers in an attacking role. Cut inventories. Abolish long runs. Smash lead times. Be instantly responsive to market forces. This is the philosophy of the flexible manufacturing system (FMS). It is the philosophy of the formidable Japanese. (Jenner, 1983).

Flexible Manufacturing Systems (FMSs). FMSs are the completion of a process that started with numerically controlled (NC) machines and has subsequently progressed through computer numerically controlled (CNC) and direct numerical control (DNC). The overall name for these developments is computer-aided design/computer-aided manufacture (CAD/CAM). FMSs integrate all previous ideas into the automatic factory (Illustration 8.7).

As can be seen in Illustration 8.9 the machines involved in the physical handling of production can be directly linked to the clerical and administrative management and information system (MIS). The manufacturing and information processes are linked together automatically with the production machines providing the necessary information as they operate.

The manufacturing machines are, of course, either special purpose or general purpose robots. Equipped with a range of tools, they can manufacture any shape of article required provided that the right tool is available and that the correct instructions are being used.

Because of the ease of reprogrammability of machines, FMS production offers the potential to provide a variety of products from one production line. In the past, the situation has generally been one where the automated production line produced many thousands of copies of the same product.

But like all computer solutions, the FMS is only a solution for certain types of problems; it is not a panacea. There appear to be two particularly

Illustration 8.7. The automatic factory

Numerical Control (NC) was first applied to any kind of metal-cutting machine. NC developed in the aircraft industry where lots of metal is machined and has extended into tube bending, cloth cutting, and so on. Traditionally, NC has used instructions that are punched as holes into paper tape. There are various problems associated with the use of NC. For example,

- NC machines are more expensive.
- NC means the automatic functioning of machines, so less-skilled people can be used to operate the machines.
- Supervisors are caught between losing some control of the production process and becoming responsible for more expensive machinery, which has therefore to be higher producing in order to financially justify itself.

In the late Sixties and early Seventies the NC control unit started to be replaced by programmable computers; this was called Computer Numeric Control (CNC). At first, minicomputers and then microcomputers were brought in to control the production machines. This step meant that the program of instructions the production machine followed was stored better and could be more conveniently altered. Additionally, the NC computer could also be used to acquire and manipulate information about what the machine was doing and thus generate management information. Automating the factory is not simply a question of putting in robots to replace humans in the physical production activities but also involves linking the production activities to information systems in order to enable management control to be automated and to allow for the greatest extent of flexibility and adaptability in the business.

The idea of CNC is easily expandable by hooking up a number of production machines to the controlling computer. This development is called Direct Numeric Control (DNC). The obvious advantage of DNC is that the operation of a sequence of machines can be controlled and harmonized.

Soon after the development of DNC came the development of computer-aided design/computer-aided manufacturing (CAD/CAM). CAD/CAM is really the second generation of DNC. A flexible manufacturing system (FMS) combines the control of the machining operations with the control of the flow of materials. Clearly in this way the ultimate in efficient factory operations can be achieved by having the right machining operations performed in the optimum sequence using both specialized and general purpose robotic machines.

However, just getting the robot aspect of factory automation working properly is difficult enough. If robots are to be integrated into factory systems their movements must be computable. The current process of training robots by using a human operator to teach the robot its movements—the robot's computer stores the movement motions for later reuse—is clearly ineffective. We must be able to specify the robot's movements by a more conventional programming process. This leads to the requirement for a simpler robot design than the present armlike structure:

> Most robots are multi-jointed arms... Six axes suffice, in theory, to move a tool or implement to any location and orient it in any position....

> Most robots are still taught their tasks by hand. But if robots are to be integrated into a computer-aided design and manufacturing operation, their movements must be computed....
>
> The computing has to be fast: with an arm-type robot you have to work out the joint angles for each new position, not just for end points but for numerous points during each of the robot's movements. This is not a difficult computation, but it involves a lot of slow-to-compute trigonemtrical functions....
>
> As a research project, GEC has built a unique robot called the Gadfly....
>
> The Gadfly is controlled by an 8086 microprocessor. An "arm"-type assembly robot (a Unimation Puma)...requires an LSI-11 minicomputer...
>
> The Gadfly swoops down cn its work from above, steered by six slanting rods....
>
> To move...in, say, a straight horizontal line, requires a co-ordinated movement of all six rods. Computing the rod extensions required for such a movement, however, is surprisingly simple. Most of the work is based on Pythagoras' theorem. (Durham, 1983)

The advantage of the Gadfly approach is that by using the gantry structure the robot can be powered by a smaller and cheaper computer, and because it does not have the mechanical massiveness of the traditional armlike robot, the machine can respond much more quickly.

Whether or not the Gadfly design is adopted is not so important as realizing that the development of factory automation requires a considerable amount of effort. The present stage of factory automation, although interesting, is only the start, because it is the connections between production operations control *and* the general information processing systems of a business that ultimately determine success or failure. Neither activity in itself is sufficient to sustain a goods producing business.

For a general introduction in this area see Gerwin (1982).

useful application areas of the FMS. The first application is in the automation of low-volume limited-variety manufacturing processes such as the production of expensive and sophisticated components. The second area, the one of current major interest, is in the production of high-volume output from a restricted selection of a wide number of possibilities. The FMS is not suitable for the high-volume, repetitious output typical of "hard," e.g., automobile, automation (Illustration 8.8). Of course, even as a good solution, the cost of an FMS is high. A DNC machine will cost around twice the price of a more conventional CNC machine.

Computer-Aided Design. As well as improving the manufacturing process itself, the computer can be used to improve the design process. Standard two-dimensional drafting onto sheets of paper can be replaced by drafting

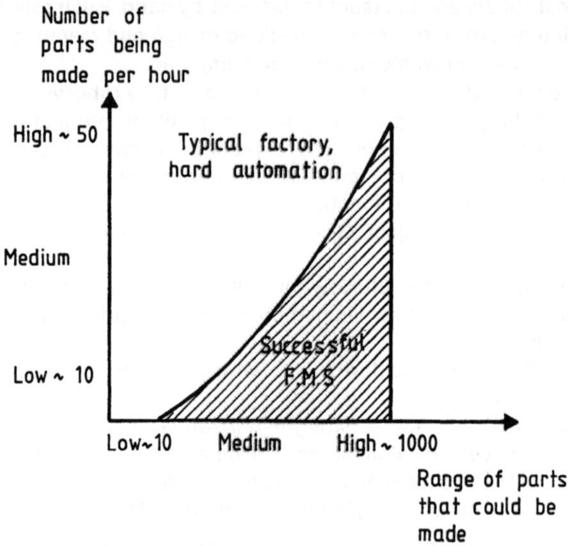

Illustration 8.8. Areas of application for a FMS

The FMS is a solution for particular kinds of problems, not a panacea for all. Successful FMS applications tend to be characterized by the production of a selected number of parts from a large possible selection.

The FMS is intended to produce a manufacturing system that can quickly respond to changing demands. There are other ways of dealing with this situation such as holding stock or only making items when demand reaches a certain level. In these latter cases the manufacturing system is controlled by administrative processes and managerial decision making. What is gained by these non-FMS approaches is less expensive manufacturing; what is lost is the ability to respond to changes quickly. [See *Computing* (1983a).]

onto a computer screen, where the two-dimensional design can be converted automatically into a three-dimensional representation. Additionally, standard items from a library of standard drawings can be drawn by the computer with only a minimum of designer specification.

Assembling. We have so far concentrated on manufacturing rather than assembly. The application of computer-controlled machines for high-dexterity assembly work seems remote since robots capable of achieving high manual dexterity are simply not available. Companies such as Briggs and Stratton who assemble small internal combustion engines operate simply by applying good management techniques and personal incentive schemes. This kind of work could be computerized successfully only by a significant redesign of the product away from a dependence on manual dexterity.

Process Control. The other aspect of factory production activity is process production. Here we are dealing with a continuous flow of raw materials used to provide products such as chemicals, paper, food, and cement. In these and similar cases, information relating to flow rate, temperature, pressure, and concentration are measured and controlled. The measurements are carried out using sensors of various kinds and transformed if necessary into suitable electronic signals by transducers. The transduced signal is then used as input information for processing according to the process computer program and will result in an adjustment being carried out to a valve or pump. The idea of process control is shown in Illustration 8.9. It is, of course, similar to the idea used in the automatic factory, the difference in application being that the process control of a continuous material flow is simpler in some ways than the control of discrete production, even if it is mass production.

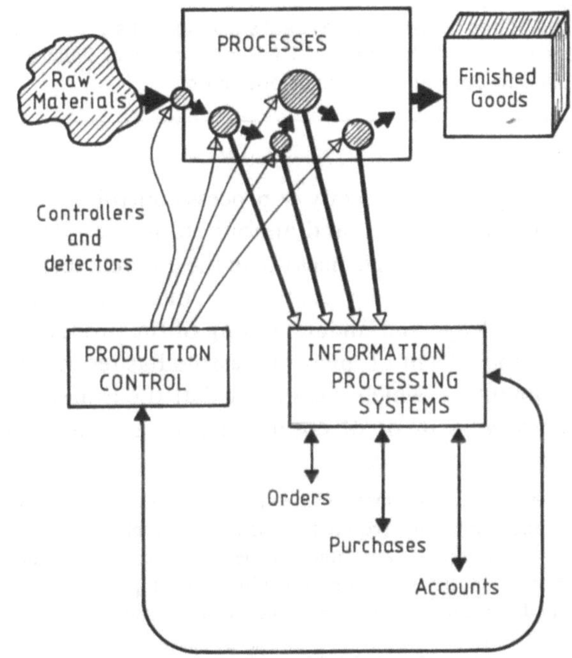

Illustration 8.9. Process control principles

The simple control loop introduced in Chapter 4 has to be extended in real-life application to allow the process controller to be linked into the general business and management information systems.

The following describes the use of a relatively small microcomputer application in process control:

> The function of the Hot Strip Mill is to turn slabs of steel into strips that are coiled for convenient storage and transportation. The work of the strip mill is divided into two sections: the roughing mill and the finishing mill. When the steel enters the strip mill it can be in the order of some 10 inches thick by 30 feet and weighs in excess of 20 tons.
>
> In the roughing mill the slab is progressively reduced and ends up a 1 inch thick bar. In the finishing mill the bars are further reduced, cooled and coiled....
>
> The advantage of the new process control system is that it is a totally dedicated system, only having one function to perform. The system has to control the water supply to the steel strips, taking into account strip speed and thickness and must be aware of which part of the strip is where at any time. Temperature requirements vary between 950° F and 1300° F and must be accurate to between ±50° F.
>
> There must be at least a 12 second gap between the strips of steel, but speed can vary. The plant is capable of processing one strip every one-and-a-half minutes. (Wright, 1983)

Some of the points noted in this extract show how this application of process control is very similar to the idea of CNC discussed in Illustration 8.7. One computer is used to control a particular operation.

Because of the greater simplicity of process control, the breakthrough to computer control was perceived and announced in the 1950s. However, the breakthrough did not materialize because of the inherent technical difficulties involved in controlling computer processes. Quite simply there is a distinct lack of formal knowledge and understanding of the processes that are to be controlled. While the advent of microprocessors has resulted in the lowering of the cost of computers, which has meant that the economics have swung even more decisively in favor of computer process control, there are still significant sources of resistance:

> Work should be aimed at systems that have increased reliability and maintainability, reduced cost and complexity, require less expertise to implement, are explainable to users with limited sophistication and knowledge, and can be implemented in an evolutionary fashion. There is need for education of potential users and for increased standardization wherever possible. (Evans, 1980)

Evans's last point is made because

> Great engineering talent, for instance, is often wasted making routine decisions on matters such as the size of valves. If some of these routine decisions could be automated, the productivity of a systems engineering team could be increased substantially. (Evans, 1980)

INFORMATION PROCESSES

Underpinning the successful operation of a business are the various information processing systems of the business. These systems may be fairly well structured, such as orders, payments, or accounting, or they may be the far less-structured general office support systems such as those involved in generating general reports, and so on.

From early on the business applications of computers were fairly well appreciated

> LEO is a machine, or rather an organized system of machines, which carries out clerical procedures at high speed and without any human intervention from beginning to end. Before the advent of LEO, which stands for Lyons Electronic Office, the machines and devices available to the office were all ancillary to the clerk. Each machine was capable of carrying out only a limited number of operations under the direct control of the clerk, the work having to be passed from machine to machine and clerk to clerk so that the overall time for a job was still governed by the speed of the clerks' working.
>
> With the development of the fully automatic high-speed computer, it has become possible for a whole procedure, starting from the original data, to be carried through at the maximum speed of which the machine is capable, with no intermediate handling of any kind whatever.
>
> Nevertheless, a fully automatic high-speed computer cannot be purchased and installed in an office as simply as equipment of more orthodox type. By its nature, it is not ancillary to the office; potentially it is the office, or rather the routine part of it. (Leo Computers Ltd., 1956)

As with other areas, the development of cheaper, more powerful computer processing has meant that the principles of application which previously were only talked about have now become practical reality.

The combination of various stages of development of processor power coupled with advancements in telecommunication has meant that there have been various fashions in having computing centralized, remote, and now dispersed.

The information processing applications can be separated into data processing and word processing.

Data Processing

The most obvious candidate for information technology is the set of number processing activities that form a fundamental basis for much of business. If a business is to be successful in the long run it must sell items at a higher price than it costs to make them. That is the concern of the accounting activity. But it is also necessary to know where the items are, or how long it will take to get some more made, etc., and all of the answers to these questions depend to a greater or lesser extent on the processing of numerical data. As was pointed out in the Introduction to this chapter, the numeric data to be processed generally will not consist of large numbers, and the processing applied to the numbers will not be particularly complicated.

Throughout the 1960s and 1970s much of business administrative data processing was centered around wage preparation and accounting. Illustration 8.10, based on studies carried out in the United Kingdom and the United States in the mid-1960s, shows the type of applications for which computers were being used.

The computers involved in these activities were christened mainframes, primarily because of their large physical size. Mainframe computers were for most of this period the only choice available until the mid-1960s and were needed anyway because of the large amount of data to be processed. These computers required special operating environments: specially trained operators, special thermal conditions, special electrical supplies. The machines were expensive to buy and to operate and so were limited at first to large organizations. Because of the expense associated with acquiring and operating them, working patterns had to a great extent to be altered to achieve the most economical use of these resources. Falling prices and the establishment of businesses selling computer time enabled an increasing number of businesses to take advantage of the benefits of data processing.

Management Information Systems. In addition to the enlargement of the realm of data processing because of falling prices, there was enlargement in the sense that the areas of application of computers were increased. The

Illustration 8.10. Number processing activities in business

Major applications carried out per installation, mid-1960s (percentage occurrence).

Application	U.S.A.	U.K.
Payroll	60	60
Sales analysis	55	45
Inventory control	50	40
Bills and invoices	45	35
Accounting	45	40
Personnel	30	30
Production	30	20
Distribution	25	15
Sales planning	20	15
Purchasing	20	15

general idea of data processing became expanded to the use of computers for providing all the information necessary for running a business. This concept was labeled as Management Information Systems. The title, usually shortened to MIS, was used preemptively to indicate a computerized information system for managers in contrast to their previous paper-based information systems. The general idea was that by using the computer's information processing capabilities managers would be provided with more and more detailed, hence better, information from which would naturally flow better management. In hindsight this approach may seem to have been rather naive, but an idea that does not work looks naive, in hindsight.

The most obvious drawback to computerized MIS stems from the ease with which a computer can generate vast amounts of printed information, or reports as they are usually called. Almost everyone who has had anything to do with a real-business MIS will be aware of the existence of large numbers of unread reports detailing different aspects of business performance. Jarvis has described these difficulties of MIS and the further problems that they lead on to in a case study report:

> Management information is the real prize of new technology. Managers have long claimed that lack of the right sort of information hinders their ability to plan and control operations properly. With the advent of computers, vast amounts of information in a myriad of forms have become readily available. Now the plea from many quarters is that there is insufficient time to pore over so many computer printouts or that in spite of everything the essential data is still not available in quite the format which would make it fully utilizable....
>
> The new management problem brought about by the new technology is: what to do with all the new data now available? The general enthusiasm expressed about how interesting it would be to know something is seldom matched by knowledge about how to use the information. (Jarvis, 1983)

White and Marajian have identified two major weaknesses with present in most MIS. The first picks up the point commented on by Jarvis, the second leads onto a further criticism.

> Firstly, computing power has outstripped information systems analysis techniques, particularly where small- or medium-sized companies are concerned. Even a small minicomputer has more than enough power to produce a plethora of unwanted reports. The second weakness is associated with the inability to input external information into an MIS and correlate this with internally generated information. Some companies have achieved this in relation to specific areas such as sales of competitors, and major economic indicators, for relevant countries. These companies are the exceptions, and the majority rely on the manager himself interpreting an increasing volume of internal information in the context of his own appreciation of the external situation. (White and Marajian, 1982)

The need to be able to use MIS in the context of the real external world leads to the serious drawback to MIS: that in the process of gathering the information, much of the real usefulness of the information is lost.

> ...it is very important to be able to get at raw or partially summarized data (which are likely to be somewhat specialized and idiosyncratic in form), to be able to rummage around in such data, and to be able to extract various fragments in various ways. Much less often is it important to have access to a global corporate data base or model that contains everything in a uniform but unrevealing fashion. This is why, even though they may be reluctant to admit it, division and plant managers commonly have their own record-keeping systems for projecting such things as work-in-progress inventory, subcontractors' accruals, and local sales results, instead of relying exclusively on corporate record keeping systems. (Vyssotsky, 1980)

Management Science and MIS. The ability to gather and process large amounts of numeric information led to a flowering of interest in management science. Management science, or operations research, is predicated on the assumption that business problems are representable in terms of mathematically analytic techniques such as linear programming and network analysis. Results of this approach have been the development of sophisticated theories of inventory control and of scheduling. This approach, while useful, can also create a situation where the users of the computer-generated information lose sight of the fact that the machine is only manipulating information given to it by people, which may therefore be wrong, according to rules that have been created by people, which also may therefore be wrong. This failure to keep things in perspective can lead to situations where people do not bother to check to see if the solutions being proferred are making sense.

What developments in information technology have to offer MIS are a reduction in the amount of paper and paper reports, a reduction in the amount of manipulation of information prior to its access by users, and an increase in the customization of MIS reports.

Information technology offers all of this through the increased accessibility of computers. Instead of having to wait for centrally produced data processing reports, the executive can use the spreadsheet and data base programs on his or her own computer to carry out immediately the manipulations that are required. It is no longer necessary to wade through volumes of paper to find a particular statistic—a few keys pressed on the computer keyboard and the information is displayed on the screen, perhaps in graphic rather than textual form. And all of the basic information can still be held centrally, so there is no need to set up complex duplications or triplications of information gathering procedures.

Transaction Analysis

After payroll preparation, the next most popular activity of information processes has been, and remains, sales analysis and inventory control.

These processes, which were inevitably cumbersome given the technology that had to be used in the 1960s and 1970s, have now progressed significantly. Previously involving the generation of paper that would then be converted into data in computer compatible form, microelectronics now offers the potential of computerization at the point where the sales information is first generated, at the sales terminal. This is known as an electronic point of sales terminal (EPOST).

In some cases the EPOST may be installed in the customer's home rather than in the shop. For ideas relating to this approach see pages 72–73 and page 181.

By using a merchandise marking technique such as bar coding the EPOST can not only note the details of the sale, and so generate a detailed customer receipt, but can also carry out the cashless electronic funds transfer from the customer's account to the business's account and generate information relating to reorders. The terminal can also carry out the reorder process itself, thus eliminating much routine managerial decision making.

There are still some formidable barriers to this approach. Currently, many EPOSTs offer no great advance over the cash till: Even when EPOSTs are developed, the cashless electronic transfer of funds can only occur when customers have bank accounts. In some countries, France, for example, the penetration of banking is high with about 90% of the population having accounts, but in other countries, Britain, for example, the penetration of banking is low with less than 50% of the population having accounts. Finally, the assumption of routine managerial decision making by computers is not to be undertaken lightly since it is extremely difficult to write computer programs that take into account all of the various factors that a good manager does.

The ideal information flow for these transaction processes is shown in Illustration 8.11. Although these approaches have been described solely in terms of consumer goods outlets, they can also be applied in any situation where transactions, financial or not, are carried out.

Real-Time Information. The technical developments in information technology have meant that in addition to becoming more personal, it has become increasingly possible to provide a system that requires immediate responses. This form of real-time data processing where the computer interacts with the operator, and hence with the real world that the computer is in some way controlling, can cause particular problems:

> Dearden has analyzed what he calls the "The Myth of Real-Time Management Information"... To watch a group of executives confronted on a screen by immediate numerical projections of their suggestions or ideas is to realize how inhibiting to reflection or deep discussion this immediate feedback can be. For many people it is so threatening that it induces mental inertia—a sort of figure-induced hypnosis. (Handy, 1976)

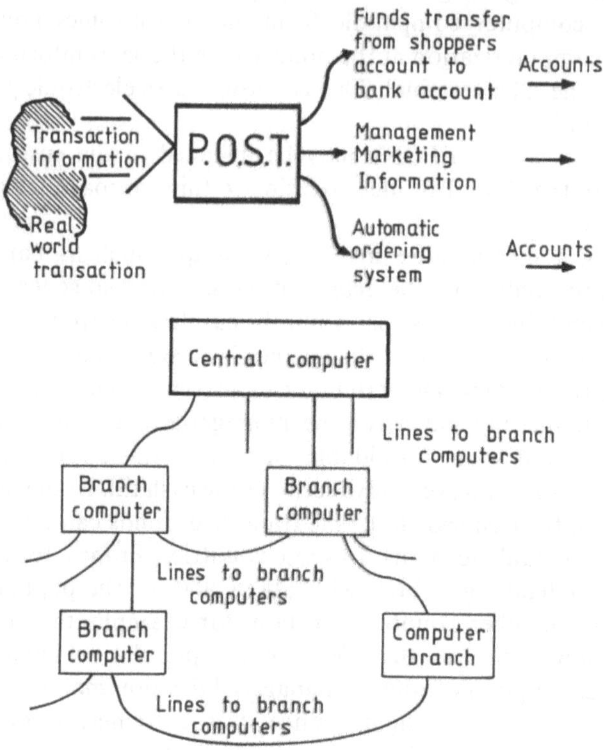

Illustration 8.11. EPOST information flow

Information concerning transactions is fed into the EPOST, perhaps semi-automatically using a bar code scanner. This information can then be used to authorize the transfer of funds from the shopper's account to the bank account of the shop. Besides this obvious financial information, the EPOST can generate the information needed for various management activities ranging from judging the efficiency of the EPOST and its operator to automatically generating stock replacement orders.

The use of EPOSTs, however, is very dependent on the cost of telecommunication, as this following extract shows:

> I recently encountered a sophisticated and well-designed point of sale (pos) system in a Belgian group of stores. The most modern pos terminals had been purchased but the link with the central dp facility was by cassette and motorcycle courier. Wideband indeed! But why not arrange telecommunications links? Because, explained the designer, it's just too expensive to contemplate with the current telecommunications costs in Belgium. (Donker, 1983)

Quite clearly in this case the value of having information coming in as the transactions are being conducted is simply not worth the cost. In business, cost and value of information systems have both to be assessed.

A typical real-business terminal arrangement is also shown here. By using branch node computers and links between branches, failures in the telecommunication links can generally be overcome, and transaction details can be sent directly from one branch to another rather than having to go all the way up through the network to the central computer before coming back down again.

In spite of the implication of Dearden's observation, which may be true for some executive decision making, there are many circumstances where real-time processing is useful and increasingly necessary. Seat reservation is a prime example of a business activity where the customer or client needs to know at the time of booking whether or not a seat is available. Indeed, any situation where there is competition for a fixed, scarce resource with a dispersed geographical demand could be dealt with by using a real-time data processing computer.

Word Processing

The emphasis on data processing was starting to be corrected by the mid-1970s by a growing realization that not all information used in a business was in numeric form. In fact, based on a process of strict character counting, probably two or three times as much information is presented in alphabetic form as in numeric form. This led to the development of word processing.

Word processing is the application of information technology to the manipulation of alphabetic rather than numeric symbols. From one viewpoint word processing is an almost completely random affair. Unlike data processing there is not just a few simple operations such as addition and subtraction to be carried out according to set programs of instructions. Viewed like this, word processing is the creation of unpredictable strings of words by individual authors. On the other hand, word processing is not a totally unpredictable affair. There can be vast amounts of textual material produced in a business that is standard, that is, the same from time to time. Letters to late-paying customers, orders, and contracts, will all tend to contain the same material with only minor variations from time to time. Clearly, the arrival of a convenient information technology that could store, provide rapid access to, and print out rapidly required information and easily accept minor amendments, could be of enormous benefit in some business situations. From this viewpoint, word processing is a repetitive, structured activity, as shown in Illustration 8.12.

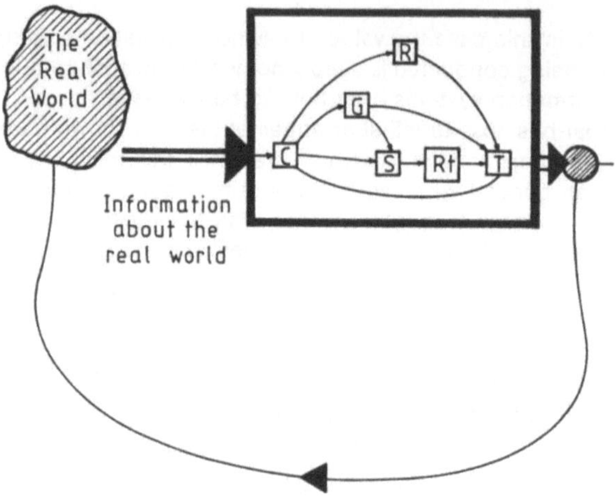

Illustration 8.12. The activities of word processing

Some of the stages of word processing can be carried out almost completely automatically, while others are almost entirely dependent on operators. It is at this stage that the difference between numeric and textual processing must be made clear.

In numeric processing, the rules being followed in the manipulation of the numbers are well known and well defined. On the other hand, the rules being followed when dealing with text manipulation are not well known. There are no simple rules that enable the generation of correct and sensible sentences. The original material has to be input into the system in full by a human operator. Later on, stored information can be retrieved and standard text created by computer program, but on the whole the main use of computers in word processing is as storage devices, enabling operators to make changes to the format of text easily and transmit it accurately and quickly to other places.

For word processors five main sequences of activities can be identified. These sequences can be labelled by the initials of the operations involved in the sequences where, C stands for Capturing data or information, R stands for Reproducing data or information, T stands for Transmitting data or information, G stands for Generating data or information, S stands for Storing data or information, Rt stands for ReTrieving data or information; (i) CRT, currently achieved, for example, by photocopying a document and then distributing it; (ii) CGT, where filed information is used to assist in the creation of a new document that is then transmitted to someone; (iii) CGS, where an incoming document is annotated and then filed; (iv) RtLC, where filed information is retrieved and then distributed and used for some purpose, perhaps in the CGT sequence; and (v) CT, where an incoming document is received and then forwarded. Since the G, S, and Rt activities are increasingly likely to be computerized, this means there will be an increasing amount of pressure to computerize the remaining T, C, and R activities because of the wasted effort in transferring from paper-based to computer-based and then back to paper-based information systems.

The biggest pressure will be on the development of the production of compatible C devices to enable information to be easily put into computer-based storage.

Computerization in the Work Place. In terms of operation, text processing is distinguished by being associated with the concept of bringing computers to the work force by bringing sophisticated equipment into the office, rather than with the concept of setting up special locations where people are brought to use the equipment.

Of course, the technical aspects of any computer-based equipment cannot be ignored, and word processing equipment that requires many terminals, memory devices, and printers will require some technically knowledgeable support, together with some special environments, if environmentally sensitive equipment is being used. However, there is much less likelihood of the existence of a large specialized administrative support function, as with data processing, since it is generally thought, maybe incorrectly, that word processing can be managed and supervised adequately by nonspecialist staff.

Differences Between Word and Data Processing. Since word processing uses the same components and principles as data processing, it is to be expected that at least superficially the equipment used in word processing will look the same as that employed in data processing. There are, however, some distinct differences. The equipment is intended to be much easier to use for word processing than for data processing applications, so the keyboard will usually have well-marked keys offering special commands and functions for cursor control, screen editing, and so on, in addition to the standard typewriter keyboard layout. The equipment itself is of a better physical design than that of computer terminals with such features as detached keyboards, adjustable screens, and an overall “friendliness” not to be found in the more traditional data processing equipment.

Convergence of Word and Data Processing

Since both data and word processing use the same equipment it is to be expected that the two activities will tend to evolve toward each other. This has happened to the extent that it is now possible to use computers as word processing machines which were originally designed for standard data processing activities. In fact, some of the manuscript for this book was prepared, as an experiment, on a Sinclair computer.

Given the obvious limitations of using any computer keyboard, let alone the limitations of a Spectrum keyboard, word processing on a general purpose computer can only be sensibly carried out for limited amounts of text. The major limitation of using a computer keyboard is the lack of the special function keys such as delete, insert, and move. All of these necessary text editing operations have to be carried out using special combinations of keys. The other important constraint when using a small computer as a word processor is the limited amount of text that can normally be handled, usually only between five and ten pages at a time.

While computeres have extended into the field of word processing, word processors have gained data processing muscle. Instead of being merely super correction typewriters, word processors are now often able to offer: records processing programs so that information can be stored and retrieved from a 'database' of some kind, a programmable math capability allowing arithmetic to be performed within text, particularly useful for generating invoices, bills, and receipts, and in some cases word processing systems support programming in high-level languages.

SUMMARY

The general areas of application of information technology are well known although the details of the particulars are not.

Products and Devices. For products and devices, the ability to select easily from a variety of program options together with the ability to time accurately, means that consumer devices, in particular, will become ever more sophisticated. Examples of these increasing abilities are microelectronic sewing machines, which can provide upward of 100 different sewing patterns, and programmable cookers.

Production and Administrative Processes. As far as processes are concerned, the emphasis is on the use of technologically based devices to replace people. However, this replacement will occur only where the substitution of information technology makes financial sense.

In production the problems of introducing information technology center around the costs of the equipment and the construction of machines that can actually do the work. No matter how much computer control is built into it, the robot is still an electromechanical device, and so has all the limitations of all other mechanical devices.

For the administrative and clerical processes, developments in information technology mean that computers are now no longer machines hidden away in special air-conditioned rooms filled solely with specialists. Computers are now out and located in ordinary offices under direct operator control. The problems of information technology here center on our inability to understand the information processing activities that we perform and to design more efficient yet more flexible computer-based alternatives.

DISCUSSION QUESTIONS

1. Think of a standard nonintelligent domestic device. In what ways could it be improved by giving it intelligence?

2. What information service would you like to have computerized and publicly disseminated? In what ways would computerization improve this service? And (most importantly) how much would you be prepared to pay for such a service?

3. To what extent does the Japanese J.I.T. (just-in-time) operations method show that computers are not needed to manage a production operation? Would it be better to spend \$ x million on computerization or \$ x million on developing and achieving a well-trained and well-motivated management and labor force?

9

REVIEW

INTRODUCTION

The purpose of this chapter is to draw together various ideas concerning information technology and the information technology age.

• Until recently production of the goods and services we consume was directly and obviously based on human skills. Each of us was either a farmer growing food, or a miner extracting coal, or a fisherman hunting fish, or, more recently, a factory worker on a production line.

Whatever we did there was a clear connection between our actions and the production or manufacture of food or some other physical item. For most of us, if not our parents then almost certainly our grandparents were involved directly in the production of food or goods. However, the development of efficient technology has caused a change. It is now quite likely that the work we do is separate from the world of physical production. It is quite likely that the work we do is concerned with manipulating information. The closest we will get to making a physical product is perhaps in writing a letter or a report. There is nothing necessarily wrong with this change, but it is different and requires thought on our part to ensure that we are doing things correctly.

• Our use of technology to help us is not new, but it is now entering an unknown era.

> The easing of human labour by technology, a process that began in prehistory, is entering a new stage. The acceleration in the pace of technological innovation inaugurated by the Industrial Revolution has until recently resulted mainly in the displacement of human muscle power from the tasks of production. The current revolution in computer technology is causing an equally momentus social change: the expansion of information gathering and information processing as computers extend the reach of the human brain. (Ginzberg, 1982)

• Although no one knows what the impact of information technology will be, we all feel that it will be enormous. The nearest experience we have had to the development of cheap computers and telecommunication has been the development of small electric motors.

> The closest analogy to the present situation is perhaps the set of problems posed by the introduction of the small electric motor. When the first factories were established in the eighteenth century the machines in them, used for weaving silk and later cotton, were powered by water. Factories were located in remote places in hills and valleys where water power was constantly available. Following the introduction of steam-powered machinery factories could be located where required, although it was economic to be near a coalfield. To provide for smaller users, belt and pulley systems were developed, and a room with a source of power could be rented adjacent to a great steam engine. Later, gas mains established a distributed source of power, but it was only with the coming of mains electricity—particularly of AC mains—and the development of the small electric motor that a convenient source of power became available to drive machinery. To see the effect, consider how different the home would be without the washing machine, vacuum cleaner, dishwasher, electric sewing machine, gramophone or electric drill. And factories would be far more seriously affected. Indeed with the small electric motor even mains power is not necessary: think of the portable gramophone, the windscreen wiper and petrol pump in the car. (Hyman, 1980)

TOPICS

People

Blue collar work. Information technology is not limited to the processing of paper. Information technology makes our machines intelligent. We are creating machines that require less human effort, intervention, and control. This clearly has implications for the manual worker.

Manual work is clearly concerned with the control of tools and machines. The blue collar worker has to control the machine to ensure that it is doing the correct things at the right time. The blue collar worker provides the feedback link between the product that is being processed and the machine that is doing the processing (Illustration 9.1).

Information technology can be used to act as a controller by detecting what state the product is in at any time, and then, by following through the stored programs of instructions, carrying out actions as appropriate by selection from the range of available choices.

The real technological problems are to construct the detecting and executing devices that can carry out the required physical actions. The limit to this use of information technology is the ingenuity of humans, and even a brief look at what has been achieved in the past will show that there are few constraints on human ingenuity (Illustration 9.2).

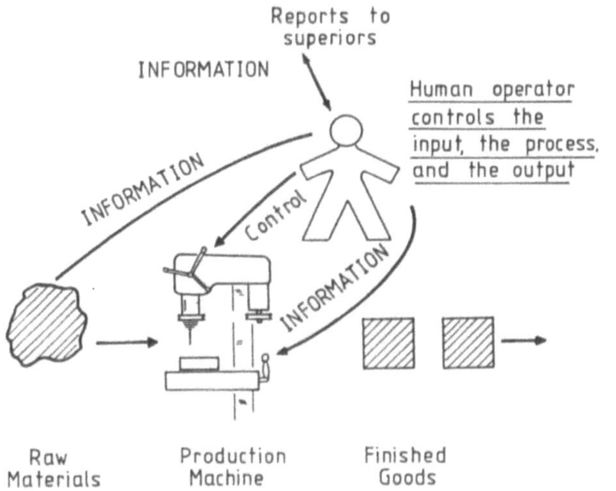

Illustration 9.1. The manual worker as a controller

The human operator is an information receiver. Information is received concerning the state of the raw materials, how the production process is performing, and whether the finished goods are what was ordered and are up to the required quality standards. All of this information will have an immediate effect in terms of the activities that will be carried out in controlling the production machine.

Additionally, the operator also provides information to, and receives information from, superiors in the organization which may also affect the controlling activities.

The conclusion must be that manufacturing processes will become less and less dependent on human workers. The speed at which this process of substitution of human labor occurs will be dependent on a complex set of factors mainly centered around the anticipated profits accruing from computerization. But while profits are clearly important, there will be constraining factors such as the limitations of information technology and limited management awareness that will slow down the process of substitution.

White Collar Work

While the blue collar worker is an obvious target because of the relative routineness of the physical work involved, white collar work has and will continue to be the subject of just as much, if not more, pressure for substitu-

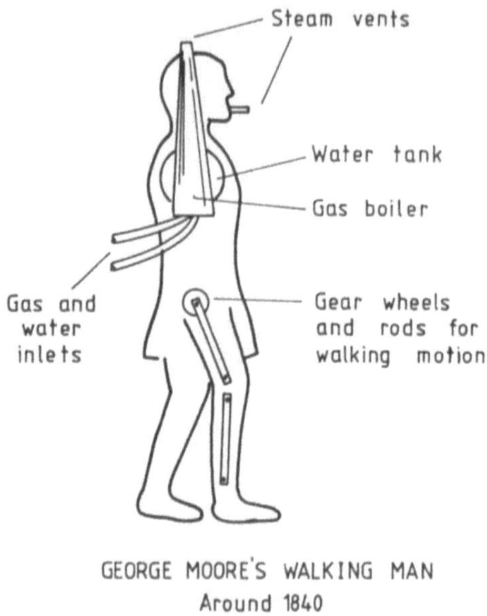

Illustration 9.2. The walking man

There are only very broad limits to the bounds of human ingenuity, as this design for a walking machine from the mid-1800s shows. Externally the machine must have looked rather strange since it looked like a man in a suit of armor with a cigar in his mouth. The "cigar" acted as a vent to allow steam to escape (there was also a vent through the top of the armored helmet).

tion. With white collar work there is the inherent advantage, as far as information technology is concerned, that the work involves the manipulation of information rather than physical items. The need to construct sophisticated transducers is thereby greatly reduced. In addition to the obvious and by now classic examples of using information technology to replace routine clerical and typing activities, there are other information jobs that can be tackled. Occupations such as lawyer, doctor, and real estate agent all have in common the routineness of information processing. These and other similar jobs are concerned primarily with deciding which out of a possibly complex set of courses of actions should be taken. As we have seen there are already situations where information technology is being used to help people performing these kinds of jobs: Portable computers to remind doctors of possible drug reactions and terminals to provide access to symptoms and disease prognosis are just two examples from the United States and France of the use of information technology in the medical field. In the United Kingdom Microtax is an example of a program that can be used on a machine as humble as a Sinclair Spectrum to help in the completion of income tax returns and the calculation of the income tax due.

Given time to develop the programs there seems to be no reason why very good professional advice should not be able to be conveniently and cheaply provided to anyone who wants it. There must, however, be an emphasis on *time.* In the 1950s computer translation from one language to another seemed to be just around the corner. We have since then learned that human languages are significantly more difficult to handle than was first thought. Although the computerization of professional services does not appear to hold the same pitfalls as human language translation, it probably does hold the same pitfalls as computer chess playing. Computer chess playing has now arrived, but some 15 to 20 years after it was anticipated because of the difficulties in getting the programs to work effectively.

In addition to the probable delays in implementing computerized professional services, there is another question to be faced. Unlike the production of physical goods, the professional advice and counselling offered by the human expert often is only marginally connected with the apparent job of the counsellor. A doctor in general practice is often confronted with problems that have got no real medical basis at all—the doctor is being consulted because he or she is a human being rather than because he or she is a doctor. The availability of machines to provide the strictly medical advice required may result in the recognition of a need for a change in the role of the doctor. Similar arguments apply to many other professional occupations.

Products

Information technology holds out the promise of products that can perform better at no greater price. The better performance stems fundamentally from the replacement of the older electromechanical technology by electronic technology. However, the use of information technology to replace older technology does create enormous problems. Many businesses have accumulated experience in one branch of technology, but this accumulated knowledge can at best be worthless and at worst be an actual hindrance when trying to substitute information technology into an existing product. The product managers must be "literate" enough to appreciate what information technology can do, and the work force must be able and willing to be retrained in new production skills.

Information technology also holds out the promise of new products. What the successful new products will be only time will reveal, but the emphasis at the moment is centered on the consumer market for entertainment.

There is one particularly significant problem with information technology products. Quite simply, the technology and products are developing at such a fast rate that we cannot use them properly. So now we face a situation where the first generation of computer telephone exchanges are starting to be replaced because they are obsolescent even though the relatively limited functions available on these first-generation products have not been fully used. The pace of development is much faster than has been encountered before, and new ways of deciding when to replace installed but obsolescent information technology equipment may be required.

Programs

While there is much excitement and glamour attached to information technology, information technology machines and devices actually need programs to make them work. So in addition to all the work being carried out designing and building new and better machines, there is vastly much more work required in order to get the machines and the devices that they control to work properly. In many, perhaps most, cases the necessary programs simply do not exist.

Processes

Although all processes are concerned with the manipulation of information, the application of information technology to processes can be seen as two distinct applications.

Manufacturing Processes. The first application of information technology is in the manufacturing process.

> The use of microelectronics, first in the form of sensors to measure various parameters of a process, followed by process calculations using microprocessors, and, finally, control by distributed or centralised computers, allows higher quality goods to be produced more reliably and at a lower cost. Through the use of microelectronics much finer control can be exercised over the various stages of a process, thus reducing the wasteful use of expensive energy, detecting at an earlier stage of manufacture any potential failures and keeping a record of the progress during the manufacture of an item. The real-time analysis of information from a complex industrial plant such as an oil refinery can now be used to control the plant dynamically, so that changes in the conditions of manufacture can be accommodated without altering the final product. (Jack, 1982)

Business Administrative Processes. The second application of microelectronic information technology is in the clerical, administrative, and management processes. Despite all the attempts of management science and word processor suppliers, among others, the automated administrative system is much further off than the automated factory.

> There is little doubt that the business functions of large- and medium-sized enterprises in the United States will be significantly changed by further growth in the use of computers. The jobs of the great majority of clerical, technical, professional, and managerial workers will be changed to some extent, and some of these jobs will be transformed beyond recognition. But the net effect on productivity may not be overwhelming. For some organisations, overall productivity may be doubled or tripled by the impact of data processing over the next twenty or twenty-five years. For others the net effect on productivity may be as little as 10 percent. To hazard a guess, the average effect for all these enterprises might be 50 percent in twenty years, or about 2 percent per year. Assuming that toward the end of the century the affected workers in these enterprises constitute 40 percent of a total U.S. workforce of about 120 million, then computer assistance will allow those 50 million workers to do what would require 75 million workers with today's methods.
>
> Such a shift might be considered revolutionary. But it will come in small steps, over a long period of time, and at a high cost, so it is unlikely to have an impact on the work force of the sort that the enclosure movement had on the English agricultural population. Rather, the effect on enterprises and employees alike is apt to show up as the ability to handle a steadily increasing load of work without a corresponding rise in the price of the goods and services that the enterprise produces. (Vyssotsky, 1980)

Productivity

The kind of changes foreseen by Vyssotsky seem to agree quite well with what appears to have happened as far as the cost of administrative overheads are concerned. Illustration 9.3 shows Illustration 2.2 once again.

Critical examination of Illustration 9.3 suggests that since the 1960s the cost of overheads, as a proportion of total business costs, have remained constant. This constancy coincides with the introduction and spread of business computers. Is this flattening off a coincidence?—it has, after all, happened before—or is it the signal of a real change occurring, a real increase in productivity?

Profits

Who actually benefits from information technology?

Superficially, information technology benefits everyone. However, experience should be enough to convince us that such a situation very rarely, if ever, occurs.

The reason for a business turning to information technology is, sensibly enough, to make bigger, in value and over time, profits. Often the generation

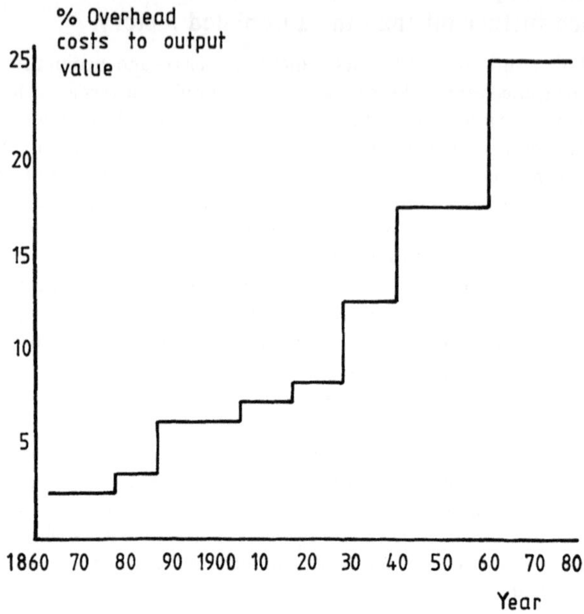

Illustration 9.3. Productivity

Overhead costs have tended to move from one plateau to another rather than in the continuous curve that was suggested in Illustration 2.2. Currently we appear to have reached a "final" plateau. Whether this really is a final plateau or whether overhead costs will soon resume an upward growth as before, or indeed start to fall—only the passage of time will reveal.

of bigger profits will also coincide with providing a better service to customers or better working conditions for employees. Often, but not necessarily always.

Customers may find that they have less of a service than before. Is standing in a queue in the rain to get money from an automatic bank teller actually an improvement in service? Does the fact that my using an Autobank card to pay my outstanding credit card debt mean I do not have to fill in a form to compensate for the fact that it actually takes me longer than before to transfer money from one account to another?

Employees will find their jobs more routinized if they simply become devices for feeding information into computers. On the other hand, if they take an interest in their new jobs and develop an understanding and enthusiasm for what they do, the intrinsic reward of their jobs can increase:

> The computer has given the operators greater autonomy through superiority of knowledge. Responsibility is increased slightly since it is they rather than an

accountant who is likely to be called upon to explain the reports which they produce. Feedback is similar. Overall the operators like being part of the new technology and respond well to the challenges which they perceive it to pose. (Jarvis, 1983)

But will this increase in intrinsic reward not only be exploited by their employers? so that, in the case quoted here, the computer operator simply replaces the accountant? Or will the employees exploit their employers' vulnerability?

Conclusions

Although information technology can be sold as a technology that can benefit everyone, and although information technology does benefit many, if not all of us, it is no service to pretend that information technology always makes life better and nicer.

Information technology is simply a technology. All technological advances mean that, compared to before the technological advance, the potential for a real mess resulting from something going wrong is increased. It is up to us to use information technology for good or ill to create profits and benefits, or losses both financial and human, as we wish.

DISCUSSION QUESTIONS

1. To what extent is computerization inevitable and beneficial? To whom and how?
2. Why will it take a long period of time for most businesses to automate and computerize their information systems? (Think in terms of the capital and training invested in current equipment, expertise, and methods.)
3. Is it likely that within the next 20 years automated corporate information systems integrating manufacturing operations with administrative and clerical processes will become available? Why?

REFERENCES

Bailey, R. W., *Human Performance Engineering,* Addison-Wesley, Reading, MA (1982).

B.I.T., Viewdata—the business choices, *Bus. Inf. Tech.,* No. 17 (1983), pp. 12–15.

Bylinsky, G., The race to the automated factory, *Fortune,* February 21 (1983), pp. 52–64.

Cawkell, A. E., Facsimile machines: results of field tests, *Inf. Tech. People,* April (1983), pp. 300–316.

Computing, Paprocki warns of limitations of FMS, November 3 (1983a).

Computing, A quote attributed to Tom Egan, Deputy Director of Projects at the Metropolitan Police, in a news story on viewdata (1983b).

Cunningham, C., *How to be Computerate.* Thames Methuen, London (1983).

Dale, R., and Williamson, I., *The Myth of the Micro,* W. H. Allen, London (1980).

Donker, M., The two conflicting realities driving IT in France, *Computing,* September 29 (1983).

Doswell, A., *Office Automation,* Wiley, Chichester (1983).

Durham, T., When elegant designs trim computation costs, *Computing,* October 6 (1983), p. 10.

Evans, L. B., Industrial uses of the microprocessor, in *The Microelectronics Revolution,* T. Forester, ed., Blackwell, Oxford (1980).

Forrester, J. W., *Industrial Dynamics,* MIT, Cambridge, MA (1961).

Gerwin, D., Do's and don'ts of computerized manufacturing, *Harv. Bus. Rev.,* March–April (1982).

Ginzberg, E., The mechanization of work, *Sci. Am.,* September (1982).

Handy, C. B., *Understanding Organizations,* Penguin, Harmondsworth (1976).

Hyman, A., *The Coming of the Chip,* New English Library, London (1980).

Jack, M. A., *The Impact of Microelectronics Technology,* Edinburgh University, Edinburgh (1982).

Jarvis, E. K. F., New information technology: One company's experience, M.B.A. report, The Strathclyde Business School (1983).

Jenner, P., Chips hit the U.K. factory, *Infomatics,* August (1983).

Jones, R. S., and Lakin, C. F., The four orders of administration, *Manage. Dec. (U.K.),* Vol. 4 (1977).

Kalthoff, R. J., and Lee, L. S., *Productivity and Records Automation,* Prentice-Hall, Englewood Cliffs (1981).

Leo Computers Ltd., The scope for electronic computers in the office, in *The Scope for Electronic Computers in the Office,* Office Management Association, London (1956).

Mann, F., in *New Patterns of Management*, McGraw Hill, New York (1961).
Nichols, A. J., An overview of microprocessor applications, in *The Microelectronics Revolution*, T. Forester, Ed., Blackwell, Oxford (1980).
Perlowski, J., The smart machine revolution, in *The Microelectronics Revolution*, T. Forester, Ed., Blackwell, Oxford (1980).
Revans, R. W., *Science and the Manager*, Macdonalds, London (1965).
Riches, H., Teletex: the facts, *Word Inf. Processing*, September (1983).
Sigel, E., Is videotext vendible?, *Datamation*, July (1983).
Stamper, R., *Information in Business and Administrative Systems*, Batsford, London (1973).
Vyssotsky, V. A., The use of computers for business functions, in *The Computer Age: A Twenty Year View*, M. L. Dertouzos and J. Moses, eds., MIT, Cambridge, MA (1980).
White, M., and Marajian, L., Information resource management, in *The International Word Processing Equipment and Software Guide 1982*, Network Communications, Lightwater (1982).
Woodward, J., *Industrial Organisation: Behaviour and Control*, Oxford University, Oxford (1970).
Wright, L., Dai turns out the steel at the Hot Strip Mill, *Computing*, September 29 (1983).

FURTHER READING

Books

Dictionary of Computing, by Frank J. Galland, Wiley, Chichester (1982).
The Future of Videotext, by Efrem Sigel, Knowledge Industry Publications (1983).
The Future with Microelectronics, by Iann Barron and Ray Curnow, Pinter, London (1979).
A History of the Machine, by Sigvard Strandh, A&W, New York (1979).
Illustrating Computers, by Colin Day and Donald Alcock, Pan-Heinemann Computers in Education, London (1982).
Information Technology: An Introduction, by Peter Zorkoczy, Pitman, London (1982).
Local Area Networks, by K. C. E. Gee, NCC Publications, Manchester (1982).
Microelectronics, A collection of Scientific American contributions, Freeman, San Francisco (1977).
Microfuture, by John Shelley, Pitman, London (1981).
The Mighty Micro, by Christopher Evans, Gollancz, London (1979).
New Office Technology, edited by Harry J. Otway and Malcolm Peltu, Pinter, London (1983).
Office Automation—A User-Driven Method, by Don Tapscott, Plenum, New York (1982).
Presentation of Computer I/O for People, by J. Abbott, NCC Publications, Manchester (1983).
Revolution in Miniature, by Ernest Braun and Stuart Macdonald, Cambridge University, Cambridge (1982).

Magazines and Journals

The following magazines contain general interest material ranging from personal computers, in general, through office and general business administration applications, to manufacturing applications and product development.

Computer Management. Monthly: computers in general, offices, and manufacturing applications.

Computing. Weekly: computers in general.

Datamation. Monthly: computers in general with a slant toward large-scale data processing.

The Economist. Weekly: business aspects of information technology.

Fortune. Weekly: business aspects of information technology.

Harvard Business Review. Bimonthly: occasional articles on various aspects of business applications in business and their management implications.

Infomatics. Monthly: computers in general, offices, and manufacturing applications.

Information Technology News. Monthly: mainly small computer systems in office applications.

Personal Computer World. Monthly: personal computer applicàtions in general.

Scientific American. Monthly: high-quality semipopularization of general science. Collected contributions on topics such as communications, microelectronics, the mechanization of work are published as separate books.

Word and Information Processing. Monthly: mainly small computer systems in office applications.

INDEX

MIX
Papier aus verantwortungsvollen Quellen
Paper from responsible sources
FSC® C105338

If you have any concerns about our products,
you can contact us on
ProductSafety@springernature.com

In case Publisher is established outside the EU,
the EU authorized representative is:
Springer Nature Customer Service Center GmbH
Europaplatz 3, 69115 Heidelberg, Germany

Printed by Libri Plureos GmbH
in Hamburg, Germany